Tony Wright is the M   and
Burntwood. A former ch   and
member of the Common   ary
Ombudsman, he has lor   ner
issues. Currently a men   tee
on Public Service, he has written several books and contributes
regularly to press, radio and television. He is married and has
three children.

WHO DO I COMPLAIN TO?

The Essential Handbook for Every Citizen

Tony Wright MP

HEADLINE

First published in 1997
by HEADLINE BOOK PUBLISHING

10 9 8 7 6 5 4 3 2 1

ISBN 0 7472 7754 0

Typeset by
Letterpart Limited, Reigate, Surrey

Printed and bound in Great Britain by
Mackays of Chatham PLC, Chatham, Kent

HEADLINE BOOK PUBLISHING
A division of Hodder Headline PLC
338 Euston Road
London NW1 3BH

Contents

Preface

All books run up debts, but this book has run up more than most. I had a clear idea of the kind of book I wanted it to be, but what I had not realised was quite what would be involved in achieving it.

It could not have been written at all without the help of a number of people. A lot of basic research was undertaken by Robin Clarke (assisted from time to time by passing volunteers) and I am extremely grateful to him for his labours. I was able to support him at a crucial period with the help of a small grant from the Joseph Rowntree Reform Trust, who were readily persuaded of the value of the project, and I owe that indispensable charity enormous thanks (and not just for this). Lucy Bailey has been absolutely invaluable in the final stages of the book, despite my promise to her that she would never have to work on it. She must get most of the credit for turning a mass of material into an orderly book – which I hope people will find coherent and easy to use. I offer her (once again) my apologetic thanks.

Two other debts must be recorded. First, there are all those people in all those organisations who responded so helpfully to our endless requests for information about their work. I hope they will now feel that they were not pestered in vain. Second, I am particularly grateful to my publisher, in the shape of Alan Brooke at Headline, who immediately understood the value of the book and shared my enthusiasm for it, while Lindsay Symons was endlessly patient and helpful. Alan's only request was that an entry on bookmakers should be included. I hope he finds it useful.

Tony Wright

Introduction

This book began life as a guide for myself. When I became a Member of Parliament a few years ago, I soon realised that I needed to know about all the various bodies (apart from MPs!) that people could complain to when they had dissatisfactions and grievances with services they had received. There are now lots of such complaints bodies, but they are only useful if people know about them. Needing a guide for myself (and not finding one), I began to put together what I wanted. This book is the result.

I hope it will be useful for everybody who wants to know who to complain to when things go wrong. Not all complaints are justified of course, but people have a right to have their complaints properly and fairly investigated and their justified grievances remedied. Complaints should also provide organisations with valuable information on how they are performing. So complaints matter.

A word about the book. In deciding what to include, the aim has been to cover the main areas (both public and private) that most people are likely to have contact with at some point, and to focus in particular on those bodies that have been set up explicitly to deal with complaints in these areas. Some very specialised areas are therefore excluded, as are the courts and much of the formal tribunal system. It is designed to be a do-it-yourself guide to the world of complaints systems.

This world is constantly changing, and there are improvements that still need to be made to the complaints systems in many areas. There are gaps and inadequacies that have to be filled if people are to be protected and their complaints dealt with properly. This is particularly the case with trade schemes of various kinds, where only members are covered and where there are often serious weaknesses in their operation. Some of the bodies and mechanisms in this guide are much more effective than others (and inclusion here does not mean that a particular complaints system is satisfactory). A complaints system should be:

- easy to access and use
- thorough and fair in its investigation

- effective in providing an appropriate response and remedy
- independent enough to command confidence

In using a complaints system, these are the sort of considerations that it is useful to keep in mind. The information given here should help with this.

Although care has been taken to make the information here as accurate and up to date as possible, there are bound to be some omissions and errors, especially as time passes. If you notice these, please do let the publishers know so that they can be put right in any future editions.

How to use this guide

This book is designed to be easy to use. The entries are arranged alphabetically, so that you simply look up the area you are interested in and you should find the appropriate body that deals with your complaint. Cross-references in **bold** type also point you in the right direction.

Each entry is set out in the same way, as follows, and gives the essential information on the body in question – from how to contact it to what you may be able to do if you are still not satisfied that your complaint has been dealt with properly:

1. *Who Can I Complain To?*

This section identifies the relevant complaints body (or bodies) and gives details of how to contact them.

2. *What Sort of Complaints Do They Deal With?*

This section describes the sort of complaints that the body is able to take up (and any complaints that it excludes from consideration). It may also include some details about procedures.

3. *How Independent Is the Complaints Procedure?*

This section attempts to identify how independent the complaints procedure is (e.g. is it internal or external? self-regulatory or wholly independent?) and the extent of any independent element.

4. *Compensation/Redress?*

This section describes whether the body is able to make recommendations and/or to compel redress measures or compensation payments as a result of its investigation of a complaint.

5. *Any Appeal?*

This section identifies whether there is a right of appeal from the body or procedure in question to another body or procedure – and, if so, what this is and how it operates.

6. *Other Options?*

This section suggests other bodies and complaints systems in the same or a related area, in case these are more appropriate, in the form of a prompt list. Cross-references to bodies and topics covered elsewhere in the book are identified by **bold** lettering whenever they occur.

NB

This section draws attention to changes in the pipeline, as well as any unusual conditions, time limits or other points to be aware of when making a complaint to the body in question.

APPENDIX

This section includes any other relevant material, e.g. other useful addresses.

If you have trouble identifying the right body to complain to, or you need some assistance in making a complaint or taking it further, there is a list at the end of the book of some of the people and organisations that should be able to help.

Much of the information here is based upon published information produced by various bodies themselves. Check with them if you are uncertain about anything or would like further details. Almost all produce leaflets about their work, some with complaint forms attached. If a certain body is not appropriate for your particular complaint, it will usually try to point you in the right direction. The same is true where there are variations between England, Wales, Scotland and Northern Ireland. Such variations are identified here where possible, but in other cases a sister body in the United Kingdom should be able to help with this.

Before using this guide, you may find it useful to read the tips that follow on making complaints. If you keep these in mind, you will have a better chance of complaining effectively, and of avoiding some of the pitfalls.

Some tips for making complaints

- Before you get to the bodies listed here, you may have to give the organisation you are complaining about a chance to sort the matter out for itself. This is only fair and sensible. Some of the bodies listed here will even insist on this before they take up your case. However, don't confuse these *internal* complaints procedures which all good organisations should have (and which the Citizens' Charter has made standard in public services) with the *external* complaints bodies which are mainly listed here. In most cases, you will turn first to internal complaints procedures and that may resolve the problem, but sometimes it will not and you will need to turn to one of the bodies here. So remember, when you have made a complaint and you are not satisfied with the response that you get from the organisation concerned (probably from someone called a 'Customer Relations Officer' or a 'Complaints Manager' or something similar), this may not be the end of the road. It may well be the moment to contact one of the bodies included here.

- There is often a time limit within which complaints normally have to be made if they are to be investigated by the bodies here. Always check on this and keep it in mind, especially if an organisation's internal response seems to be dragging on. If there are special reasons why your complaint to a body listed here is outside the normal time limit, then make sure you say so.

- When you complain, it is usually a good idea to put your complaint in writing. This makes sure it gets into the system. If your initial complaint to an organisation is by telephone, make sure you find out to whom you are talking and what they will do – and keep a note of all this, along with the date and time. A phone call is often the best way to find out who to write to in an organisation – the higher up the better as a general rule. Ask for positive and prompt action.

- Complaints should always be as clear and concise as possible. Avoid telling your life story and concentrate on the essentials. A factual chronology (incidents, dates, responses, etc.) on a separate sheet is often useful. A firm but courteous tone is best. An invitation to put something right may be more fruitful than a threat to string someone up from the nearest lamppost. Try to be clear about what you are asking for (an apology? compensation? system improvements?) and that it is reasonable and deliverable.

- Keep a record as you go along, including copies of letters you send and the replies you get, telephone calls made and other relevant information. Not only will this support what you say if challenged, but it will give you the essential information you need when you take your case to one of the complaints bodies in this guide.

- Don't give up. If you seem to be getting nowhere with the organisation concerned, try other fronts. Tell them you are taking your complaint elsewhere. Good organisations should tell you what your next port of call might be, but do not rely on this. This is the moment to contact one of the external bodies listed here, or to seek advice and help from one of the sources given at the end (such as the Citizens Advice Bureau and/or your MP). Sometimes this also has the effect of making an organisation show renewed interest in a complaint.

- Always try to make sure that you are taking the most appropriate course of action and that you have thought about the alternatives. For example, if you opt for one of the *arbitration* or *conciliation* schemes offered by many trade bodies (which only cover scheme members, of course), make sure you understand the scope and costs and how it may affect your legal rights. If you approach one of the *ombudsmen* or *regulators*, be aware that they differ in their powers, in what they can investigate and in how they operate. Finally, although this book is about how to pursue complaints without using the *courts*, sometimes going to law may be the best course of action or the last resort (especially if you use the low-cost and more user-friendly small claims procedures in the county court). Going to court is one way to pursue complaints. This book provides information about other ways. You will need to decide which course of action makes most sense in your particular case.

Good luck!

Using the system: what happens when you complain?

Many of the bodies listed in this directory publish summary case studies of complaints they have handled. The following examples are taken from recent Annual Reports.

Parliamentary Ombudsman
(*see* **Government Departments**)

Failure to uprate a claim to benefit

Complaint   A woman was widowed on 21 November 1990. She made a claim to sickness benefit. Since she did not satisfy the national insurance contributions conditions, the DSS local office investigated her entitlement to IVB under the special provisions of the Social Security Act. They established that she was entitled to IVB from 22 November 1990. Social Security benefits are normally uprated in April each year. In 1991 and 1992 DSS failed to make enquiries of their Records Branch at the appropriate time to ensure that the woman received her increased benefit from the due date. In September 1992 her Member of Parliament complained to DSS about their failure to uprate the woman's benefit on time. Despite assurances that steps would be taken to prevent any future recurrence, the 1994 uprating of her benefit was also subject to error and prolonged delays.

Result   I criticised DSS for errors, delays and their generally poor handling of the woman's claim. In particular I criticised them for the fact that, despite their assurance to the Member that more control would be taken of the woman's case, they still failed properly to administer her affairs.

DSS apologised for the shortcomings identified in my report and have taken steps to avoid recurrence of that poor service.

Press Complaints Commission (see **Press**)

Complaint	Mrs A. Anderson, Headteacher, Eastfield Primary School, Penicuik, Midlothian, complained that an article in the Edinburgh *Evening News* headlined 'Fury over Nazi school play' contained critical quotations from a person who had not seen the performance.
Result	The newspaper published a clarification and apology.

Pensions Ombudsman (see **Pensions**)

Complaint	Employer and scheme declined to stand by incorrect estimate of benefits given to the member prior to her voluntary early retirement.
Result	Complaint **upheld**. There is an employer's responsibility to ensure that an accurate estimate is provided to a member before an irrevocable decision has to be taken. This is particularly true where the employer encourages an employee to leave employment. Minor adjustments to previously quoted figures are acceptable if final salary details not known. Major errors by schemes or employer are not acceptable excuses for reducing previous estimates of benefits which have been relied upon by the member. There was no reason

for the member to suspect that the estimate was incorrect. Award of increased lump sum and pension of a value of £8,300 plus compensation of £200.

Local Government Ombudsman   (*see* Schools 2 Local Government)

Exclusions from School

Complaint   Another area of education which causes distress for everyone involved is the exclusion of a child from school. Exclusions are only to be used as a last resort and, if the exclusion is to be permanent, parents have the right to appeal to an independent panel. In one case, although the child had been permanently excluded, the education authority failed to follow the correct procedure and the parents were therefore denied this right. The family were placed under considerable stress because other schools were reluctant to admit the child, despite the recommendation of a social worker and an educational psychologist that an early placement was necessary.

Result   I am pleased to be able to report that the authority accepted the finding of maladministration and injustice and compensated the complainants for the loss of six months' education for their son.

Equal Opportunities Commission   (*see* Discrimination)

Complaint   Three women lance-corporals had taken voluntary redundancy from the army only to find they were being paid £6,000 less each to go than male soldiers of the same rank.

Originally the three women got computer forecasts telling them they would get redundancy packages ranging between £13,800 and £15,000 (based on length of service). Then they were told there had been an error because the computer calculations assumed they were male soldiers.

When the MOD realised they were women soldiers the redundancy packages were cut by £6,000 each.

The EOC agreed to back the women, and the case was argued under European equality law because the Armed Forces were exempt from the Equal Pay Act.

Result   The MOD settled the cases five days before they were due to be heard for payments totalling £20,000. The court ordered the MOD to pay half of the EOC's legal costs.

Banking Ombudsman   (*see* **Banks**)

Complaint   Mr M and his wife purchased a house with a bank mortgage. Following divorce proceedings, they could not agree on a selling price for the house and mortgage payments went into arrears. With the encouragement of Mr M, the bank sold the property for £205,000. The conveyancing work was carried out by solicitors instructed by the bank. Mr M accepted that the bank was entitled to recoup its solicitors' fees from the proceeds of sale but complained about the amount charged, which was £1,853.75, plus VAT of £324.40.

The bank's solicitors said their fees were calculated by charging £663 for time spent at £68 per hour, a 25% mark-up of £166 and a further 'value element' of £1,025, representing 0.5 per cent of the sale price.

Mr M's own solicitors said that they would have charged between £700 and £800 plus VAT for a straightforward sale of this nature, which was about the same as the bank's solicitors had charged, excluding the 'value element'.

Result

The Ombudsman decided that it was neither usual nor reasonable to have charged the 'value element' in addition to an hourly rate and a mark-up. He, therefore, awarded Mr M, as one of the two joint mortgagors, the sum of £512.50, representing one-half of the 'value element'.

Tax Adjudicator   (*see* **Tax**)

Tax Law – repayment supplement

Complaint

Mr D complained about the Inland Revenue's delay in repaying money that was due to him. He also complained that the Inland Revenue should have paid him repayment supplement for the whole period that they had held his money.

The Inland Revenue were investigating the accounts of a company in which Mr D was a director. The Inland Revenue inspector informed the company's agents that she intended to send Mr D an estimated Schedule E assessment. Mr D agreed to pay £25,000 tax to stop interest accumulating. About 10 months later, the inspector told the agents that, after consulting an Inland Revenue Head Office specialist, she had decided that the actual Schedule E liability was much lower than she had estimated, and that the amount overpaid would be refunded. The agents asked that repayment supplement cover the entire period that the Inland Revenue had held Mr D's money.

The Inland Revenue delayed in making the refund to Mr D. When the agents queried the delay, they were told that the Inland Revenue's Head Office were considering the agent's request for repayment supplement. Shortly afterwards, the Inland Revenue made a refund to Mr D. One month later, they sent Mr D repayment supplement, but this did not cover the entire period that they had held his money.

Result

We agreed that there had been delays in making the refund to Mr D. We also felt that the Inland Revenue should have kept Mr D better informed about the position with his refund. The Inland Revenue apologised to Mr D for the poor service he had received.

The A-Z Directory

A

Accountants 1
(Certified)

1. *Who Can I Complain To?*

Legal Department
Chartered Association of Certified Accountants (ACCA)
29 Lincoln's Inn Fields
London WC2A 3EE

Tel: 0171 396 5928
Fax: 0171 396 5968

2. *What Sort of Complaints Do They Deal With?*

a. Complaints of professional misconduct against Certified Accountants, ACCA students, and certain non-members (such as partners in mixed practices) who have expressly agreed to be bound by ACCA's rules. 'Misconduct' includes, but is not confined to, any act or failure to act likely to bring discredit to an individual accountant, ACCA or the accountancy profession.

b. If a member has given advice which later turns out to have been wrong, and as a result of which loss has been suffered, you should normally address your claim to the firm's professional indemnity insurers (but see 4 b, below).

c. ACCA does not intervene in fee-related disputes as it considers that the courts are the proper forum for such matters.

d. Complaints should be made in writing to ACCA's Legal

Department, and include any supporting evidence. Given the above remit, there are no conditions or time limits on making a complaint. The usual duration of an investigation is six months.

3. *How Independent Is the Complaints Procedure?*

ACCA is a self-regulating Recognised Professional Body. If the Legal Department decides a complaint is sufficiently serious, they will refer it to ACCA's Investigations Committee, a committee of ACCA's Council made up of senior members of ACCA and lay members, including lawyers, which sits in private.

In serious cases the Investigations Committee may decide to refer the complaint to the Disciplinary Committee, made up as before of ACCA and lay members, including lawyers, which operates as a tribunal. Hearings are normally open to the public.

An independent lay observer (solicitor) is paid to oversee both procedures.

4. *Compensation/Redress?*

a. ACCA's main function is to ensure proper standards of professional conduct by its members. Disciplinary action against certified accountants found guilty of a breach of ACCA's code of professional conduct can include reprimands, fines, suspension and expulsion.

b. ACCA cannot provide financial compensation for any loss suffered, unless the claim falls within the scope of its *Financial Services Compensation Scheme*. This is a 'rescue fund' set up to compensate investors who have lost money as a result of dealings with a certified accountant who has subsequently gone bust   *see* **Financial Services**

Contact ACCA for more details.

5. *Any Appeal?*

a. No appeal is possible by you against the orders of the Disciplinary Committee. If the member disagrees with the finding(s) or order(s) of the Disciplinary Committee, he or she may appeal to the Appeal Committee; if they are unsuccessful a second time the penalties may be more severe.

b. There is a theoretical right to judicial review of Disciplinary Committee hearings, although no attempt has ever been successful.

c. If you are unhappy about the outcome of ACCA's procedures, you can still pursue a claim through the courts.

6. *Other Options?*

Association of Authorised Public Accountants
Chartered Institute of Management Accountants
Institute of Chartered Accountants (England and Wales)
Institute of Chartered Accountants (Scotland)

For general advice on complaints about financial services
see **Financial Services**

Legal action   *see* **Where to get help**

Accountants 2 (Chartered)

1. *Who Can I Complain To?*

England and Wales

Director of the Professional Conduct Department
Institute of Chartered Accountants in England and Wales
   (ICAEW)
Gloucester House
399 Silbury Boulevard
Central Milton Keynes MK9 2HL

Tel: 01908 248100
Complaints Helpline: 01908 248048
Fax: 01908 248002

Scotland

> Director of Legal Services
> Institute of Chartered Accountants of Scotland (ICAS)
> 27 Queen Street
> Edinburgh EH2 1LA
>
> Tel: 0131 225 5673
> Fax: 0131 225 3813

Northern Ireland

> The Secretary
> Institute of Chartered Accountants of Ireland (ICAI)
> Chartered Accountants House
> 87–89 Pembroke Road
> Dublin 4
>
> Tel: 00 3531 668 0400
> Fax: 00 3531 668 5685

2. *What Sort of Complaints Do They Deal With?*

a. Complaints about professional misconduct and/or conduct discreditable to the profession of accountancy by Chartered Accountants, including complaints against Chartered Accountants licensed by their Institute as insolvency practitioners. You should complain directly to the accountant concerned in the first instance. If you are still unhappy, you may then refer the matter to the relevant Institute. Complaints should be made in writing and will normally relate to the conduct of clients' affairs. There are no conditions or time limits. The Institutes also have jurisdiction over members who have come adversely to the notice of the authorities (for example in the Criminal Courts or in relation to the Company Directors Disqualification Act 1986).

b. The Institutes do not get involved in complaints about professional fees, which are a legal matter, although if you and the member agree, they can appoint an Independent Arbitrator

(Auditor of Fees in Scotland) to arbitrate on the matter. The system is designed to offer a quick, cost-effective alternative to litigation, but is not free: the Arbitrator's fees are charged at an hourly rate and will be apportioned by him. Arbitration decisions are legally binding. Application forms can be obtained from the Legal Services Department of the relevant Institute.

c. If a member has given advice which later turns out to have been wrong, and as a result of which loss has been suffered, you should normally address your claim to the practice concerned together with a request that it notifies its professional indemnity insurers of the possible claim.

d. Claims for compensation relating to the investment services provided by accountants where the firm has become insolvent are handled by the Chartered Accountants' Investment Business Compensation Scheme (see *NB*, below).

e. Complaints are initially allocated to an Investigation or Conciliation Officer as appropriate; if conciliation is unsuccessful a case may then be transferred to an Investigation Officer. After this stage complaints are handled progressively by the Investigations Committee and the Disciplinary Committee.

f. Serious cases of discreditable conduct with a 'public interest' angle, such as those involving significant amounts of money (a recent example being the Barings case), can be referred (by the ICAEW and ICAS only) to the Joint Disciplinary Scheme. It is up to the Institute dealing with the complaint to identify such cases; members of the public cannot themselves refer cases to the JDS. Similar breaches of the ICAI code of conduct are referred to a Special Disciplinary Scheme.

3. *How Independent Is the Complaints Procedure?*

The Institutes are self-regulating professional bodies. They are recognised as the statutory regulatory authorities (Recognised Professional Bodies) for Chartered Accountants under the

Financial Services Act 1986, the Insolvency Act 1986 and the Companies Act 1989.

All Professional Conduct Committees include not less than 25 per cent lay (i.e. non-accountant) members.

If the Investigations Committee decides to bring charges before the Institute's Disciplinary Committee, the Investigations Committee then assumes the role of complainant and you will be represented by a lawyer member of the Secretariat. The proceedings of the Disciplinary Committee are similar to those of a tribunal, and are held before a panel of three persons (chaired by a QC in Scotland, a solicitor in Ireland). You will not be asked to attend the hearing unless called as a witness by either side.

4. *Compensation/Redress?*

a. The Disciplinary Committees of the Institutes have the power to expel, fine or reprimand (and in Scotland and Ireland to suspend) members for any proven misconduct or other action that makes them liable to disciplinary proceedings.

b. The Institutes cannot provide financial compensation for any loss suffered, unless the claim falls within the scope of the Chartered Accountants' Investment Business Compensation Scheme (see *NB*, below).

5. *Any Appeal?*

a. If you are unhappy with the Investigation Committee's decision not to refer your case to the Disciplinary Committee you may appeal to the Reviewer of Complaints.

b. No appeal is possible by you against the orders of the Disciplinary Committee. If the *member* disagrees with the finding(s) or order(s) of the Disciplinary Committee, he or she may appeal to the Appeal Committee; if they are unsuccessful a second time the penalties may be more severe.

c. There is a theoretical right to judicial review of Disciplinary

Committee hearings, although no complainant has ever tried this.

6. *Other Options?*

- Unless you have already agreed to arbitration over the same matter, you can pursue a claim for financial compensation through the courts. For more information about arbitration and legal action   *see* **Where to get help**
- The other main professional body for publicly practising accountants is the Chartered Association of Certified Accountants   *see* **Accountants 1**
- Your accountant may be a member of one of the other professional bodies below, although options ii to iv mainly cover in-house (employed) accountants. All of these operate broadly similar complaints procedures.

    i. Association of Authorised Public Accountants
   ii. Chartered Institute of Management Accountants
  iii. Chartered Institute of Public Finance and Accountancy
   iv. Institute of Chartered Secretaries and Administrators

Banking Ombudsman   *see* **Banks**

Building Societies Ombudsman   *see* **Building Societies**

Personal Investment Ombudsman   *see* **Investment 1**

Investment Ombudsman   *see* **Investment 3**

Insurance Brokers Registration Council   *see* **Insurance 1**

Insurance Ombudsman   *see* **Insurance 2**

Pensions Ombudsman   *see* **Pensions**

For general advice about financial services *see* **Financial Services**

NB

- The Chartered Accountants' Investment Business Compensation Scheme handles claims relating to losses from investment business conducted by chartered accountants in cases where the firm is unable to pay compensation because it has gone out of business. Claims must relate to investment business carried out by firms authorised by one of the Institutes of Chartered Accountants under the **Financial Services Act 1986**, and the relevant advice must have been given *after 28 August 1988*. A legal liability must exist. The maximum claim is £50,000 or the legal liability, whichever is lower, and the claim must be made within *six months* of discovering the firm's insolvency. For information contact:

Secretary to the Compensation Committee
Chartered Accountants' Compensation Scheme
PO Box 433
Moorgate Place
London EC2P 2BJ

Tel: 0171 920 8100

Advertising

1. *Who Can I Complain To?*

The Advertising Standards Authority
2–16 Torrington Place
London WC1E 7HW

Tel: 0171 580 5555
Fax: 0171 631 3051

2. *What Sort of Complaints Do They Deal With?*

a. Advertisements in newspapers, magazines, posters, direct marketing, sales promotions, cinema, video cassettes, teletext (excluding ITV text services).

b. Whatever is written or shown in an advertisement or promotion that is not considered to be 'legal, decent, honest, or truthful'. This includes cases in which:

- claims are factually wrong
- the advertisement is misleading
- the advertisement is likely to cause offence
- the advertisement is socially irresponsible
- the advertisement is commercially unfair

c. The ASA does *not* handle complaints about advertisements on commercial radio or television.

3. *How Independent Is the Complaints Procedure?*

The ASA is a self-regulatory body governed by a code of practice written by advertising industry representatives. However, the ASA's Council is essentially independent in that the majority of its membership has no advertising interests.

4. *Compensation/Redress?*

If the ASA finds in your favour, then it will act to have the advertisement or promotion changed or withdrawn. Compliance with ASA guidelines is a standard condition for advertisements to be accepted by any of the media in 2a.

The outcome of every complaint investigation is published in the Authority's Monthly Reports. The ASA has no power to award financial compensation.

5. *Any Appeal?*

a. The ASA will only reconsider your complaint if you can present new information which had not been previously considered.

b. Advertisers will find it very hard and/or expensive to persist in issuing a misleading advertisement if the Authority has found against them. If they do try to ignore the ruling, the ASA will exercise further sanctions, and may refer the case to the Director General of Fair Trading (see *NB*, below).

c. You may take your complaint to the Director General of Fair Trading yourself, but he will only use his powers if he considers the ASA (or other existing channel) has not adequately dealt with it, and if the nature of the complaint comes under his remit (see below).

6. *Other Options?*

a. Complaints about advertisements for investments or investment business, issued by persons authorised under the **Financial Services Act 1986**, may also be directed to the Securities and Investment Board (SIB)   *see* **Financial Services**

b. Complaints about advertisements for medicines may also be directed to:

   Department of Health Medicines Control Agency
   Control Tower
   Market Towers
   1 Nine Elms Lane
   London SW8 5NQ

   Tel: 0171 720 2188

c. Complaints about racial or sexual discrimination in an advertisement may also be directed to the Equal Opportunities Commission   *see* **Discrimination**

d. To complain about advertisements broadcast via:

   Commercial television   *see* **Broadcasting 2**

   Commercial radio   *see* **Broadcasting 3**

e. To complain about: the quality of advertised goods not being as described; the safety of goods; the accuracy of prices or measures quoted; the safety of advertised food and drink, etc.   *see* **Goods & Services**

f. To complain about, or claim compensation in relation to, mail order companies advertising in national newspapers
                         see **Mail Order**

g. If you wish to stop receiving *any* direct mail *see* **Direct Mail**

NB

The role of the Director General of Fair Trading

Complaints about seriously misleading advertisements – *except* for those covered by the ITC (independent TV), Radio Authority (independent radio) or SIB (authorised investment businesses) – may also be made to the Director General of Fair Trading (DGFT). He will refer it to the ASA if they have not already received it.

Unlike the ASA, the DGFT has the legal power, under the Control of Misleading Advertisements Regulations 1988, to stop advertisements by means of a court injunction (in Scotland, an interdict) if: 'in any way, including its presentation [an advertisement] deceives or is likely to deceive the persons to whom it is addressed or whom it reaches and if, by reason of its deceptive nature, it is likely to affect their economic behaviour or, for those reasons, injures or is likely to injure a competitor [of the advertiser]'. Advertisements might, for example, contain false statements, conceal or omit important facts, make insincere promises and/or create a false impression.

The DGFT *cannot* act if a complaint is about taste or decency, the quality of advertised goods, a personal advertisement, or does not come under the above definition of 'misleading'. Neither can he award compensation.

In theory the ASA can pass on complaints about misleading advertisements to the DGFT if an advertiser fails to comply with its instructions. In practice, almost all complaints are resolved by the ASA.

You can write to the Director General at:

Office of Fair Trading
Field House
15–25 Bream's Buildings
London EC4A 1PR

Tel: 0171 242 2858

Appointments (Public)

1. *Who Can I Complain To?*

Office of the Commissioner for Public Appointments (OCPA)
Room 62/2
Horse Guards Road
London SW1P 3AL

Tel: 0171 270 6032
Fax: 0171 270 1981
e-mail: ocpa@gtnet.gov.uk

2. *What Sort of Complaints Do They Deal With?*

a. Written complaints about Ministerial appointments to the boards of Executive Non-Departmental Public Bodies (ENDPBs) and National Health Service bodies. These kinds of bodies are also known as Quangos (Quasi Non-Governmental Organisations). At the time of the Nolan Report on Standards in Public Life it was estimated that such bodies had almost 9,000 board members and were spending some £40bn a year.

b. According to the Commissioner's Code of Practice, all appointments to ENDPBs and NHS bodies must be based on the following seven principles:

   i. Ministerial Responsibility
   ii. Merit
   iii. Independent Scrutiny – no appointment may be made without first being scrutinised by an independent panel or by a group including independent members
   iv. Equal Opportunities
   v. Probity – board members 'must be committed to the principles and values of public service and perform their duties with integrity'
   vi. Openness and Transparency – the appointments process

'must be transparent and information must be provided about appointments made', including the political activity, concurrent appointments and pay (including fees) of the successful candidate

vii. Proportionality – i.e. large powerful bodies with big budgets are expected to require more elaborate and expensive appointments procedures than small, less powerful ones

Political activity should not be an acceptable criterion for appointment except in specified circumstances: for example, if party political representation is a statutory requirement. Candidates are expected to 'subscribe to the objectives of the body in which they are interested'.

c. Complaints might therefore be about:

- the way someone, or a group of people, has been appointed
- the fact that a particular person has, or has not, been appointed to a particular board
- the failure to adequately advertise a vacancy and/or publicise the fact that anyone may nominate anyone, including themselves, for consideration on a selection list
- the lack of independence of scrutiny panels, etc.

d. The OCPA will acknowledge your complaint within 3 working days of receipt, and should be able to answer it fully within 20 days.

e. In the first instance, the OCPA will ask the relevant government department to comment and suggest a reply. If the department's response suggests cause for concern, the Commissioner may then ask for further information and a fuller explanation.

3. *How Independent Is the Complaints Procedure?*

The role of Commissioner for Public Appointments was created in 1995. The Commissioner is appointed by HM The

Queen by Order in Council (on the recommendation of the Privy Council), to independently monitor, regulate and provide advice on departmental procedures for Ministerial appointments. The Commissioner has the right to investigate all these appointments.

4. *Compensation/Redress?*

If the Commissioner considers that a complaint is justified, he will raise the matter with the Minister concerned. There is no legal redress, but a summary of complaints is published in the Commissioner's Annual Report.

5. *Any Appeal?*

Not at the time of writing.

6. *Other Options?*

For more information about equal opportunities, including racial, sexual and age discrimination   *see* **Discrimination**

For more information about 'open government'
see **Information 1**

The Parliamentary Ombudsman   *see* **Government Departments**

NB

- There are no time limits for making a complaint.
- All the procedures described are very new, and under constant review.
- The Public Appointments Unit (PAU) maintains a register of people willing to be considered for public appointment to any public body. Their experience, interests, time commitments and other relevant information are recorded and searches are then made on request. The PAU welcomes applications from everyone regardless of age, status, etc. If you would like to nominate yourself or someone else for

inclusion on the register, you can get an application form from the PAU at:

PAU
Cabinet Office
Horse Guards Road
London SW1P 3AL

Tel: 0171 270 6210/6217
Fax: 0171 270 6053

Most government departments also maintain lists, although they are less widely publicised. Contact the department in question for more information about these.

- The Women's National Commission publication *Stepping Out in Public: A Woman's Guide to Public Appointments* can be obtained free from:

Women's National Commission
Caxton House
Tothill Street
London SW1H 9NF

Tel: 0171 273 5486

Architects 1 (Chartered)

1. *Who Can I Complain To?*

Professional Conduct Office
Royal Institute of British Architects (RIBA)
66 Portland Place
London W1N 4AD

Tel: 0171 580 5533
Fax: 0171 255 1541

2. *What Sort of Complaints Do They Deal With?*

a. Complaints about members of the Royal Institute of British Architects, known as Chartered Architects. A member will usually have the initials RIBA, FRIBA or ARIBA after their name. About 70 per cent of all architects registered in the UK are RIBA members.

b. The RIBA may look at any complaint about a member, but is primarily concerned with those of a professional and ethical nature such as allegations of:

- dishonesty or lack of integrity
- improper conduct of a client's affairs or inadequate liaison with the client
- abuse of confidentiality or lack of discretion
- allowing other interests to conflict with those of the client, without prior disclosure to the client
- improperly obtaining commissions

The RIBA has a written Code of Professional Conduct with which members are required to comply. This is available on request.

c. The RIBA is normally *unable* to:

- provide or obtain compensation for a member's shortcomings
- give legal advice or assistance
- give advice or assistance relating to specific building or architectural matters
- represent a complainant's interests against a member
- investigate matters other than misconduct, such as negligence or a financial dispute

For details about conciliation and arbitration services (for contractual and compensation disputes) available to clients of RIBA members, see below.

d. The Professional Conduct Committee sits only every six weeks, so it may take some time for your complaint to be dealt with.

3. *How Independent Is the Complaints Procedure?*

The Institute is a private, self-regulatory professional body with no independent element. The Professional Conduct Committee is composed of practising architects, but undertakes to investigate all complaints thoroughly and impartially.

4. *Compensation/Redress?*

The RIBA has no powers to compel a member to pay you compensation, or otherwise enforce its ruling.

Members who are found to have broken the RIBA Code may be disciplined under the RIBA By-laws and receive a warning (which may be published), a suspension, or, in extreme cases, be expelled from the RIBA. Expulsion from the RIBA does *not* stop an architect legally doing business.

5. *Any Appeal?*

No.

6. *Other Options?*

- If your complaint is a very serious one, you should contact the Architects' Registration Council of the United Kingdom (ARCUK) after or at the same time as complaining to the RIBA (the RIBA will also refer serious complaints to ARCUK itself). If your architect is not a member of the RIBA, ARCUK is your only option   *see* **Architects 2**
- If your dispute relates to contract law and/or you wish to claim compensation, the RIBA will try and help resolve matters via *conciliation* or *arbitration*.

  If both parties agree, the relevant regional office of the RIBA can arrange informal conciliation for a fee of no more than £100 + VAT per party. If you agree to conciliation, a binding settlement will be drawn up for you to sign at the end, which may result in mutually acceptable redress and/or compensation. If agreement cannot be reached, arbitration will be suggested.

Many architectural contracts contain an arbitration clause, stating that disputes must be resolved by legally binding independent arbitration. Contracts issued by RIBA members will normally stipulate that the RIBA's President should be responsible for appointing any arbitrator. Such clauses may save money by avoiding the courts (although the costs of independent arbitration can also be significant), but are not usually binding on individual consumers if the amount of compensation claimed comes within the county court limit. If you agree to arbitration, or are contractually bound to go to arbitration over a compensation claim, the decision of the arbitrator is final and legally binding.

- For more information on conciliation and arbitration
  see **Where to get help**
- For advice about taking legal action   *see* **Where to get help**

NB

- The RIBA's complaints procedures are currently under review. Its role is also expected to change in relation to that of ARCUK, with new legislation currently in the pipeline
  see **Architects 2**
- A leaflet, *Guidance on Complaints against Chartered Architects*, is available from the RIBA.
- If you decide to obtain a second opinion, the RIBA's Clients' Advisory Service can help you select another architect. A second opinion may not be free.

Architects 2 (Registered)

1. *Who Can I Complain To?*

Architects' Registration Council of the United Kingdom (ARCUK)
73 Hallam Street
London W1N 6EE

Tel: 0171 580 5861

Note: The name and constitution of this body is changing in April 1997 (see NB, below) when the complaints procedure will be somewhat simplified and strengthened in favour of the consumer. The following details therefore apply only until then.

2. *What Sort of Complaints Do They Deal With?*

a. All serious complaints about registered architects. Everyone calling themselves an architect within the UK has to be registered with the Architects' Registration Council of the United Kingdom (ARCUK).

b. ARCUK will discipline a registered architect if their behaviour is judged to have been 'disgraceful'. The definition of disgraceful relates to ethical matters and includes cases of extreme professional misconduct – for example: undisclosed major conflicts of interest; severely improper handling of correspondence or money. ARCUK may also act where an architect has been found guilty of a criminal offence, but does not need a criminal conviction to strike an architect off.

c. The only case in which ARCUK will bring a prosecution is when someone who is not registered is calling themselves an architect. It does not get involved in disputes covered by contractual law.

d. The Council currently publishes a Standard which registered architects are supposed to comply with.

3. *How Independent Is the Complaints Procedure?*

ARCUK is an independent statutory body funded from registration fees. Complaints are currently dealt with, in the first instance, by a Professional Practice Committee, which may refer them to the Discipline Committee and/or the Council if sufficiently serious. The Discipline Committee has 50 per cent lay membership.

4. *Compensation/Redress?*

a. ARCUK is empowered by Act of Parliament to terminate the registration of any person it finds guilty of 'disgraceful conduct' in their capacity as an architect.

b. It has no powers of redress, and cannot award compensation. However, the threat of being struck off, and therefore effectively put out of business (although see *NB*, below), may be enough to make an architect put things right.

5. *Any Appeal?*

Yes, in serious cases, to the High Court.

6. *Other Options?*

- If your architect is a member of the RIBA, you may wish to refer your complaint to them first. The RIBA's code of practice is more rigorous than that of ARCUK, so behaviour adjudged by ARCUK to fall short of 'disgraceful' (or of the new definitions of 'unacceptable' or 'serious incompetence') may be enough to get a RIBA member disciplined or even expelled. When ARCUK decides to discipline a member of the RIBA the RIBA will usually resume their own investigation of the case, or instigate one if they have not already done so   *see* **Architects 1**
- For advice about taking legal action   *see* **Where to get help**
- Many architectural contracts contain arbitration clauses, which state that disputes must be resolved by legally binding independent arbitration. Such clauses may save money by avoiding the courts (although the costs of independent arbitration can also be significant), but are not usually binding on individual consumers if the amount of compensation claimed comes within the county court limit. For more information on arbitration   *see* **Where to get help**

NB

- The law relating to the regulation of architects will change on 1 April 1997, when the **Housing Grants Construction and**

Regeneration Act 1996 comes into effect. ARCUK will then become the *Architects' Registration Board* (ARB). The governing body will change to a smaller board with a majority of members who are not architects. A new Professional Conduct Committee will be set up to investigate complaints, which will operate independently of the board, and which will also have a majority of lay members. The criteria for disciplinary action will be changed, to 'unacceptable' rather than 'disgraceful' conduct, and extended to include 'serious professional incompetence'. Under the new Act the ARB is also required to publish a Code of Standards of Professional Conduct and Practice.

- Although all 'architects' have by law to be registered, you do not have to be registered to do the *work* of an architect, and neither do people calling themselves 'architectural designers', 'architectural engineers', etc. (which may include struck-off architects). The only redress against such practitioners is via the courts.

Auctioneers

- Auctioneers do not have to be registered and are not subject to any special statutory regulation. Anything can be sold at auction, the four main areas of business being: real estate; livestock; plant and machinery; and fine art and antiques. Cars, bankruptcy stock, house clearance and other second-hand furniture, wine, and office equipment including computers are also widely bought and sold at auction.
- Take care if you buy anything at auction, because you have fewer rights under consumer law than when you buy from an ordinary trader. Auctioneers, unlike other sellers, can refuse to accept responsibility for the quality of goods they auction (the rule is usually 'buyer beware'). Look out for exclusion clauses and read any notices and catalogues carefully. Note any conditions of sale, such as buyer's premium, terms and method of payment, deposits, and time limits for removal of goods. Once the hammer has fallen, you cannot back out of the deal. Be extra careful if you are buying from a temporary auction centre (for example, many second-hand car auctions), as it may be difficult to contact the auctioneer after the sale.

- If you want to complain about an auctioneer, you should first find out if they are a member of a professional association. Auctioneering frequently overlaps with other professional activities, and most established auctioneers are members of one, or both, of the following professional bodies, which have entries elsewhere in the book:

The Incorporated Society of Valuers and Auctioneers
see **Valuers & Auctioneers**
The Royal Institution of Chartered Surveyors *see* **Surveyors**

- *See also* **Estate Agents 1** and **2**
- Some specialist auctioneers will be members of small specialist trade associations (Scottish livestock auctioneers, for example, are usually members of the Institute of Auctioneers and Appraisers in Scotland, Tel: 01467 623700). However, these associations may not have any formal complaints procedures.
- If your complaint is about an auctioneer who is not a member of any professional body, you should contact your local Trading Standards Officer   *see* **Goods & Services**

B

Banks

1. *Who Can I Complain To?*

The Office of the Banking Ombudsman
70 Gray's Inn Road
London WC1X 8NB

Tel: 0171 404 9944
Fax: 0171 405 5052
LO-call: 0345 660902 (local-rate calls within UK)
e-mail: banking.ombudsman@obo.org.uk

2. *What Sort of Complaints Do They Deal With?*

a. Complaints against High Street Banks and companies that
are members of the Ombudsman Scheme, about events that
have occurred within the previous *six years*, or since the
bank joined the Scheme, if later. You should first have
exhausted the internal complaints procedure of the bank in
question, which will probably mean taking your complaint
as far as their head office.

b. Complaints about all types of business normally transacted
through bank branches: current, deposit or savings accounts,
cheques, standing orders, direct debits, automatic cash
machines, bank credit cards, etc. Loans, mortgages and
overdrafts are covered (but only where the bank has been at
fault, not when you are questioning the bank's commercial
judgement). The Ombudsman can also deal with complaints
about telephone banking and about credit cards issued
where no account is held at a bank branch, complaints about

bank executor trustee services and with some complaints about bank services relating to taxation and insurance where these have been provided at ordinary branch level.

c. The Ombudsman *cannot* deal with claims of more than £100,000. Neither can he become involved where the complaint is about the bank's commercial judgement, general interest rate or other policies, or the way a bank has exercised its discretion under a will or trust, *unless* there has been some maladministration or unfair treatment.

d. He *cannot* investigate complaints that are being, or have been, dealt with by a court or similar body.

e. Complaints are accepted from personal customers, sole traders, partnerships, clubs and trade unions. Limited companies can only use the Banking Ombudsman Scheme for complaints relating to events *after* 26 January 1993 and if their turnover is *under* £1 million a year.

3. *How Independent Is the Complaints Procedure?*

The Ombudsman is independent of the members of the Scheme. He is a senior lawyer appointed by, and responsible to, an independent Council.

4. *Compensation/Redress?*

a. If after an investigation the Ombudsman decides in your favour, he will attempt to get the bank to settle the matter to your satisfaction. If the matter cannot be settled amicably the Ombudsman has the power to make a binding award of compensation of up to £100,000 against the bank.

b. Occasionally the Ombudsman may decide it is more appropriate that your case be resolved by a court of law. In rare cases of legal significance the Ombudsman may agree to the case being transferred to a court, if the bank agrees to pay your legal costs.

c.   There is a 'rescue fund' specifically for customers of banks that have gone bust: see *NB*, below.

5. *Any Appeal?*

You have the right to reject the Ombudsman's proposals at any stage and to pursue the matter in another way, for example through the courts.

6. *Other Options?*

If at any stage the Ombudsman comes to the conclusion that your complaint should be dealt with under some other complaints procedure, for example by another Ombudsman, he will usually pass on your papers himself.

Building Societies Ombudsman	*see* **Building Societies**
Insurance Ombudsman	*see* **Insurance 2**
Investment Ombudsman	*see* **Investment 3**
Pensions Ombudsman	*see* **Pensions**
Personal Investment Authority Ombudsman	*see* **Investment 1**
Chartered Association of Certified Accountants	*see* **Accountants 1**
Institute of Chartered Accountants	*see* **Accountants 2**
Insurance Brokers Registration Council	*see* **Insurance 1**
For advice about taking legal action	*see* **Where to get help**

NB

In the event of a bank becoming insolvent the *Deposit Protection Scheme* is obliged to pay each depositor up to 90 per cent of the bank's total liability, up to a maximum of £18,000 (or ECU 20,000). Multiple accounts in the same name will be aggregated, but in joint accounts each holder will be entitled to £18,000 protection. The Scheme does not protect secured deposits,

deposits made by an individual who has profited from the bank's financial difficulties, deposits made by other authorised banks or building societies or deposits made by companies or individuals who are related to the insolvent bank. Any interest earned on the account up to insolvency is protected. In the event of an authorised bank becoming insolvent the Deposit Protection Board will write to each customer informing them how to make a claim. To find out about the Fund, contact:

**Deposit Protection Scheme
19 Old Jewry
London EC2R 8HA**

Tel: 0171 601 5062

Barristers

1. *Who Can I Complain To?*

In England and Wales only

**The Secretary of the Professional Conduct Committee (PCC)
General Council of the Bar
3 Bedford Row
London WC1R 4DB**

**Tel: 0171 242 0082
Fax: 0171 831 9217**

Note: The Bar Council's complaints procedures are due to be reformed in April 1997. See NB *for details of these changes, and for who to complain to in Scotland and Northern Ireland.*

2. *What Sort of Complaints Do They Deal With?*

a. Complaints against all barristers, whether practising or not. Only people who have been called to the Bar by the Inns of Court may call themselves (and practise as) barristers in England and Wales. Complaints may relate to events occurring within the UK or abroad. The Council will only investigate allegations of personal conduct 'disreputable to a barrister' or which might 'bring the profession into disrepute'. Examples of such conduct include:

- dishonesty
- criminal offences
- delay in dealing with papers
- failure to follow instruction
- inadequate representation of the lay client in court
- rudeness to the judge or clients, or misleading the court
- other serious matters which might bring into question a barrister's fitness to practise their profession

b. Complaints are investigated by the Professional Conduct Committee (PCC). If the PCC considers there is a prima-facie case of professional misconduct, it will do one of three things:

    i. The most serious cases are referred to a Disciplinary Tribunal.

    ii. Cases not serious enough to warrant a barrister being disbarred, and involving no dispute over facts, may be referred to Summary Procedure.

    iii. Finally, cases involving less serious breaches of the code of conduct may be referred to various Informal Panels.

3. *How Independent Is the Complaints Procedure?*

a. The General Council of the Bar is a non-statutory self-regulatory body. Its code of conduct is, however, deemed to be approved under the **Courts and Legal Services Act 1990**.

b. The Professional Conduct Committee of the Bar Council consists of thirty barristers and two lay representatives, currently appointed by the Bar Council. Cases cannot be dismissed unless both lay members of the PCC agree (but see *NB*, below, for how this will change from April 1997).

c. Disciplinary Tribunals are run by the Inns of Court and usually chaired by a judge. They also include three barristers and one lay person, who are not necessarily members of the PCC.

d. Summary Procedures are conducted by three barristers and

one lay person, this time chaired by a QC, drawn from past and present members of the PCC.

e. Informal Panels consist of a QC plus two barristers drawn from present members of the PCC.

4. *Compensation/Redress?*

a. Disciplinary Tribunals can do any, or a combination, of the following things to discipline a barrister:

- disbar them (they will then be unable to practise)
- suspend them for any length of time
- fine them up to £5,000
- issue a formal reprimand
- order the refund of fees
- advise them as to future conduct

b. Summary Hearings can:

- suspend a barrister for up to 3 months
- fine them up to £500
- reprimand/order refunds/advise, etc.

c. Informal Panels can only admonish barristers and/or advise them as to future conduct.

d. At present, Tribunals and Summary Hearings have no powers to award compensation; they can only reduce or waive a barrister's fee, and this happens rarely. This is due to change in April 1997 (see *NB*, below).

e. The Legal Services Ombudsman has the power to award compensation (see below).

5. *Any Appeal?*

a. A case may be re-opened by the Professional Conduct Committee, but only if new evidence is made available. A re-opened case is most likely to be looked at by the original team.

b. If you are unhappy with the way your complaint has been dealt with, you can appeal to the Legal Services Ombudsman. If you decide to do this, you must approach the Ombudsman *within 3 months* of the PCC's final decision
see **Legal Profession**

It is comparatively rare for the Committee to re-open investigations and you should not delay submitting an appeal to the Ombudsman in the hope that the Professional Conduct Committee will re-open the matter.

6. *Other Options?*

- It may be worth talking to your solicitor before approaching the Bar Council, to see if they can help you negotiate a reduced fee or otherwise resolve the matter at an early stage.
- You may have a civil claim for damages against a barrister for negligent advice – if, for example, he or she missed a limitation date, resulting in financial loss on your part. If you think you have been badly represented in court, you will not be able to claim compensation for any losses this may have caused (see *NB*, below, on 'advocates' immunity'), but you may be able to make a judicial appeal. In either case, you should seek legal advice
see **Where to get help**

NB

- The Bar Council is planning to reform this procedure in April 1997. The three main changes will be:

  a. A lay Complaints Commissioner will be appointed by the Bar Council, via advertisement and interview. He or she will oversee the investigation of complaints and will dismiss cases where there is obviously no prima-facie case. If the Commissioner thinks there is a prima-facie case, or is in doubt, the matter will be sent to the PCC which will act as before now: it may dismiss or it may refer the complaint to one of the panels.

  b. A new kind of panel – Adjudication Panels – will be

established to deal with 'inadequate professional service' only. Inadequate professional service is a new category of unsatisfactory conduct, less serious than 'misconduct', and is where a barrister has provided services for a lay client which fall significantly below what could be expected from a barrister.

c. In cases of 'inadequate professional service' the Bar Council will be able to order a barrister to apologise and/or to repay or reduce fees. Where a client has suffered loss which is recoverable at law (i.e. through the small claims court) all panels will also be able to award compensation of up to £2,000. Compensation will not be available for hurt feelings, or where the advocates' immunity rules apply.

- You cannot sue a barrister for compensation for losses alleged to result from their conduct in court: for example, over whether they should have brought a particular witness before the court or not, or over the way they have presented your case. This is known as advocates' immunity. Complaints about inadequate representation are, however, taken extremely seriously by the Bar Council, and may result in a barrister being disbarred, particularly if it is decided that he or she has deceived the court.

- The Northern Irish and Scottish Bars are completely separate from the Bar of England and Wales (and each other), and have their own slightly different complaints procedures: contact them for details.

In *Northern Ireland* complaints should be addressed to:

> **Chief Executive**
> **Bar Library**
> **Royal Courts of Justice**
> **PO Box 414**
> **Belfast BT1 3JP**

> Tel: 01232 562349
> Fax: 01232 562350

In *Scotland* complaints should be addressed to:

The Dean
Faculty of Advocates
Advocates Library
Parliament House
Edinburgh EH1 1RF

Tel: 0131 260 5658
Fax: 0131 225 5341

Bookmakers

1. *Who Can I Complain To?*

The Sporting Life Green Seal Service
The Sporting Life
1 Canada Square
Canary Wharf
London E14 5AP

Tel: 0171 293 3905
Fax: 0171 293 3904

2. *What Sort of Complaints Do They Deal With?*

a. Disputes about the settlement of bets placed on sporting events of all kinds, where the Rules of the bookmaker in question state that the Green Seal Service has been adopted as the independent arbitration service in the event of a dispute. Most bookmakers have adopted the Green Seal Service, which is run by the *Sporting Life* newspaper.

b. As usual, complaints should first be taken up with the individual bookmaker concerned. Disputes at horserace meetings are usually referred immediately to the (impartial) ring inspector, who may be able to resolve the matter on the spot.

c. If your bet was with a racecourse bookmaker, and your complaint arises after you (or the bookmaker) have already left the meeting, it may be easier to contact the bookmaker through the relevant trade association. Not all bookmakers are members of trade associations, but most racecourse businesses are members of one of the regional associations affiliated to the National Association of Bookmakers (NAB), who will be able to point you in the right direction:

National Association of Bookmakers
298 Ewell Road
Surbiton
Surrey KT6 7AQ

Tel: 0181 390 8222
Tel: 0181 339 9940

A bookmakers' trade association may offer to arbitrate in a dispute, but none of them have independent complaints procedures or binding codes of practice for their members.

d. The Green Seal Service *cannot* investigate:

- disputes involving spread betting
- complaints about the way a betting shop or racetrack stand is run, regarding, for example, the size of queues or setting of prices
- allegations of fraud, drugging or other illegal practices at the sports event in question

e. Complaints should be made in writing, and include a clear copy of the disputed betting slip.

3. *How Independent Is the Complaints Procedure?*

The Green Seal Service is totally independent. It is run by the *Sporting Life* as a service to both punters and bookmakers, with a panel of *Sporting Life* staff and outside experts. Each case is judged individually and on its own merits; no precedents are set. On rare occasions, when a decision cannot be agreed by the panel, the *Sporting Life*'s editor will give the final judgement.

The Service has no legal standing but it is accepted by the betting industry and is included in the Rules of many bookmakers as an official arbitrator.

4. *Compensation/Redress?*

a. If the panel decides that the punter has a valid case, or to recommend a compromise, it will either write to the bookmaker direct, stating the reasons for its ruling, or ask the punter to return to the betting shop with the ruling (which is published in the paper). Bookmakers almost always abide by a Green Seal decision against them, which is usually that a punter should be paid a sum of money as winnings.

b. The Green Seal Service has no powers to enforce a judgement. If a bookmaker refuses to pay out on a bet after the panel has ruled that he should do so, it can only ask that he removes the *Sporting Life*'s name from his Rules as an official arbitrator. The Service will then refuse to offer advice in the future. If this happens, you may not be able to get the money that is due to you, as gambling debts are not recoverable at law. There are a couple of alternative options if you want to take things further (see *Other Options?*, below).

c. If the panel feels that the punter is wrong, and the bookmaker's settlement of a bet is in fact correct, it will publish a reply explaining the reasons for the settlement.

5. *Any Appeal?*

a. Not formally, although the Green Seal Service panel will always re-examine a case if new information is brought to its attention.

b. Unresolved complaints about horserace bets may be referred to Tattersalls Committee (see below).

6. *Other Options?*

● Disputes about betting at horserace meetings can be referred to Tattersalls Committee at any time. The Committee acts under the authority of the Jockey Club (JC) and consists of ten members, four of whom are bookmakers (one retired) and six of whom are other people with an interest in horseracing, recommended by the JC or existing members of the Committee, and including ex-stewards, racehorse owners and JC officials. They can be contacted at:

Tattersalls Committee
PO Box 13
19 Wilwyne Close
Grosvenor Road
Caversham
Reading
Berkshire RG4 0EP

Tel: 01734 461757

There is a charge for this service, related to the amount in dispute. Because of the legal situation, Tattersalls Committee is also unable to enforce its judgements, but, if it rules against a bookmaker (or punter) who then refuses to pay up, they will be reported to the Jockey Club as a defaulter and banned from working at (or attending) future race meetings. The Jockey Club can only enforce betting bans on premises controlled by it, i.e. at race meetings themselves; it has no powers to close down off-course betting shops (or to stop off-course betting by defaulting punters).

- Complaints involving spread betting should in the first instance be made to the compliance officer of the company in question, and may then be referred to the Securities and Futures Authority   *see* **Investment 2**
- You may object to a bookmaker's permit on the grounds that he is unfit to hold a licence. If you decide to do this, you should contact the bookmaker's local Magistrates' Court, where his betting permit will come up for annual renewal some time during the year. You will be asked to deposit a written objection. Bookmakers' licences require them to display and abide by a set of Rules, and to be of sound financial standing, among other things. A Green Seal Service or Tattersalls Committee judgement against a bookmaker will be influential in licence renewal cases.

- The National Association for the Protection of Punters (NAPP) is a consumer organisation and information service for betting customers. They may be able to help you argue your case:

  > NAPP
  > PO Box 1329
  > London SW1V 2HY

- If you have reason to believe something illegal has taken place, such as fraud or drugging, you should go to the police.

NB

- There are no time limits attached to making a complaint, but it should be noted that bookmakers are only obliged to keep records for *six months*, after which they may be destroyed.
- On many occasions, disputes are caused by a simple misunderstanding of the bookmaker's Rules, which all bookmakers must display, and which may vary from bookmaker to bookmaker. Many adjudications on betting disputes are published in the *Sporting Life* for the information of all readers.

Broadcasting 1 (BBC)

1. *Who Can I Complain To?*

Serious complaints should be made in writing to:

> The Head of Programme Complaints
> Programme Complaints Unit
> BBC Broadcasting House
> London W1A 1AA

2. *What Sort of Complaints Do They Deal With?*

a. Serious complaints about all radio and television programmes broadcast by the BBC.

b. Where you think there has been a specific and serious injustice or inaccuracy.

c. Where you think there has been a serious breach of accepted broadcasting standards as laid out in the BBC's *Producers' Guidelines*, including standards relating to:

   ● bad language or the portrayal of sex and violence
   ● other matters of taste and decency including the coverage of disasters
   ● bias, including racism, sexism and political bias in BBC presentation

d. Allegations of defamation, breach of copyright and complaints regarding other legal matters, including the balance of political coverage during election periods, can also be made to the Complaints Unit in the first instance.

3. *How Independent Is the Complaints Procedure?*

The procedure is internal but independent of programme makers' areas of the organisation. The Governors' Complaints Committee includes appointed members from outside the industry.

4. *Compensation/Redress?*

If the Programme Complaints Unit agrees with some or all of what you have to say, the BBC will find ways of making the appropriate acknowledgement or correction. This may be on-air if a significant unfairness or seriously misleading error of fact is found to have occurred, or in the relevant trade press if the impact is confined to a small professional circle.

Matters of law will be handled by the BBC's legal department.

5. *Any Appeal?*

If you are not satisfied after the Programme Complaints Unit has looked at your complaint, you may appeal to the Governors' Complaints Committee. This is the final stage of the procedure within the BBC.

6. *Other Options?*

Non-BBC programmes

Independent Television Commission	*see* **Broadcasting 2**
Radio Authority	*see* **Broadcasting 3**

Higher levels of appeal:

Broadcasting Complaints Commission	*see* **Broadcasting 4**
Broadcasting Standards Council	*see* **Broadcasting 5**

NB

- The *Producers' Guidelines* are available in bookshops. They are periodically revised to reflect changes in law and public opinion.
- Many programmes broadcast by the BBC are now made by independent production companies, but they are all covered by the BBC's complaints procedure.

Appendix

Other useful BBC phone numbers and addresses

- Immediate and minor complaints can be made by telephoning: **0171 580 4468**
- General comments, queries or criticism can be directed in writing to:

BBC Viewer & Listener Correspondence
Fourth Floor
Villiers House
The Broadway
Ealing
London W5 2PA

or by telephoning:

The Television Information Office: **0181 743 8000**

The Radio Information Office: **0181 580 4468**

Minicom number (TV comments only):   **0181 576 8988**

- Complaints about BBC Education programmes may be made on: **0181 746 1111**
- For radio and television reception advice, contact:

    BBC Engineering Information
    Villiers House
    The Broadway
    Ealing
    London W5 2PA

    Tel: 0181 231 9191

- 'Right to reply' and public access programmes include:

Biteback   **0181 741 3715**

Points of View   **0181 576 4560**

Broadcasting 2
(Independent/Commercial TV)

1. *Who Can I Complain To?*

The Independent Television Commission (ITC)
33 Foley Street
London W1P 7LB

Tel: 0171 255 3000
Fax: 0171 306 7800

2. *What Sort of Complaints Do They Deal With?*

a. The ITC is the public body responsible for licensing and regulating all non-BBC television services operating in or from the UK: Channel 3 (ITV), Channel 4, Channel 5, a range of cable and satellite services and text and data services.

b. The ITC receives complaints from viewers if they believe that a programme has broken the ITC's Programme Code concerning taste, decency, the portrayal of violence, privacy or impartiality.

3. *How Independent Is the Complaints Procedure?*

The ITC is an independent public body and replaced the Independent Broadcasting Authority (IBA) and the Cable Authority under the Broadcasting Act 1990.

4. *Compensation/Redress?*

The programme company may be asked to broadcast an apology, not to repeat the programme, or to make cuts where appropriate. If the ITC believes that the breach of its code has been serious enough, then it can impose financial penalties, shorten or revoke the programme maker's licence.

5. *Any Appeal?*

No.

6. *Other Options?*

BBC Programme Complaints Unit   *see* **Broadcasting 1**

Broadcasting Complaints Commission   *see* **Broadcasting 4**

Broadcasting Standards Council   *see* **Broadcasting 5**

Broadcasting 3
(Independent/Commercial Radio)

1. *Who Can I Complain To?*

The Radio Authority
Holbrook House
14 Great Queen Street
London WC2B 5DG

Tel: 0171 430 2724
Fax: 0171 405 7062

2. *What Sort of Complaints Do They Deal With?*

a. Complaints against independent or 'commercial' radio stations. The Authority does not deal with complaints against any of the BBC's radio services   *see* **Broadcasting 1**

b. Complaints about:

- programming, advertising and transmission
- bias or inaccuracy of news, misleading information or material which is generally likely to offend

3. *How Independent Is the Complaints Procedure?*

The Authority is the independent licensing and regulatory body for commercial radio in the UK, although it is funded by the industry. Its seven members are appointed by the Department of National Heritage.

4. *Compensation/Redress?*

The Authority will take up the matter with the radio station and if the complaint is upheld may:

- admonish the company and/or request an apology and/or a correction, on-air if appropriate
- impose a penalty and/or fine, or a shortening of the station's licence, or the revocation of the licence

5. Any Appeal?

No.

6. Other Options?

- An alternative body to complain to about matters of taste and decency is the Broadcasting Standards Council (BSC), which has the power to have an adjudication published in the press, but cannot revoke a radio station's licence

  see **Broadcasting 5**
- To complain about unjust or unfair treatment or infringement of privacy in an independent radio programme you should contact the Broadcasting Complaints Commission (BCC)   *see* **Broadcasting 4**
- To complain about BBC radio programmes

  see **Broadcasting 1**

NB

- Complaints should be made *within 42 days* of the programme being broadcast, as after this time tapes may be destroyed.
- The BSC and the BCC are due to merge in April 1997. This will not affect the remit or powers of the Radio Authority.

Broadcasting 4 (Treatment)

1. *Who Can I Complain To?*

The Secretary
The Broadcasting Complaints Commission (BCC)
Grosvenor Gardens House
7 The Sanctuary
London SW1P 3JS

Tel: 0171 233 0544 (shared with the BSC – make sure to ask for the BCC)
Fax: 0171 222 3172

2. *What Sort of Complaints Do They Deal With?*

a. Complaints about television and radio programmes and teletext transmissions broadcast on *all* terrestrial, cable and satellite channels.

b. Allegations of:

  * 'unjust or unfair' treatment in a broadcast programme
  * unwarranted infringement of privacy in, or in connection with, the obtaining of material for a broadcast programme

c. The Commission will *not* normally investigate complaints which are already subject to court (e.g. libel) proceedings.

3. *How Independent Is the Complaints Procedure?*

The BCC is an independent statutory body set up under the **Broadcasting Act 1990.**

4. Compensation/Redress?

a. Where a complaint is upheld, and the complainant would like some public redress (which may not be the case in infringement of privacy cases), a summary will normally be published in the national or regional press as appropriate. The Commission may also direct the broadcaster to broadcast a summary of the adjudication on the same channel as, and normally at a similar time to, the programme which was subject to the complaint.

b. The Commission has no powers to compel a broadcaster to apologise or to award financial compensation.

5. Any Appeal?

No.

6. Other Options?

BBC Programme Complaints Unit	*see* **Broadcasting 1**
Independent Television Commission	*see* **Broadcasting 2**
Radio Authority	*see* **Broadcasting 3**
Broadcasting Standards Council (BSC)	*see* **Broadcasting 5**
For advice on legal action	*see* **Where to get help**

NB

● The BSC and the BCC are due to merge in April 1997. This is not expected to affect the complaints procedures.

Broadcasting 5 (Standards)

1. *Who Can I Complain To?*

The Director
Broadcasting Standards Council (BSC)
7 The Sanctuary
London SW1P 3JS

Tel: 0171 233 0544 (shared with the BCC – make sure to ask for the BSC)
Fax: 0171 233 0397

2. *What Sort of Complaints Do They Deal With?*

a. Complaints about any television and radio programmes that have already been broadcast (it does not have powers of preview and cannot investigate programmes that have yet to be shown).

b. Complaints relating to the portrayal of violence and sexual conduct, and matters of taste and decency (such as bad language or the treatment of disasters).

3. *How Independent Is the Complaints Procedure?*

The BSC is an independent statutory body established under the **Broadcasting Act 1990.**

4. *Compensation/Redress?*

The Council issues a regular bulletin of its findings to the media, and may require a summary of its findings to be placed in the press or broadcast at the broadcaster's expense.

5. *Any Appeal?*

No.

6. *Other Options?*

BBC Programme Complaints Unit	*see* **Broadcasting 1**
Independent Television Commission	*see* **Broadcasting 2**
Radio Authority	*see* **Broadcasting 3**
Broadcasting Complaints Commission	*see* **Broadcasting 4**

NB

- There is a time limit of *two months* after transmission for complaints to be considered.
- The BSC and the BCC are due to merge in April 1997. This is not expected to affect the complaints procedures.

Builders

1. *Who Can I Complain To?*

National House-Building Council (NHBC)
Buildmark House
Chiltern Avenue
Amersham
Bucks HP6 5AP

Tel: 01494 434477
Fax: 01494 728521

Note: The NHBC scheme only covers new houses. For complaints about repairs, alterations, extensions, etc. to existing buildings see Other Options, below.

2. *What Sort of Complaints Do They Deal With?*

a.   Complaints about building work and claims for the cost of repairs that come under the remit of NHBC's 'Buildmark' warranty and insurance scheme for new homes.

The majority of new homes built each year in the UK are subject to the Buildmark warranty. This means that NHBC inspectors have conducted spot checks during construction to ensure that the builder is complying with the Council's standards. On completion, and provided it is satisfied that its standards have been 'substantially complied with', the NHBC will issue the house with a Ten Year Notice (Buildmark certificate). This notice brings the full benefits of cover into operation.

b.   If you buy a new house under the Buildmark warranty, you are protected in three ways:

   i.   If you are buying a new house 'off plan' (speculatively built), or are having a house 'custom built' under the scheme – whereby a registered builder agrees to complete building work to the NHBC's technical requirements – the warranty protects against loss of deposit and/or the additional cost of completion by another builder if the original builder goes bankrupt *before completion* of the property. If this happens you should *contact the NHBC* direct.

   ii. For the *first two years* after the property is completed, it is the builder's responsibility to put right, at his own expense, any defects arising from a failure to comply with the NHBC's minimum standards. If this happens you must *complain to the builder* in writing.

      If a dispute arises between you and the builder, only then should you *contact the NHBC* and request their free conciliation service. Under conciliation the NHBC agrees to act as an independent third party to decide whether breaches of its standards have occurred and what remedial action, if any, the builder needs to take to comply with those standards.

   iii. From the *third to the tenth year*, insurance cover is provided for 'major damage' caused by structural faults, and for drainage system defects which result from a failure to comply with the NHBC's technical requirements. You should *contact the NHBC* direct about such problems; they will then visit the property to assess the claim.

c. If at any stage of the process a dispute remains unresolved – for example after an attempt at conciliation under part ii, or if you do not agree with the NHBC's assessment of your claim under part iii and have exhausted the internal complaints procedure of the NHBC (by writing to the Director of Claims at NHBC's Head Office) – you can refer the matter to independent arbitration.

d. The definition of 'major damage' and the conditions *not* covered under part iii are set out in the Buildmark warranty document, which you should examine carefully, as with all insurance policies.

e. It is important to notify the appropriate person (your builder or the NHBC) of any defects in the property as soon as possible after the problems become apparent. Failure to do so may jeopardise your chances of making a successful claim.

f. The Buildmark scheme does *not* cover any work done after the date on which the Ten Year Notice was awarded, nor discrepancies between what you wanted and what the contractor has built (under custom build contracts), nor builders who are not registered with the NHBC.

3. *How Independent Is the Complaints Procedure?*

a. The NHBC is the self-regulatory body of the private housebuilding industry, funded by the fees paid by registered builders. It is governed by an independent council with members drawn from a wide range of professional, commercial and consumer organisations associated with the housebuilding industry. Although builders form the largest single group, they have no overall majority.

b. The NHBC arbitration scheme is completely independent
    of the NHBC, and is run by the Chartered Institute of
    Arbitrators. The Arbitrator appointed is usually a qualified
    architect, surveyor or engineer. You should be aware that
    arbitration in building cases can get very expensive,
    although a simplified procedure has recently been intro-
    duced with the aim of bringing average costs down.

4. *Compensation/Redress?*

a. Under the scheme you should recover your deposit, or any
    additional costs of completing a house to NHBC standards,
    if the original builder goes bust before construction is fin-
    ished.

b. As long as the builder *and* the house being built are
    registered with the NHBC, problems arising from non-
    adherence to NHBC standards and revealed by NHBC
    inspection during or on completion of construction (before
    the Buildmark is awarded), or noticed by you during the
    first two years, should be rectified within a 'reasonable
    time' and at the builder's expense. (If you are having a
    house custom built, you should take extra care – see *NB*,
    below.)

c. If the builder is still trading and fails to carry out repairs,
    the NHBC will, in certain circumstances, have the job done
    (and then recoup the costs from the builder). If the builder
    has become insolvent during the first two years of cover,
    the scheme includes insurance to cover the cost of repairs.

d. All 'major defects' emerging during the first ten years
    should be put right one way or another. 'Major defects' are
    only as defined under the scheme and must be caused by a
    builder's failure to comply with the NHBC's technical
    specifications.

e. The Buildmark scheme does *not* cover you for any added
    expense incurred if unforeseen repairs mean you have to wait
    to take initial possession of your home. Once the Ten Year
    Notice has been issued, the *only* costs you are covered for are

those of alternative accommodation (if this is necessary) during repairs, and of certain professional (e.g. surveyor's) fees agreed in advance.

f. If you go to arbitration you may be awarded consequential costs and expenses in addition to amounts for repair (and/or, occasionally, structural devaluation where repair would be disproportionately expensive and is not necessary for safety reasons). The Arbitrator will also decide how the costs of arbitration itself, including his or her own fees, should be divided between the parties.

5. *Any Appeal?*

a. If you are unhappy with the way the NHBC has assessed any insurance claim under the scheme, and are not taking your case to arbitration or to court, you can ask the Insurance Ombudsman Bureau to investigate. The Ombudsman can confirm or vary the decision, and can make awards for inconvenience as well as financial loss   *see* **Insurance 2**

b. If you decide not to accept the decision of the Insurance Ombudsman you can still go to arbitration, or to court.

c. The outcome of arbitration is normally legally binding on both sides.

6. *Other Options?*

a. About 15 per cent of new homes built every year are warranted by Zurich Municipal under a similar scheme, linked to their own register of house builders.

Zurich also offers a policy called 'Custom Build', designed solely for those building their own homes. It offers a greater level of protection than their standard scheme (including more frequent inspections) and is issued in the name of the householder not the builder, on the basis that many excellent small builders never become 'registered house builders'.

They can be contacted at:

Zurich Building Guarantees
Zurich Municipal
Hermes House
6 Southwood Crescent
Farnborough
Hants GU14 0NL

Tel: 01252 522000
Fax: 01252 372989

b. If your complaint is about repairs, modifications or extensions to an existing property *and* you have already taken out a guarantee under the scheme run by the National Register of Warranted Builders, you will be covered: if your builder goes bust before completion; for the first two years against defective workmanship and materials; and for another three years against major structural defects. Claims are assessed by an independent loss adjuster, and ultimately arbitration is available (from the independent Institute of Arbitrators, as above).

If you are *not* covered by this guarantee (which is neither obligatory nor automatic, and costs 1% of the gross price of the building contract) it is still worth finding out if your builder is on the register, which is run by the Federation of Master Builders. If they are, the FMB will attempt to resolve any dispute, with the added leverage that it may, in extreme cases, remove a builder from its register. To check if your builder is registered contact:

The Federation of Master Builders
Gordon Fisher House
14/15 Great James Street
London WC1N 3DP

Tel: 0171 242 7583
Fax: 0171 404 0296

c. If:

● you decide not to go to arbitration, *or*
● your new house is not covered by a warranty scheme, *or*

- your house is more than ten years old, *or*
- your complaint is about a custom built house being different to what you wanted, *or*
- the builder who has carried out your repairs, modifications, etc. is not on the NRWB

your only option is legal action under contract law
see **Goods & Services**
Where to get help

d. For more information on arbitration   *see* **Where to get help**

see also **Architects 1**

Architects 2

Surveyors

NB

- If your house is being 'custom built', i.e. to order and often to a unique design on your own land, you must be extra careful. Simply using an NHBC-registered builder is not a guarantee that your house will be built to NHBC standards, or that you are covered by the Buildmark warranty if things go wrong. If you want your house to be covered by the NHBC scheme, you must ensure not only that the builder is registered, but that they have registered your house for Buildmark cover with the NHBC. If you are in any doubt, call the NHBC Members' Department (on the number given above) to check. It is also a good idea to check out other recent work done by the builder (as registered builders are not systematically re-vetted by the NHBC after initial registration), and to take legal advice to make sure it is written into your building contract that the house is to be built to NHBC standards under the Buildmark scheme. An alternative is the Zurich Custom Build scheme (see above).
- Without a warranty from either the NHBC or Zurich Municipal it can be difficult to get a mortgage on a new home. *This does not mean that such warranties are a substitute for an independent surveyor's report*, and the NHBC has stressed that 'issue of cover is not itself a guarantee that a property is completely free from defects'.

Building Societies

1. *Who Can I Complain To?*

The Office of the Building Societies Ombudsman
Millbank Tower
Millbank
London SW1P 4XS

Tel: 0171 931 0044
Fax: 0171 931 8485

2. *What Sort of Complaints Do They Deal With?*

a. Complaints about UK building societies, or organisations associated with them. As with other Ombudsman schemes, you should first address your complaint to the particular building society you have been dealing with. If you are not satisfied with their response, you can then refer the matter to the Ombudsman. You should do this within *six months* of the time you first became aware of the matter, not including the time taken by the internal complaints procedure of the society.

b. If you think a building society has infringed your legal rights, has treated you unfairly, or has been guilty of maladministration (including inefficiency or undue delay) in a way that results in you losing money or suffering inconvenience.

c. The Ombudsman generally deals with complaints about the operation or termination of building society accounts relating to:

- mortgages and other loans
- savings accounts
- banking services, including cheques, standing orders, direct debits, automatic cash dispensers and foreign exchange
- trusteeship
- executors

d. Complaints will *not* be dealt with if the complainant is not personally affected by the building society's actions (unless they are acting on behalf of a personally affected complainant with written authorisation), or if the complaint is made on behalf of a limited company.

e. For complaints about financial loss incurred because a building society has gone bust, see *NB*, below.

3. *How Independent Is the Complaints Procedure?*

The Scheme is funded by the industry, but is legally required under the **Building Societies Act 1986** to act impartially and fairly. The Ombudsman reports to a special Council which has a majority of members representing public or consumer interests. All societies are required to be members of the Scheme.

4. *Compensation/Redress?*

The Ombudsman can award up to £100,000 for financial loss, expense and inconvenience. He may also direct the society to contribute towards your out-of-pocket expenses in bringing a complaint. He has no power to fine a society or impose any other penalty.
See also *NB*, below.

5. *Any Appeal?*

No, but you may be able to take legal action against the society if you have not accepted the Ombudsman's Final Decision. If you accept his Decision, both parties are normally bound by it.

6. *Other Options?*

Banking Ombudsman	*see* **Banks**
Insurance Ombudsman	*see* **Insurance 2**
Investment Ombudsman	*see* **Investment 3**

Pensions Ombudsman   *see* **Pensions**

Personal Investment Authority   *see* **Investment 1**

Insurance Brokers Registration Council   *see* **Insurance 1**

Credit Reference Agencies   *see* **Credit Reference Agencies**

Estate Agents   *see* **Estate Agents 1** *and* **2**

For advice about taking legal action   *see* **Where to get help**

NB

In the event of a building society becoming insolvent the *Building Societies Investor Protection Fund* is obliged to pay each depositor or investor 90 per cent of the client's 'protected investment', up to a maximum of £18,000. The 'protected investment' is the first £20,000 of the client's shares or deposits. Multiple accounts in the same name will be aggregated, but in joint accounts each holder will have a protected investment of £20,000. The Fund does not protect deferred shares, certificates of deposit or Permanent Interest Bearing Shares. To find out about the Fund, contact:

Building Societies Investor Protection Fund
15 Great Marlborough Street
London W1V 2LL

Tel: 0171 437 9992

C

Charities

1. *Who Can I Complain To?*

The Charity Commission for England and Wales

London

St Alban's House
57–60 Haymarket
London SW1Y 4QX

Tel: 0171 210 4477
Fax: 0171 210 4545

Taunton

Woodfield House
Tangier
Taunton
Somerset TA1 4BL

Tel: 01823 345000
Fax: 01823 345003

Liverpool

2nd Floor
20 Kings Parade
Queens Dock
Liverpool L3 4DQ

Tel: 0151 703 1500
Fax: 0151 703 1555

The geographical areas served by these three offices are listed in the Appendix at the end of this entry. Complaints should be addressed to the appropriate office.

The Charity Commission only covers England and Wales. For Scotland and Northern Ireland contacts, see *Other Options?*, below.

2. *What Sort of Complaints Do They Deal With?*

a. The Commission mounts investigations into the running and integrity of charities only when there is good reason to do so. It will consider complaints where there is evidence suggesting that:

- the way a charity is run is putting its funds at risk
- the funds and assets of the charity are being used or applied in breach of trust
- the trustees are misleading the public or the Commission in a material way
- the trustees are improperly receiving unauthorised benefits from the charity
- proper accounts are not kept
- fund-raising or administrative costs are too high
- the charity is undertaking improper political activities (see *NB*, below)

b. It will *not* use its powers of investigation to resolve internal disputes between members of a charity or its trustees, where no grounds for investigation exist. Neither will it get involved in legal proceedings taken against a charity, including those for debt collection, unless the Attorney-General asks it to do so.

c. Complaints should be made in writing to the appropriate Commission office, including full details of the allegation, with an estimate of the value of property you believe has been misused if appropriate, and details of any attempts you have made to put right what you believe to be misconduct.

d. The Commission will not normally accept anonymous complaints. It will respect confidences as far as possible, unless and until it decides to publish the results of an investigation, or information given in confidence is required under a Court Order during legal proceedings.

e. It is a criminal offence knowingly or recklessly to supply false or misleading information to the Commission. Anyone able to give information in good faith, however, is encouraged to do so.

f.   You will normally be told within one calendar month of receipt of your complaint whether the Commission intends to carry out an investigation. You will also be told the outcome of the investigation, and in long cases you will be kept informed of progress at least every six months.

3. *How Independent Is the Complaints Procedure?*

a.   Most investigations are carried out by the staff in the Commission's Investigation Division, assisted by lawyers and accountants. Specialists may also be consulted. Investigators are under a duty to act fairly and impartially, and have the power to obtain and copy all relevant information and documents from the charity, its advisers and bankers.

b.   The Charity Commission's task is to seek to preserve the integrity of charity. Up to five Commissioners are appointed by the Secretary of State for National Heritage. They are answerable to the courts for their legal decisions and their interpretation of charity law, and to the Secretary of State for National Heritage and Parliament for the effective performance of the Commission as a government department. There have to be at least three Commissioners, two of whom must be qualified lawyers. The powers and functions of the Commissioners are set out in the **Charities Act 1993**.

4. *Compensation/Redress?*

a.   If an investigation finds misconduct or mismanagement the Commission can:

- suspend and/or remove trustees and employees
- appoint new or additional trustees
- freeze bank accounts
- prohibit all further fund-raising
- stop further actions by the trustees in dealing with the charity's property
- refer the matter to the appropriate authorities for them to consider legal proceedings for the recovery of charity property or to compensate the charity for any loss

- refer the matter to the police, the Serious Fraud Office, the Inland Revenue or another public body

Some of these actions can be taken only if the Commission is satisfied that there is a risk to charity property.

b. In less serious cases, the Commission may simply give a charity a warning and ensure that any problems are sorted out. If necessary, the Commission can continue to monitor the future activities of the charity.

5. *Any Appeal?*

If you are not happy with the way the Charity Commission has handled your complaint, you can write to the Customer Complaints Manager at the office you have been dealing with. All complaints of this kind will initially be dealt with by a senior member of staff, and can also be reviewed by another senior manager.

6. *Other Options?*

- If you are concerned about any aspect of misconduct or mismanagement in the administration of *Scottish charities* or charities registered in England and Wales and operating in Scotland, contact:

> **The Director**
> **Scottish Charities Office**
> **Crown Office**
> **25 Chambers Street**
> **Edinburgh EH1 1LA**
>
> Tel: 0131 226 2626
> Fax: 0131 226 6912

The SCO operates under the aegis of the Lord Advocate, who has similar powers of investigation and redress to those of the Charity Commission. A leaflet, *The Supervision of Charities in Scotland*, is available from this office. Charities in Scotland are registered with the Inland Revenue.

- In *Northern Ireland* there is neither a Charity Commissioner nor a register of charities. The Department of Health and Social Services is the charity authority for Northern Ireland but has less power than the Charity Commission to investigate or take action against charity trustees.

  The Royal Ulster Constabulary are more involved with charities in Northern Ireland than the police are in England and Wales, and the Department can ask the Attorney-General or the High Court to take action where appropriate.

  If a complaint involves any question of criminal activity, it should be brought to the attention of the RUC. If there is no question of criminal activity, you may either apply directly to the High Court, under section 29 of the **Charities Act (Northern Ireland) 1964,** asking them to take action, or ask the Department of Health and Social Services to look into the matter. The Department's address is:

  > **Department of Health and Social Services**
  > **Charities Branch**
  > **Annexe 3**
  > **Castle Buildings**
  > **Stormont Estate**
  > **Belfast BT4 3RA**
  >
  > Tel: 01232 522780
  > Fax: 01232 523203

- If, after complaining via the Commission's Customer Complaints system, you are still unhappy about the way your complaint has been handled, or about the way an investigation has been conducted, you might wish to approach the Parliamentary Ombudsman (via your MP)
  see **Government Departments**

NB

- One of the more difficult principles to apply in practice is the extent to which charities may engage in political activities. Charities are *not* allowed to have political 'purposes', which are defined as 'purposes designed to promote the interests of a political party, or to seek or oppose changes in the law or government policy or decisions, whether in this country or abroad'. However, the trustees of a charity *may* do some things of a political nature as a means of achieving the purposes of the charity, i.e. 'any political activity undertaken by trustees must be in furtherance of, and ancillary to, the charity's stated objects and within its powers'. The Charity Commission has produced a leaflet clarifying this, called *Political Activities and Campaigning by Charities*, and obtainable from any of its offices.

● If you are involved with a charity yourself and wish to complain about the service you or your charity have received from the Commission, you should complain to the Secretariat at the London office. The procedure for dealing with this kind of complaint is that set out under 5, above.

Appendix

Distribution of work for each office, based on charities' areas of benefit/operation:

1.   London Office

National and Overseas charities based in: all the Boroughs in the Greater London area.

   Local charities based in: Bedfordshire, Buckinghamshire, Cambridgeshire, East Sussex, Essex, Greater London, Hertfordshire, Kent, Norfolk, Northamptonshire, Suffolk, Surrey, West Sussex.

2.   Taunton Office

National and Overseas charities based in: Bedfordshire, Buckinghamshire, East Sussex, Hertfordshire, Kent, Surrey, West Sussex.

   Local charities based in: Avon, Berkshire, Cornwall, Devon, Dorset, Dyfed, Gloucestershire, Gwent, Hampshire, Hereford and Worcester, Isle of Wight, Mid Glamorgan, Oxfordshire, South Glamorgan, West Glamorgan.

3. **Liverpool Office**

   National and Overseas charities based in: Cambridgeshire, Essex, Norfolk, Northamptonshire, Suffolk.

   Local charities based in: Cheshire, Cleveland, Clwyd, Cumbria, Derbyshire, Durham, Greater Manchester, Gwynedd, Humberside, Lancashire, Leicestershire, Lincolnshire, Merseyside, North Yorkshire, Northumberland, Nottinghamshire, Powys, Shropshire, South Yorkshire, Staffordshire, Tyne and Wear, Warwickshire, West Midlands, West Yorkshire.

- All *Welsh* general charities, operating throughout Wales but not elsewhere, are dealt with in the *Liverpool* office.
- All *charities administered by the National Health Service* are dealt with by the NHS Charities Review Section in the *Liverpool* office.
- All *charities in connection with the Armed Forces* are dealt with by the Services Charities Section in the *Taunton* office.

Child Support Agency

1. *Who Can I Complain To?*

Stage 1

Child Support Officer at the office you have been dealing with

Stage 2

Child Support Appeal Tribunals (CSAT)
8th Floor
Anchorage Two
Anchorage Quay
Salford Quays
Manchester M5 2YN

Stage 3

> **The Office of the Child Support Commissioners** (CSC)
> **Harp House**
> **83 Farringdon Street**
> **London EC4A 4BT**

2. *What Sort of Complaints Do They Deal With?*

a. If you disagree with a Child Support Officer's (CSO's) decision there are three stages of appeal, as indicated above. Initial requests for review of a CSA decision should be sent to the address appearing on the letter of notification you will have been sent, and will be dealt with by a (different) CSO. If you are still unhappy after such a review, you can appeal to the Child Support Appeal Tribunal. The last stage within this system is further appeal to the Child Support Commissioner on a point of law.

b. Any absent parent, parent with care or a child in Scotland (see *NB*, below) who is unhappy about a CSO's decision can complain via this system.

c. *Stage 1*

> i. You can apply for your case to be *reviewed* if you believe that, at the time of making the decision, the CSO dealing with your case
>
> - did not know a relevant fact
> - was mistaken about a relevant fact
> - was wrong in law
>
> ii. If this is so, you should write to the address that appears on your notification, stating why you disagree with the decision. This kind of review is called a 'Section 18' ('Section 20' in *Northern Ireland*) or 'Second Tier' review and will only take place if, after reading your complaint, a second CSO believes one of the above mistakes may have been made. You must complain *within 28 days* of the date written at the top of the decision letter.

iii. Second Tier reviews have to be carried out by a different CSO from the one who made the original decision with which you disagree. If a review is carried out, all relevant people will be notified and given the opportunity to make observations.

d. *Stage 2*

i. You can *appeal* to the Child Support Appeal Tribunal (CSAT) if you are unhappy because:

- a second CSO decided not to review your case
- the CSO did not change the maintenance assessment after review
- of the way the maintenance assessment was changed

ii. Review by a CSO is necessary as a preliminary to appeals to the CSAT except in one special case, where this stage may be skipped. This is where the CSO gives a 'reduced benefit direction' to the Benefits Agency, telling it to reduce the amount of benefit received by a parent with care, in an attempt to make the parent cooperate with them in setting maintenance for the child or children. If a CSO has issued such a direction about you, you may appeal direct to a CSAT.

iii. If you decide to appeal, you should do so in writing to the address given above. *You have 28 days to appeal, beginning on the date on which the decision is posted to you (which will be at the top of the decision letter) and ending on the day your signed letter of appeal is received by the Independent Tribunal Service.* Do *not* send your appeal to the CSA as this will delay the process and you may run out of time.

iv. Your letter should include:

- what decision you wish to appeal against
- the date of that decision
- the reference number quoted on the letter from the CSO
- why you think the decision is wrong

v. Make sure you sign and date your letter of appeal. You

may appeal yourself, or authorise someone else to on your behalf. Unless the person you authorise is a barrister, advocate or solicitor, you will still need to sign the letter of appeal yourself. At the actual hearing you may also be represented by anybody you feel can best put forward your views.

vi. At the tribunal, all the participants (usually you or your representative, the other party to the appeal or their representative, and a Presenting Officer representing the CSA) have a chance to present their case with any evidence, call any witnesses they want, and question any of the witnesses, including each other. Everyone is also expected to answer questions from tribunal members, if asked. At the end of the tribunal the Chair summarises the evidence.

vii. The CSAT's role is to establish the facts of the case and then to apply the relevant law. You have a right to appeal to the CSAT and, unlike in court, you do not have to pay any costs even if your appeal is not successful.

viii. A decision by a CSAT can be set aside if there is a good reason to do so, for example if relevant papers were delayed or not sent to the tribunal. If you think there is a reason for the CSAT decision to be set aside you should write as soon as possible to the clerk of the tribunal saying why. If the decision is set aside your appeal will be heard again.

e. *Stage 3*

i. If you disagree with the decision of a CSAT, you can appeal *on a point of law only* to a Child Support Commissioner (CSC). You need to obtain leave to do so from either the Chairman of the CSAT or from a Commissioner.

ii. An error in a point of law is where, for example, the CSAT:

- failed to apply the correct law
- wrongly interpreted the Acts or Regulations
- breached the rules of natural justice
- took into account irrelevant matters and did not consider relevant matters

- didn't record adequately in writing the reasons for their decisions
- gave a decision supported by insufficient or no evidence
- found the facts in such a way that no person acting judicially and properly instructed as to the relevant matters could have come to the determination under appeal

You cannot appeal simply because you do not agree with facts or opinions.

iii. You should apply in writing to the CSAT Chairman for leave to appeal *within three months* of being notified of the tribunal's decision (special forms for doing this will be available at the tribunal). If the Chairman refuses leave, you then have *42 days* to apply direct to the Commissioner at the address above.

iv. All applications for leave to appeal should include:

- your name and address
- a copy of the tribunal decision you wish to appeal against
- the reasons on which you base your appeal
- a copy of your refusal from the Chair if you are now applying to the Commissioner
- your written authority for anybody (other than a legal professional) who is going to represent you, and
- the address of your representative if you wish any correspondence to be sent to them rather than you

v. If the Chairman of the CSAT grants you leave to appeal, you then have *42 days* to appeal to the CSC office. Your appeal must contain all the above information plus a copy of the Chair's decision granting leave to appeal. If the Commissioner grants you leave to appeal, your application for leave will usually be treated as your appeal.

vi. Most appeals to a Commissioner are decided on written evidence and without an oral hearing, but you may request one if you wish. If one is held it will be in public unless the Commissioner decides there are special reasons for keeping it private.

vii. If the Chief CSC thinks your appeal involves an important and difficult question of law, it may be dealt with by a tribunal of Commissioners (i.e. three). If the tribunal cannot agree, the decision will be that of the majority.

3. *How Independent Is the Complaints Procedure?*

At *Stage 1* the CSO review procedure is internal.

At *Stage 2* CSATs are heard by the Independent Tribunal Service, which is completely independent of the CSA. The tribunal consists of a chairman who is a lawyer, and two other members from the local community.

At *Stage 3* Child Support Commissioners are independent law officers, usually judges, completely separate from the CSA.

4. *Compensation/Redress?*

a. If at review, appeal or further appeal the investigating body finds in your favour, the maintenance decision will be adjusted as appropriate.

b. You will be informed in writing of the decisions at every stage, including reasons except at *Stage 3* if everyone concerned has agreed that the Commissioner does not have to provide any.

c. You will be able to claim travelling and other unavoidable expenses incurred as a result of appealing to a tribunal. You should check with the Commissioner's office to see if expenses will be paid for a *Stage 3* appeal.

5. *Any Appeal?*

a. There is *no* appeal against a decision not to set aside a CSAT decision.

b. There is *no* right of appeal against a refusal of leave to appeal to a CSC, and the Commissioner does not have to give any reasons for the decision to refuse your application. If you think a refusal is wrong there is a small possibility you might be able to seek judicial review; you should take legal advice about this.

c. If you have been through the whole system and are still unhappy, you *may* appeal to the Court of Appeal or Court of Session in Scotland, but *only on a point of law*. If you wish to do so, you must apply to the Commissioner (or the Tribunal of Commissioners) for leave to appeal *within three months* of the date on which you were given written notice of the decision. If this is refused, you then have *only six weeks* to apply directly to the Court of Appeal or Court of Session for leave of appeal. If you are granted leave to appeal, you have *six weeks* to lodge your appeal. You should always seek legal advice in such cases   *see* **Where to get help**

6. *Other Options?*

If you think there has been 'maladministration' in the handling of your case, you may ask your MP to refer it to the Parliamentary Ombudsman   *see* **Government Departments**

NB

- Children of 12 or over who live in Scotland may apply for child support maintenance, and may therefore ask for reviews and appeal, in their own right.
- You can also apply for your case to be reviewed if your circumstances have changed in a way that will affect the amount of maintenance (if any) that should be paid. If you think this has happened, ask for a 'change of circumstances review'.
- A 'periodic review' will normally be carried out automatically once an assessment has been in force for 104 weeks (two years).
- It is important to try and keep to all the deadlines mentioned. Late appeals to a CSAT may only go ahead at the discretion

of the Tribunal Chair. Only in exceptional circumstances may a Chairman's refusal to extend the time limit be set aside. If you miss any of the deadlines in *Stage 3*, you may still apply direct to the Commissioner, but he will only accept your application if he thinks there are 'special reasons' for the delay.

- You can withdraw an appeal at any time and you will not be penalised.
- The Agency, the Independent Tribunal Service and the Commissioners will not, without written consent, disclose addresses of any of the parties involved or other information which could lead to them being located. They may, however, pass on information to Housing Benefit or Council Tax Benefit authorities or to other courts or tribunals in connection with your case.
- This entry is based on information given in Child Support Agency leaflet number 2006, *A Guide to Reviews and Appeals*, available from any CSA Centre.

Companies House

1. *Who Can I Complain To?*

Stage 1

The relevant **section head** at the office you have been dealing with.

The addresses and phone numbers of the seven regional offices are listed in the Appendix at the end of this entry – ask them for the name of the appropriate member of staff

For central enquiries:	**Tel: 01222 380801**
For complaints about Post Search:	**Tel: 01222 380111**
or (for Scottish registered companies)	**Tel: 0131 535 5800**

Stage 2

The Chief Executive at the Cardiff office (for England and Wales) *or*
The Registrar for Scotland at the Edinburgh office.

Stage 3

> **The Complaints Adjudicator for Companies House**
> **PO Box 2**
> **Fakenham**
> **Norfolk NR21 0RJ**

2. *What Sort of Complaints Do They Deal With?*

a. Most complaints to Companies House are about errors and omissions in and legibility of microfiched documents. There is a special form for such complaints, ML7.

b. Complaints about any other aspect of Companies House performance or standards of service should receive a reply within 10 working days.

c. Complaints are handled progressively as indicated above. Problems which remain unresolved at any stage should be referred in writing to the address given for the next stage.

3. *How Independent Is the Complaints Procedure?*

Stages 1 and 2 are internal.
   The Adjudicator is a lawyer who acts as an impartial referee.

4. *Compensation/Redress?*

a. Errors in microfiche information should be corrected within 5 working days unless documents need to be resubmitted, in which case they should be corrected within 20 days.

b. Refunds are available if it is found that a company search undertaken in a Companies House search room is delivered outside the published target time.

c. In general, if the internal complaints procedure or the Adjudicator finds a complaint to be justified, the matter should be put right and you may receive an apology where appropriate.

d. If the investigation of a complaint reveals that a company director has failed to comply with the legal obligation to provide accurate and complete information to Companies House, they may be prosecuted and, if found guilty, fined up to £5,000 for every offence.

5. *Any Appeal?*

a. If you are still dissatisfied after complaining to the Adjudicator you can complain to:

> **The Minister for Company Affairs**
> **Department of Trade and Industry**
> **Ashdown House**
> **123 Victoria Street**
> **London SW1H 0ET**

b. Alternatively (or *after* complaining to the DTI), and only if your complaint relates to maladministration, you can ask an MP to refer your case to the Parliamentary Ombudsman
see **Government Departments**

Appendix

Regional Offices of Companies House

London

> **55–71 City Road**
> **London EC1Y 1BB**
>
> Tel: 0171 253 9393

Manchester

> **75 Mosley Street**
> **Manchester M2 2HR**
>
> Tel: 0161 236 7500

Birmingham

> **Central Library**
> **Chamberlain Square**
> **Birmingham B3 3HQ**
>
> Tel: 0121 233 9047

Leeds

> **25 Queen Street**
> **Leeds LS1 2TW**
>
> Tel: 0131 535 5800

Cardiff

> **Crown Way**
> **Cardiff CF4 3UZ**
>
> **Tel: 01222 388588**

Edinburgh

> **37 Castle Terrace**
> **Edinburgh EH1 2EB**
>
> **Tel: 0131 535 5800**

Glasgow

> **7 West George Street**
> **Glasgow G2 1BQ**
>
> **Tel: 0141 221 5513**

Conveyancers (Licensed)

1. *Who Can I Complain To?*

The Council for Licensed Conveyancers
16 Glebe Road
Chelmsford
Essex CM1 1QG

Tel: 01245 349599
Fax: 01245 348380

2. *What Sort of Complaints Do They Deal With?*

a. The Council must investigate any complaint made against a licensed conveyancer whether the person making the complaint has used the services of a licensed conveyancer or not. All conveyancers must be licensed.

b. Complaints considered include allegations of any kind of professional misconduct, including:

- conflicts of interest
- fee disputes

- failure to respond to professional correspondence
- generally acting unprofessionally

c. Complaints *not* considered include claims for damages due to negligence, which are covered by the Council's Professional Insurance arrangements.

3. *How Independent Is the Complaints Procedure?*

The Council is a self-regulatory body, created by statute. It currently has 15 members, 8 of whom are licensed conveyancers, 7 of whom are nominated, including two nominated by the Department of Trade and Industry. The Investigating Committee is made up of a mixture of licensed conveyancers and nominated members, to include at least one of those nominated by the DTI.

4. *Compensation/Redress?*

a. The Investigating Committee has the power to refer a licensed conveyancer to the Disciplinary and Appeals Committee. The Disciplinary Committee has the power to order that a conveyancer's licence is suspended, withdrawn permanently or for a period of time, or re-issued subject to conditions.

b. If the Investigating Committee decides that an inadequate service has been provided, the Council has the power under the **Courts and Legal Services Act 1990** to order a licensed conveyancer to:

- put matters right at their own expense
- take other necessary action at their own expense
- refund part or all of any fee already paid for the service, and/or waive the right to recover part or all of any fee
- pay compensation of up to £1,000

It should be noted that these powers of redress only apply to the client of a licensed conveyancer, not to complainants other than the client.

5. *Any Appeal?*

Not within the CLC, but see *Other Options?*, below.

6. *Other Options?*

- If you are not satisfied with the decision of the Council's Investigating Committee, you may refer the complaint to the Legal Services Ombudsman. You must do this *within three months* of the date of the notification of the Committee's decision

  see **Legal Profession**

- If the person you have used does not have a licence to practise as a conveyancer, you should contact a Trading Standards Officer   *see* **Goods & Services**

Council Tax

1. *Who Can I Complain To?*

Stage 1

For valuation appeals: The **Listing Officer** at your local branch of the **Valuation Office Agency** (the address is listed on your council tax bill, and in the phone book under 'Valuation Office')
For all other appeals: **Your local council** (at the address on your council tax bill)

Stage 2

Valuation Tribunal (at the address given to you in *Stage 1*)

Note: For details of how the procedure described differs in Scotland, *and for how to complain about domestic rates in* Northern Ireland, *see* Other Options?, *below.*

2. *What Sort of Complaints Do They Deal With?*

There are four main kinds of *appeal* against decisions connected with Council Tax:

a. *Valuation bands*

 i. You may appeal against the valuation band your home has been assigned to if:

 - there has been a material increase in the value of your home since initial valuation and you disagree with the new valuation (this will happen after the sale of an improved property, but not before)
 - there has been a material reduction in the value of your home since initial valuation (because of partial demolition, adaptation for disability, or deterioration in the local area) and you either want to ask for a revaluation, or disagree with the new valuation (which will not happen automatically)
 - you start or stop using part of your dwelling for business purposes, or the balance between domestic and business use changes
 - the Listing Officer has altered a valuation list without an appeal having been made by a taxpayer
 - you think that a decision by a Valuation Tribunal or the High Court about another property is relevant to your home and, in your view, means that the entry in the list for your property should be changed

 ii. Normally you can appeal a council tax banding only if you are:

 - the person liable to pay the council tax
 - the person who would be liable if the dwelling were not exempt *or*
 - the owner of the dwelling.

 iii. Council Tax valuations are based on the price a property would have fetched if it had been sold on 1 April 1991. You *cannot* appeal on the basis that fluctuations in the housing market have either reduced the absolute market value, or affected the relative market value, of your home.

iv. If you think the banding is wrong, you should write to the Listing Officer for your area at the local branch of the Valuation Office Agency, explaining why you believe the list is wrong and how you think it should be altered. You should *not* contact your council.

v. If the Listing Officer does not agree with your proposal and you cannot agree on an alternative, or if no decision has been made at the end of six months, the Listing Officer must refer your proposal to a Valuation Tribunal.

vi. You can also appeal to a Valuation Tribunal if the Listing Officer has rejected your proposal as invalid (i.e. not made correctly).

b. *Liability*

i. You may appeal against the council's assessment of your council tax liability if:

- you disagree with the council's decision that your home is chargeable
- you disagree with the council's decision that you are liable for the council tax on your home
- you disagree with certain aspects of the calculation of your bill, such as the fact that a discount has not been applied or that no reduction for disabilities has been given

ii. If you think you have grounds on which to appeal, you should first write to your council at the address given on your bill or notification of exemption.

iii. If you are still dissatisfied you may refer your appeal to a Valuation Tribunal. You must do this *within two months* of the council's decision, or *four months* if you hear nothing.

c. *Penalties*

If you want to dispute an imposed penalty, you will normally have *two months* to appeal directly to a Valuation Tribunal. You may choose to discuss the matter with your council first.

d. *Completion notices*

Completion notices identify the day from which a new

building becomes a dwelling, or on which a conversion is completed. If you receive a completion notice with which you disagree, you should appeal directly to the Valuation Tribunal, within *four weeks* of receiving the notice. You may choose to discuss the matter with your council first, if there is time.

If your case is referred, or if you decide to appeal directly to a Valuation Tribunal, you will be sent a booklet explaining the tribunal's procedures. Where possible Valuation Tribunals are held locally and last no more than a day. They are free.

3. *How Independent Is the Complaints Procedure?*

Complaints to Listing Officers and council officials are dealt with internally.

Valuation Tribunals are appointed by the local authority, but operate completely independently of both the council and the Valuation Office Agency.

4. *Compensation/Redress?*

a. *Valuation bands*

If a Listing Officer agrees with your proposal, they will alter the valuation list, and your council will be required to revise your council tax bill and adjust your payments if necessary. Similarly, if your complaint goes to a tribunal which finds in your favour, your bill and payments will be adjusted as necessary.

b. *Liability*

If the council or tribunal finds in your favour, your bill and payments will be adjusted as necessary.

c. *Penalties*

If the council or tribunal finds in your favour, your penalty will be quashed.

d. *Completion notices*

If the council or tribunal finds in your favour, the notice will be adjusted as necessary.

5. *Any Appeal?*

a. A Valuation Tribunal's decision is normally final, although you may appeal to the High Court on a point of law. If you wish to do this you should get legal advice

see **Where to get help**

b. If you are unhappy about the way the Valuation Office has dealt with you, and have exhausted their internal complaints procedure, you can complain to the Revenue Adjudicator

see **Tax**

c. If you are unhappy about the way the council has dealt with you, you can complain to the Local Government Ombudsman   *see* **Local Government**

6. *Other Options?*

a. In *Scotland* the procedure is similar, except for the following differences:

● Appeals against *valuation bands* should be made to your local **Assessor's Department** (the Valuation Office Agency does not operate in Scotland). The address will be in your local phone book and also available from the relevant regional or islands council, which is responsible for appointing the assessor.

● In Scotland, **Valuation Appeal Committees** fulfil the same role as Valuation Tribunals in England and Wales. Similar time limits apply.

● For general enquiries about the council tax in Scotland, write to:

> **Council Tax Enquiries**
> **The Scottish Office**
> **Area 3-J**
> **Victoria Quay**
> **Edinburgh EH6 6QQ**

b. *Northern Ireland* still has domestic rates. To complain about:

- *Valuation bands*, contact the local office of the **Valuation and Lands Agency** (in your local phone book)
- *Rates collection*, contact the office concerned in the first instance, and then, if necessary, write to:

>   **Chief Executive**
>   **Rate Collection Agency**
>   **Oxford House**
>   **49–55 Chichester Street**
>   **Belfast BT1 4HH**

- *Liability and ratings policy*, write to:

>   **Department of Finance and Personnel**
>   **Rating Policy Branch**
>   **Rosepark House**
>   **Upper Newtownards Road**
>   **Belfast BT4 3NR**

- If you are still unhappy after any of these stages, you can ask your MP to refer your case to the Northern Ireland Ombudsman   *see* **Government Departments**

c.   To appeal an assessment of Council Tax Benefit
                                          see **Social Security**

NB

You must continue to pay your council tax bill while any appeal is outstanding.

Courts

1. *Who Can I Complain To?*

Stage 1

The Chief Clerk at the address of the court concerned

Stage 2

The Courts Administrator

The name of the Chief Clerk and the name and address of the relevant Courts Administrator will be displayed in court, and printed on leaflets displayed in every court office. The address of the court will also be in the phone book, and the Chief Clerk will be able to tell you the Courts Administrator's address.

Stage 3

Customer Service Unit
Court Service
Southside
105 Victoria Street
London SW1E 6QT

Tel: 0171 210 8500
Fax: 0171 210 1687

Note: The procedure described applies only to courts in England and Wales. For who to complain to in Scotland and Northern Ireland, see the Appendix *at the end of this entry.*

2. *What Sort of Complaints Do They Deal With?*

a. Complaints about any aspect of the court service in England and Wales which cannot be resolved on the spot should be made in writing to the Chief Clerk. You should give as much detail about your complaint as possible – for example, dates, events, and, if relevant, the details and number of your case.

b. Complaints might include objections to the way you have been treated, the way business has been conducted, or the way court officials have behaved in any part of the court system. You can complain whether you have come into contact with the court as a plaintiff, defendant, witness, juror or member of the public.

c. Complaints are escalated through the system as indicated. If you are unhappy with the Chief Clerk's response, you can write to the Courts Administrator, who will investigate your complaint. If you are still not satisfied, you can write to the Customer Service Unit of the Court Service asking them to carry out an independent investigation.

d. If you believe you have lost money or incurred costs as a result of a mistake by a member of the court staff, write to the Chief Clerk enclosing proof of any financial loss. The Chief Clerk will review the circumstances and send your claim to the Courts Administrator with a report. Large claims may be passed on again to the Customer Service Unit.

e. At all stages your complaint should be acknowledged within 2 working days of receipt and answered within 20 working days. If legal advice is needed regarding a financial claim, a final reply will be sent within 40 working days.

f. The system described cannot investigate a judge's decision. Such a complaint can only be investigated by another, more senior, judge on 'appeal' (see below).

3. *How Independent Is the Complaints Procedure?*

The system is internal to the Courts Service, although there is a commitment to fresh and impartial investigation at each successive stage.

4. *Compensation/Redress?*

a. If the Chief Clerk decides your complaint is fair, you will receive an apology and an explanation of what is being done to avoid a similar mistake happening again.

b. The Courts Administrator can make compensation payments of up to £1,000 if you can prove you have lost money because of a mistake by court staff. The Customer Service Unit may make awards of any amount.

5. Any Appeal?

Yes, you can ask your MP to refer your case to the Parliamentary Ombudsman if you think there has been 'maladministration' in the handling of your complaint   *see* **Government Departments**

6. Other Options?

- If you wish to complain about the conduct or behaviour of a *judge* (and not just because a decision has gone against you), you may write to:

    The Lord Chancellor
    The House of Lords
    London SW1A 0PW

- If you are unhappy with the way the *Crown Prosecution Service* (CPS) has handled a case, you should write first to the Branch Crown Prosecutor at the CPS office concerned. If they cannot deal with your complaint to your satisfaction, you can ask the Chief Crown Prosecutor of the Area to conduct an independent review. If you are still unhappy after this, the final stage is to write to the Director of Public Prosecutions at:

    Director of Public Prosecutions
    50 Ludgate Hill
    London EC4M 7EX

    Tel: 0171 334 8505

see also **Barristers**

Solicitors

Legal Profession

Police

Prisons

- Appeals against judicial decisions are part of the legal process. If you are considering an appeal, you should talk to your solicitor or take other legal advice   *see* **Where to get help**

Appendix

Who to complain to in Scotland

Stage 1 and *Stage 2*

As above. Complaints will be replied to *within 28 days*.

Stage 3

Administration Unit
Scottish Court Service
Hayweight House
23 Lauriston Street
Edinburgh EH3 9DQ

Tel: **0131 229 9200**

Who to complain to in Northern Ireland

Stage 1 and *Stage 2*

As above. Complaints will be replied to *within 28 days*.

Stage 3

Communications Unit
The Northern Ireland Court Service
Windsor House
9–15 Bedford Street
Belfast BT2 7LT

Tel: **01232 328594**

Credit Reference Agencies

1. *Who Can I Complain To?*

Stage 1

The relevent **credit reference agency**. There are now only two main agencies:

CCN Group Ltd
Consumer Affairs Department
PO Box 40
Nottingham
Nottinghamshire NG7 2SS

Equifax Europe (UK) Ltd
Dept 1E
PO Box 3001
Glasgow G81 2DR

Stage 2

a.   The **Data Protection Registrar (DPR)**
     for the address and more details   *see* **Information 2**

b.   **Director General of Fair Trading (DGFT)**
     Field House
     15-25 Bream's Buildings
     London EC4A 1PR

     Tel: 0181 398 3405

2. *What Sort of Complaints do they deal with?*

a.   *Stage 1*

     i. If you are trying (or have tried) to get credit for up to
         £15,000, you have a legal right to know the name and
         address of any credit reference agency that a lender has
         asked for details about you. To find this out, simply write
         to the lender who refused you credit and ask. This should
         be done *within 28 days* of the last time you contacted the
         lender about the credit deal. The lender must tell you the
         name and address of the agency within seven working days
         from receipt of your letter.

     ii. You should then write to the credit agency enclosing £1,
         giving your full name and address, including your post
         code. You should also include any other addresses you
         have lived at during the previous six years. If you run a
         business, give its name and address too. The agency must

send you your file, if held, within seven working days from receipt of your letter.

iii. You can ask for the details on your file to be amended if it contains information about *other people* with whom you have no financial connection. Agencies are only allowed to give lenders information about:

- you
- people with the same name, or a very similar name, living at your address
- other family members living in your household
- people with the same name or a very similar name who have in the past lived with you at your current or last address
- other people who have, in the past, lived with you as part of your family at your current or last address

iv. They must *not* report financial information about other people:

- if they have not lived at your current or last address as a member of your family at the same time as you
- if the agencies have information which makes it reasonable to believe that you have no financial connection with them

v. If there is information on your file about people in your family with whom you have no financial connection, or people who have never been part of your family, you can write to the agency to disassociate yourself from them. The agency may wish to make some enquiries or checks to make sure that you are not just trying to avoid a bad credit record. However, unless the agency has good reason to doubt what you tell it, it must not continue to give lenders information about the other people you have mentioned. You need only write to the agency which supplied you with your file, as 'disassociation' information will be shared between the two main agencies.

vi. You may also get your file amended if it contains information which is *incorrect*. In such a case you should write to the agency, asking it to either remove or change the mistake. The agency should respond to you within 28 days saying what action it has taken. If within 28 days the agency tells you that it will not remove or change the entry, you can, within a further 28 days send it a 'notice of correction' to be added to your file. A notice of correction is a statement of up to 200 words. It is your opportunity to tell your side of the story. What you say is up to you, but the agency can reject your notice if it thinks it is incorrect, defamatory, frivolous or scandalous, or is for any other reason unsuitable.

vii. If the agency amends your file or adds the notice of correction, it must send the details to any lender who has asked about you in the six months immediately preceding the receipt by the agency of your request for your file. The new information must be used in the future.

viii. If the notice of correction relates to information *other* than a judgement or decree, it may not be held by the other credit reference agencies, and will not be automatically corrected by your notice. You may therefore wish to obtain your file from the other agencies and correct them if necessary.

b. *Stage 2*

i. If a credit reference agency refuses to accept your instruction to *disassociate* your records from those of other specified people you should complain to the Data Protection Registrar. For more about how to complain to the DPR, including the address,   *see* **Information 2**

ii. If an agency to which you have sent a *notice of correction* refuses to add it to your file, it must refer the matter to the Director General of Fair Trading for a final decision. Within 14 working days of receiving a request from an agency the Director General will invite you to comment, and should make a decision within two months of receiving information from both parties. The DGFT will usually refer your case to the DPR if you are not satisfied with the version of your notice of correction which is finally accepted, or if your complaint involves matters other than accuracy (e.g. disassociation).

iii. If the agency does not reply to your letter enclosing your *notice of correction* within 28 days of receiving it, or if the agency refuses to accept it, you can ask the DGFT to intervene in the dispute yourself.

3. *How Independent Is the Complaints Procedure?*

a. Credit reference agency complaints procedures are internal.

b. The Data Protection Registrar and the Director General of Fair Trading are independent.

4. *Compensation/Redress?*

a. If at any point the agency accepts your complaint, it should adjust your file as requested.

b. Under the **Data Protection Act,** the DPR has the power to fine, and ultimately to de-register any organisation that keeps personal data on computer and refuses to appropriately amend a personal file. You also have the right to claim compensation under the Data Protection Act

see Information 2

c. The DGFT may attempt to redraft a notice of correction that has been refused by an agency, and ultimately has the power, under the **Consumer Credit Act,** to order agencies to correct or delete inaccurate information. You cannot obtain compensation under the Consumer Credit Act.

5. *Any Appeal?*

Not beyond the DPR and DGFT, as described.

6. *Other Options?*

● For more information about complaining to the Data Protection Registrar   *see* **Information 2**
● *See also*   **Security and Privacy 1**
   Goods & Services

D

Direct Mail

1. *Who Can I Complain To?*

Mailing Preference Service
FREEPOST 22
London W1E 7EZ

Tel: 0171 738 1625

2. *What Sort of Complaints Do They Deal With?*

Unwanted postal advertising (direct or 'junk' mail).

3. *How Independent Is the Complaints Procedure?*

The MPS enforces the Advertising Standards Authority Code of Practice as it relates to unsolicited mail.

4. *Compensation/Redress?*

The MPS will probably send you a form to fill in, after which unrequested mail should stop within 3–6 months.

5. *Any Appeal?*

If unrequested mail continues to arrive, you should forward it to the MPS. They will then ask the advertiser in question to stop.

6. *Other Options?*

- The company that is sending you unwanted mail.
- If you want to complain about a particular direct mail advertisement   *see* **Advertising**

NB

You will need to update your MPS form every five years.

Discrimination

Racial Discrimination

The **Race Relations Act 1976** makes it unlawful to discriminate against another person because of their race, colour, nationality, or ethnic or national origin. The Act recognises that racial discrimination can occur in such areas as employment; education; housing; advertising; and the provision of goods, services and facilities, but does not make it a criminal offence. It does give individuals the right to take legal action, either at an industrial tribunal (for employment matters) or at a designated County Court (Sheriff Court, in Scotland) if they think they have been discriminated against.

Your rights under the Race Relations Act are complex. If you think you have been subjected to racial discrimination, you should contact the Commission for Racial Equality (CRE) for advice. The CRE is the official body set up under the Race Relations Act to advise and assist people with complaints involving racial discrimination. It can be contacted at:

Commission for Racial Equality

London (Head Office)

**Elliot House
10–12 Allington Street
London SW1E 5EH**

Tel: 0171 828 7022

Manchester

**Maybrook House
  (5th Floor)
40 Blackfriars Street
Manchester M3 2EG**

Tel: 0161 831 7782

Birmingham

Alpha Tower (11th Floor)
Suffolk Street Queensway
Birmingham B1 1TT

Tel: 0121 632 4544

Leicester

Haymarket House
(4th Floor)
Haymarket Shopping
Centre
Leicester LE1 3YG

Tel: 0116 251 7852

Leeds

Yorkshire Bank Chambers
(1st Floor)
Infirmary Street
Leeds LS1 2JP

Tel: 0113 243 4413

Scotland

Hanover House
45–51 Hanover Street
Edinburgh EH2 2PJ

Tel: 0131 226 5186

Wales

Pearl Assurance House
(14th Floor)
Greyfriars Road
Cardiff CF1 3AG

Tel: 01222 38889

The CRE will help you complete a questionnaire (which will also be sent to the person you are complaining about, to get their side of the story) to help decide whether you should take your case to court. There are some circumstances in which the CRE will be able to represent you in court, and pay your costs.

NB

● It is important to get advice from the CRE as soon as possible after the incident you wish to complain about. In general you have only *three months* in which to complain to an industrial tribunal and *six months* to complain to a

County (or Sheriff) Court, although if you have applied to the Commission for assistance, these time limits are extended by one month.

- The Race Relations Act does not apply in Northern Ireland at the time of writing, although its provisions are in the process of being extended. Discrimination in employment matters on political or religious grounds is covered by the Fair Employment (Northern Ireland) legislation.

Sex Discrimination

The **Sex Discrimination Act 1975** makes it unlawful for a member of one sex to be treated less favourably than a member of the other simply because of their sex. The Act recognises that sex discrimination can occur in such areas as employment; education; housing; advertising; goods, services and facilities, but does not make it a criminal offence. It does give individuals the right to take legal action, either at an industrial tribunal (for employment matters) or at a designated County Court (Sheriff Court, in Scotland) if they think they have been discriminated against.

Under the **Equal Pay Act 1970**, women are entitled to equal pay with men (and vice versa) when doing work that is the same or broadly similar and, under the amended Act, to equal pay for work of equal value.

Your rights under these two Acts are complex. If you think you have been subjected to sex discrimination, you should contact the Equal Opportunities Commission (EOC) for advice. The EOC is the official body set up to advise and assist people with complaints involving sex discrimination. They can be contacted at:

Equal Opportunities Commission

England	*Wales*
Overseas House **Quay Street** **Manchester M3 3HN**	**Caerwys House** **Windsor Lane** **Cardiff CF1 1LB**
Tel: 0161 833 9244 Fax: 0161 835 1657	Tel: 01222 343552 Fax: 01222 641079

Scotland

> **Stock Exchange House**
> **7 Nelson Mandela Place**
> **Glasgow G2 1QW**
>
> **Tel: 0141 248 5833**
> **Fax: 0141 248 5834**

Northern Ireland

> **22 Great Victoria Street**
> **Belfast BT2 7BA**
>
> **Tel: 01232 242752**
> **Fax: 01232 331047**

The EOC will help you complete a questionnaire (which will also be sent to the person you are complaining about, to get their side of the story) to help decide whether you should take your case to court. Very occasionally, the EOC will be able to represent you in court, and pay your costs.

NB

- Once you have decided to take legal action, don't delay. There are various time limits – sometimes as little as *three months* from the date of the incident you want to complain about – within which you must make your complaint.
- Sexual harassment at work may amount to sex discrimination, in which case you will be able to complain to an industrial tribunal. Serious sexual harassment may constitute unlawful assault; indecent assault, in particular, is a serious criminal offence.

Disability Discrimination

The **Disability Discrimination Act 1995** creates a right not to be discriminated against on grounds of disability in the field of employment, and a right of disabled access to goods and services, including premises. It also allows the Government to set minimum access criteria for new public transport vehicles, and requires that schools, colleges and universities provide information to disabled people about the accessibility of their facilities.

The employment section of the Act, together with parts of the goods and services provisions, will come into operation in December 1996. The remaining areas will come into force over the next ten years.

The Act establishes the National Disability Council to advise

Government on issues and measures relating to the elimination of discrimination. There is no statutory body analogous to the CRE or EOC able to give advice on disability discrimination matters. If you are already in contact with a specialist disability organisation (such as the RNIB, Scope, etc.), they should be able to help. Alternatively contact:

> **RADAR** (Royal Association for Disability and Rehabilitation)
> **250 City Road**
> **London EC1V 8AF**
>
> Tel: 0171 250 3222
> Fax: 0171 250 0212
> Minicom: 0171 250 4119

Discrimination on Other Grounds

There is no British legislation against discrimination on the basis of age, sexual orientation, or beliefs (but see note on Northern Ireland, above). However it is arguable that discrimination on grounds of sexual orientation is sex discrimination (this will be decided in a test case pending before the European Court of Justice at time of writing). In certain cases, discrimination on grounds of age may be indirect sex discrimination, and discrimination on grounds of beliefs may be unlawful if it is linked to racial discrimination. It is always worth seeking legal advice if you think you have been discriminated against, as European law in the areas of human, civil and political rights is more far-reaching than domestic law, and it may be possible to petition or appeal to a European body.

● For advice on age discrimination, contact:

> **Third Age Challenge Trust (TACT)**
> **St James' Walk**
> **Clerkenwell Green**
> **London EC1R 0BE**
>
> Tel: 0171 336 7477

If your complaint is about the *difference* in the age at which men and women become entitled to certain services, discounts, etc., you should contact the Equal Opportunities Commission at one of the addresses above.

- For general advice on sexual orientation discrimination contact:

    Stonewall
    16 Clerkenwell Close
    London EC1R 0AA

    Tel: 0171 336 8860

    The following organisation provides help, advice and tribunal representation for lesbians and gay men facing discrimination in the workplace:

    Lesbian and Gay Employment Rights (LAGER)
    Unit 1G, Leroy House
    436 Essex Road
    London N1 3QP

    Tel: 0171 704 8066 (women)/**6066** (men)

- For general advice on civil and political rights write to:

    Liberty
    21 Tabard Street
    London SE1 4LA

see also **Employment**

Schools 1

Further Education

Higher Education

Advertising

Housing Benefit/Council Tax Benefit

Where to get help

European Union

Double Glazing

1. *Who Can I Complain To?*

Glass and Glazing Federation (GGF)
44–48 Borough High Street
London SE1 1XB

Tel: 0171 403 7177
Fax: 0171 357 7458

2. *What Sort of Complaints Do They Deal With?*

a. Complaints about the service and quality of work provided by companies that are members of the GGF, if the company concerned cannot resolve your complaint itself. The GGF covers approximately 60 per cent of businesses involved in the installation of replacement windows, conservatories and other glazing products.

b. The GGF deals with complaints from private individuals who have personally entered into a contract with a member. You can complain to the GGF about any of the following:

- not being made aware that you can, or being told that you cannot, change your mind about a contract (signed anywhere other than the company's business premises) within seven days
- a company going bust before completing (or beginning) a job but after banking your deposit
- installed glazing not being safe
- installed glazing not being of the same type or quality as the samples you chose from *if* this was what you were led to expect at the time
- installed glazing not conforming to the description in the advertisement you chose from
- discourteous or otherwise unacceptable conduct by employees of a member company

c.   You *cannot* complain to the GGF if

- a job has cost more than you expected, if an hourly rate but not a completion date was firmly agreed in advance
- you knew (or should have known) you could change your mind within seven days, but only did so more than seven days after signing a contract

d.   The GGF will attempt to resolve disputes via its own free conciliation service. If a solution cannot be reached, disputes may then be referred to independent arbitration. Arbitration is not free.

3. *How Independent Is the Complaints Procedure?*

a.   The GGF acts as a voluntary self-regulatory body in relation to its members. The conciliation service is internal to the GGF, although all conciliators are committed to impartiality.

b.   The GGF arbitration scheme is operated by the Chartered Institute of Arbitrators, which is completely independent.

4. *Compensation/Redress?*

a.   The GGF Code of Ethical Practice offers some safeguards *in addition* to your rights under consumer law. For example, it requires its members to allow customers a seven-day 'cooling-off' period for *all* contracts negotiated away from business premises, whether you invited the sales call or not. (The law requires this cooling-off period only if a salesman is uninvited.) If you changed your mind within this period, you should therefore get a full refund of any deposit and be freed of all contractual obligations.

b.   The GGF also operates a Deposit Indemnity Fund, underwritten by Commercial Union, to compensate customers who lose deposits placed with member companies which then go into receivership. Deposits are covered up to 25 per cent of the contract price or £2,500, whichever is the lower.

c. Ultimately, the GGF can de-register a company that fails to comply with its Code of Practice.

d. An independent arbitrator may award damages up to the value of the claim. The costs of arbitration are paid by the member regardless of the award. Consumers pay a nominal sum, the amount of which depends on the size of the claim being made.

5. *Any Appeal?*

- Arbitration is usually legally binding.
- If you decide not to go to arbitration, you retain the right to claim compensation through the courts.

6. *Other Options?*

- If the company you have been dealing with is not a member of the GGF, or if you decide not to go to arbitration, your only option is to pursue the matter through the courts
  see **Where to get help**
- If your windows are made of plastic, your contractor may be a member of the following trade association, who may be able to help:

    British Plastics Federation
    6 Bath Place
    Rivington Street
    London EC2A 3JE

    Tel: 0171 457 5000

- For more information on your legal rights as a consumer
  see **Goods & Services**

Drycleaning & Laundry

1. *Who Can I Complain To?*

Customer Advisory Service
Textile Services Association Limited (TSA)
7 Churchill Court
58 Station Road
North Harrow
Middlesex HA2 7SA

Tel: 0181 863 7755/9177
Fax: 0181 861 2115

2. *What Sort of Complaints Do They Deal With?*

a. Complaints from private individuals about items being lost or damaged by domestic laundry and/or drycleaning companies that are members of the TSA, and which cannot be resolved by the company concerned. The TSA does *not* handle complaints about services provided by launderettes or coin-operated drycleaning establishments, or about drycleaners and launderers that are not members of the TSA.

b. The TSA's Code of Practice is *in addition to* your legal rights. Launderers' and drycleaners' legal liability for loss and damage is dependent on there having been 'negligence', i.e. a breach of a duty or obligation, whether imposed by law or by an express or implied term in a contract. Professional cleaners are also expected to have specialised knowledge of the techniques they employ, and to recognise any risks (of, for example, using a particular process on a particular fabric) which would be 'generally recognised by others in the industry'.

c. Cleaners are not legally obliged to pay compensation for items lost or damaged by fire or burglary whilst in their custody, unless the fire or burglary was caused by the cleaner's negligence. TSA members *do*, however, undertake to pay fair compensation for items lost or damaged through fire or theft, however caused, in cases where the item is not covered by the customer's own insurance policy. This is an example of the TSA code going further than the protective remit of the law.

d. Similarly, cleaners are not legally obliged to pay compensation for unavoidable delays in returning items to customers. The TSA *does*, however, recommend its members to 'consider favourably, in the interest of good customer relations, making a reduction in the standard process charge for the article concerned'. If, on the other hand, a cleaner *knows* that (or is 'reckless' as to whether) he is making a false statement when he tells you your items will be ready within a particular time, he is committing an offence under the Trades Descriptions Act and you may be able to claim compensation through the courts (see *Other Options?*, below).

e. Cleaners *cannot* be held responsible for damage caused by:

- faulty manufacture, e.g. colours that run, relaxation of stretch imparted during manufacture, inadequate seaming, incorrect care labelling, etc.
- prior misuse by the customer, e.g. drying of razor blades on towels, excessive use of bleach, spillage of acids or other corrosive liquids on fabrics, etc.
- normal but unrecognised wear, e.g. weakening of curtains by exposure to light

f. The TSA will attempt to settle any dispute with a cleaner informally. If this is impossible, it will usually suggest an assessment of the garment by an Independent Test House (for addresses see the *Appendix* at the end of this entry). Tests are carried out on a 'loser pays basis', so that you will have to pay for the test if the test house decides in the cleaner's favour, and the cleaner will have to pay if the test goes against them. The cost of a test will vary depending on the article, fabric and problem under investigation, and you are advised to get several estimates before deciding which test house to use.

g. Both you and the cleaner will be asked to write to the test house with an explanation of the condition of the garment, including relevant details of its history (from you) and of any cleaning and finishing processes carried out (from the cleaner). Whoever sends in the garment for inspection will be expected to make the report available to the other party.

3. *How Independent Is the Complaints Procedure?*

The TSA is a self-regulatory body committed to the maintenance of industry standards. It is funded by members' subscriptions.

The test houses are independent companies.

4. *Compensation/Redress?*

a. In law, a launderer or cleaner who loses or destroys a customer's article through his or his employees' negligence is liable for the market value of the article at the time it is lost or destroyed, allowing for depreciation but reflecting to some extent the cost of replacement at current costs. If the article is only damaged and is capable of adequate repair, the launderer/cleaner is only liable for the cost of that repair (if this is less than the cost of replacement).

b. If an independent test finds the cleaner to be at fault, you will therefore receive compensation. The amount will be decided by the cleaner, according to standard valuation tables. The amount of any 'voluntary' compensation for fire, theft or lateness is at the discretion of the cleaner, in negotiation with the customer concerned.

c. Cleaners failing to comply with the TSA's Code could in theory be removed from membership, although this rarely happens. The TSA does make annual anonymous assessment visits to branches of every member company, and will recommend improvements where these are thought necessary.

5. *Any Appeal?*

No.

If you do not agree with the offer of compensation, you may wish to pursue a claim through the courts.

6. *Other Options?*

The TSA complaints procedure does not affect your rights under consumer law, under which you can seek redress through the courts at any time. This is also your only option if the drycleaner or launderer you have a problem with is not a member of the TSA
see **Goods & Services**
see also **Where to get help**

NB

- Cleaners are legally entitled to dispose of uncollected items after six months, as long as they have a notice prominently displayed saying that this will happen, or tell you so at the time you leave any items with them.
- If you are having a particularly valuable or unusual item cleaned, it is a good idea to tell the cleaner in advance how much you consider it to be worth. The cleaner is always within his rights to refuse to accept an article for cleaning.

Appendix

Independent Test Houses

British Leather Confederation
Kings Park Road
Moulton Park
Northampton NN3 1ED

Tel: 01604 494131/2

Drycleaning Technology Centre
25A Brook Street
Ilkley
West Yorkshire LS29 8AA

Tel: 01943 816545

British Textile Technology Group
Wira House
West Park Riding Road
Leeds LS16 6QL

Tel: 0113 259 1999

Fabric Care Research Association
Forest House Laboratories
Knaresborough Road
Harrogate
North Yorkshire HG2 7LZ

Tel: 01423 885977

Scot Innovation & Development Ltd
Netherdale
Galashields
Selkirkshire TD1 3EY

Tel: 01896 2196

E

Electrical Installation

1. Who Can I Complain To?

**National Inspection Council for Electrical Installation
    Contracting** (NICEIC)
Vintage House
37 Albert Embankment
London SE1 7UJ

Tel: 0171 582 7746
Fax: 0171 820 0831

2. What Sort of Complaints Do They Deal With?

a. All electrical work carried out by NICEIC Approved Contractors must conform to the current edition of the **Regulations for Electrical Installations (BS 7671: 1992)** and all other relevant British Standard Codes of Practice. In addition approved contractors are required to use materials of good quality, and to employ competent electricians with adequate supervision.

b. You can complain to the NICEIC if you have reason to believe that an electrical installation does not conform to the Council's technical standard (i.e. is 'unsafe or unsound') and:

   • the contractor is on the NICEIC Roll of Approved Electrical Installation Contractors

You will probably be asked to complete a Notification of Complaint form.

c.   The NICEIC does *not* deal with complaints:

- about contractual or commercial matters, such as the price charged for work
- about anything other than electrical safety
- where anyone has already tried to correct the problems complained about
- which are the subject of current or impending litigation
- about anything which falls outside the Council's technical standards
- about work in progress, or work completed *more than three years* ago

d.   If your complaint is relatively minor and the facts are not in dispute, the NICEIC will attempt to resolve the problem informally. In other cases, arrangements will be made for a NICEIC Inspecting Engineer to carry out an on-site inspection. You or your representative will be expected to attend the inspection, as will a representative of the approved contractor.

e.   After the inspection the NICEIC Inspecting Engineer will forward a report to the approved contractor; a general indication of the Council's findings will be sent to you. If the report shows that the contractor has not complied with the Council's technical standard, he will have to correct any problems at his own cost. Another inspection will be made after this work is completed.

f.   If the original contractor refuses to honour the requirement to put things right, and you are still within the *first 12 months* after a completed (certified) installation is put into service, or after the 'inspection and test' section of the Completion Certificate was signed (whichever is first), the NICEIC 'Guarantee of Standards Scheme' automatically comes into effect, whatever the value of your contract.

Under the Guarantee Scheme the Council will appoint another approved contractor to carry out essential remedial work if the original contractor defaults.

g. The Guarantee Scheme does *not* apply to:

- the work of approved contractors who are covered by a Trade Association Guarantee
- contractual problems covered by a customer's own insurance
- work carried out by approved contractors that have closed their businesses or gone into liquidation
- consequential and/or contingent liabilities, including personal injury or death, arising from the work of an approved contractor being below the required standards
- problems with any electrical equipment that is not part of a fixed installation

3. *How Independent Is the Complaints Procedure?*

The NICEIC is a non-profit-making organisation, registered as a charity, set up to protect consumers against unsafe and unsound electrical installations. The Council acts as the industry's voluntary regulatory body, and is funded from registration fees.

4. *Compensation/Redress?*

a. If the original contractor is still in business and agrees to comply with NICEIC's requirements, any problems caused by deviations from the NICEIC's standard and arising in the first three years will be put right at no extra cost.

b. If the original contractor refuses to carry out the necessary remedial work, and you have complained within the first 12 months after completion, the NICEIC will arrange for the problems to be sorted out at no extra charge, up to a cost of £10,000.

c. Contractors who refuse to carry out required remedial work, and those whose work consistently falls below the required standards (as revealed by regular re-inspection), are removed from the Roll.

d. The NICEIC has no power to award compensation.

5. *Any Appeal?*

No, but if you disagree with the NICEIC's decision in your case, you may wish to pursue the matter through the courts (see *Other Options?*, below).

6. *Other Options?*

a. The following trade associations operate schemes guaranteeing a minimum standard of work, and will try to sort out complaints about members' work:

Electrical Contractors Association	**Electrical Contractors Association of Scotland**
ESCA House	**Bush House**
34 Palace Court	**Bush Estate**
London W2 4HY	**Mid Lothian EH26 0SB**
Tel: 0171 229 1266	**Tel: 0131 445 5577**

b. The NICEIC requirements and Guarantee of Standards Scheme, and any other trade association schemes, provide benefits *in addition* to your legal and statutory rights. If your original contractor has gone bust, or the relevant time limits have passed, or you want to claim damages, or if the contractor you have used is not a member of any trade association or on the NICEIC Roll, your only option is to take legal action.

- For more information on your rights as a consumer (including how to complain about electrical appliances)
  see **Goods & Services**
- For more information on taking legal action
  see **Where to get help**

Electricity

1. *Who Can I Complain To?*

Stage 1

Your local **Office of Electricity Regulation** (OFFER) and your local **Electricity Consumers' Committee** (ECC)
ECCs are at the same address as regional offices of OFFER.
(The addresses are listed in the *Appendix* at the end of this entry.) Complaints should usually be addressed to OFFER in the first instance – but see below.

Stage 2

The Director General of Electricity Supply
OFFER Head Office
Hagley House
Hagley Road
Birmingham B16 8QG

Tel: 0121 456 2100
National Minicom helpline (for those with hearing difficulties): **0345 697128**

2. *What Sort of Complaints Do They Deal With?*

a. Both OFFER and the ECCs will look into complaints about electricity companies which cannot be satisfactorily resolved by the company concerned. OFFER's role includes ensuring that electricity companies meet their legal requirements and comply with the Codes of Practice and Standards of Performance which the Director General (DG) has set for the electricity companies concerned. Complaints might therefore include:

- being cut off unreasonably or in contravention of a Code of Practice
- being refused an electricity supply
- unacceptable terms and conditions of electricity supply

- bill estimate disputes
- metering disputes
- unreliable supply
- unacceptable service – e.g. unreliable metering visits, inadequate maintenance
- inadequate advice or information
- unavailability of meter tokens

b. Codes of Practice cover such areas as dealing sympathetically with customers in financial difficulties, as well as special protection during the winter months for old, sick and disabled customers. Public electricity suppliers are, however, entitled to disconnect supply for non-payment of electricity bills and can impose conditions (such as a security deposit) on a new or recommended supply where there is a history of bad payment.

c. Neither OFFER nor the Consumers' Committees have any responsibilities in relation to problems arising from the sale and use of electrical appliances or with electrical work inside the home.

d. OFFER's regional offices investigate all complaints that come in. If they cannot resolve a problem straight away, they may pass it on to the local ECC. ECCs monitor the services provided by local electricity companies closely and may be able to resolve disputes informally: for example, electricity companies often accept ECC recommendations on compensation. You can also contact your local ECC direct, and they may be the best body to approach if your complaint does not involve a company actually breaking the law.

e. If a complaint is complex, or involves new issues of policy or legal interpretation – for example, an allegation of discrimination against a particular group of consumers – the regional office will pass a complaint on to the Director General. You can also contact the DG direct if you are not happy with a regional OFFER's response.

3. *How Independent Is the Complaints Procedure?*

a. OFFER is the independent statutory body set up under the

Electricity Act 1989 to regulate the electricity industry. Under the Act, the Director General of Electricity Supply (also known as the DG of OFFER) has various powers and duties relating to the protection of customers and the promotion of competition within the electricity industry (see below).

b. ECCs are independent of both the electricity companies and OFFER, although they work closely with, and share administrative support with, OFFER's regional offices. They were set up under the 1989 Act specifically to represent the interests of electricity consumers. Each ECC has between ten and twenty members, plus a chair, appointed from people in the local community by the Director General of OFFER. They have no statutory powers.

4. *Compensation/Redress?*

a. An electricity company may accept an ECC recommendation to put things right and/or pay compensation.

b. If OFFER finds a company to be in breach of its legal obligations, it can compel the electricity supplier to take the necessary action to put things right. This may include an explanation, an apology and/or a change in policy and procedure.

c. The Director General (and any branch of OFFER acting on his behalf) has the specific statutory powers to:

- make an electricity supplier reconnect (or prevent a supplier disconnecting) a customer when it has contravened its 'duty to give and to continue to give a supply'
- make an electricity supplier meet a 'reasonable request' from a potential customer for a supply
- determine whether terms and conditions of supply are 'reasonable' and enforce a decision on the supplier

d. If an electricity company is contravening one of the Codes of Practice or failing to maintain the agreed Standards of Performance and refuses to comply with OFFER's directions, the DG will take enforcement action under the company's licence conditions, with the ultimate sanction of legal action to withdraw the licence in question.

e. OFFER has no power to award compensation. It may, however, help customers to negotiate an out-of-court settlement with an electricity company, with the help of the ECC if necessary.

5. Any Appeal?

a. You may be able to claim compensation through the courts.

b. Decisions of the Director General of Electricity Supply are subject to judicial review on a point of law.

In both of the above cases you should get legal advice
see **Where to get help**

c. If you are unhappy with the way OFFER has investigated your complaint, you can ask your MP to refer your case to the Parliamentary Ombudsman
see **Government Departments**

6. Other Options?

see also **Electrical Installation**

Goods & Services

Appointments

NB

● It is planned that, after 1998, all customers (not only business customers) will be able to choose which electricity company they buy their electricity from. This will increase competition, and will also affect the role of ECCs in liaising between customers and suppliers.

Appendix

OFFER and the Electricity Consumers' Committees can be contacted at the following addresses:

Eastern Region

4th Floor
Waveney House
Handford Road
Ipswich
Suffolk IP1 2BJ

Tel: 01473 216101

North Western Region

5th Floor
Boulton House
17–21 Chorlton Street
Manchester M1 3HY

Tel: 0161 236 3484

East Midlands Region

Suite 3C
Langford House
40 Friar Lane
Nottingham NG1 6DQ

Tel: 0115 950 8738

South Eastern Region

1–4 Lambert's Yard
Tonbridge
Kent TN9 1ER

Tel: 01732 351356

London Region

11 Belgrave Road
London SW1V 1RB

Tel: 0171 233 6366

Southern Region

30–31 Friar Street
Reading
Berkshire RG1 1DX

Tel: 01734 560211

Merseyside & North Wales Region

4th Floor
Hamilton House
Hamilton Place
Chester CH1 2BH

Tel: 01244 320849

South Western Region

Unit 1
Hide Market
West Street
Bristol
Avon BS2 0BH

Tel: 0117 954 0934

North Eastern Region

> 1st Floor
> St Cuthbert Chambers
> 35 Nelson Street
> Newcastle-upon-Tyne
> NE1 5AN
>
> Tel: 0191 221 2071

Yorkshire Region

> Symons House
> Belgrave Street
> Leeds LS2 8DD
>
> Tel: 0113 234 1866

South Wales Region

> 5th Floor
> St David's House
>   (West Wing)
> Wood Street
> Cardiff CF1 1ES
>
> Tel: 01222 228388

Scotland

> Regent Court
> 70 West Regent Street
> Glasgow G2 2QZ
>
> Tel: 0345 697187

Employment

1. *Who Can I Complain To?*

a. In *England*, *Wales* and *Scotland* complaints should be made to your local **Office of the Industrial Tribunals**. Complaint forms are available from your local Job Centre.

> **National helpline** (local rate calls): **0345 959775**

b. *Northern Ireland*

> **Industrial Tribunals and the Fair Employment Tribunal**
> **Long Bridge House**
> **20–24 Warring Street**
> **Belfast BT1 2EB**
>
> Tel: **01232 327666**

2. *What Sort of Complaints Do They Deal With?*

a. The following is a list of the main areas of employment rights which may be considered by an industrial tribunal. You are strongly recommended to obtain the booklet(s) indicated (with reference number where relevant) next to the category you are concerned about before proceeding with your complaint. All booklets are available free from your local Job Centre unless otherwise stated:

- Breach of contract See general booklet ITL1

- Deduction from wages PL 810 (Rev 3): *The law on the payment and deduction of wages*

- Disability discrimination (see *NB*, below)

- Equal pay PL 743: *Equal pay – A guide to the Equal Pay Act*

- Guarantee payments PL 724: *Guarantee payments*

- Health and safety activities PL 716 (Rev 2): *Individual rights of employees*

- Insolvency of employer PL 718 (Rev 1): *Employee's rights on the insolvency of employer;*

  Insolvency of employers safeguard of occupational pension scheme contributions (available from DfEE Redundancy Payments Offices)

- Itemised pay statement PL 704 (Rev 2): *Itemised pay statement*

- Maternity rights PL 958 (Rev 1): *Employment rights for the expectant mother*

- Medical suspension PL 705 (Rev 1): *Rights on suspension from work under health and safety regulations*

- Occupational pension schemes See general booklet ITL1

- Race discrimination

  Guide to the Race Relations Act 1976 (available from the Home Office)

- Redundancy

  PL 833 (Rev 3): *Redundancy consultation and notification*;

  PL 808 (Rev 3): *Redundancy payments*

- Rehabilitation of offenders

  A guide to the Rehabilitation of Offenders Act 1974 (available from HMSO and other bookshops)

- Rights for shop workers

  PL 960: *Sunday Trading Act 1994 New Employment Rights for Shopworkers*;

  PL 973: *Sunday Betting – New Employment Rights for Betting Workers*

- Sex discrimination including sexual harassment

  Guide to Sex Discrimination Act 1975

- Time off

  Safety representatives and Safety Committees (HSE booklet obtainable from HMSO and other bookshops);

  PL 702 (Rev 1): *Time off for public duties*;

  PL 703 (Rev 2): *Facing redundancy? – time off for job hunting or to arrange training*

- Trade union membership/non-membership rights

  ACAS Code of Practice 3: Time off for trade union duties and activities (obtainable from HMSO and other bookshops);

  PL 871 (Rev 4): *Union membership and non-membership rights*;

PL 865 (Rev 1): *Unjustifiable discipline by a trade union*;

PL 944: *The payment of union subscriptions through the check off*

- Transfer of undertakings

PL 699 (Rev 3): *Employment rights on the transfer of an undertaking*

- Unfair dismissal (including dismissal for exercise of statutory rights or for health and safety reasons)

PL 712 (Rev 10); *Unfairly dismissed?*;

PL 714 (Rev 4): *Fair and unfair dismissal: a guide for employers*;

PL 869 (Rev 2): *Industrial action and the law: a guide for employees, trade union members, and others*;

PL 870 (Rev 2): *Industrial action and the law: a guide for employers, their customers and suppliers*

- Written reasons for dismissal

PL 707 (Rev 6): *Rights to notice and reasons for dismissal*

- Written statement of employment and particulars

PL 700 (Rev 2): *Written statement of employment particulars*;

PL 700A: *Example form of written statement of employment particulars*

b. Your trade union, a Citizens Advice Bureau, the Free Representation Unit or a Law Centre should be able to give you advice or help with your application, and may also be able to represent you *see* **Where to get help**

c. If your case concerns equal pay, or any kind of discrimination, you should seek advice from the appropriate body *see* **Discrimination**

d. Tribunal hearings are relatively informal, but usually proceed with each party:

- giving evidence
- calling witnesses to give evidence
- questioning their own witnesses and those brought by the other party
- addressing the tribunal

The procedures are summarised in the general booklets ITL1 *England and Wales* and ITL1 *Scotland* available from your local Job Centre. For general enquiries about tribunal *procedure only* you can also call the free helpline on **0800 221111**.

e. In most cases the tribunal will send copies of all relevant documents to the Advisory, Conciliation and Arbitration Service (ACAS). ACAS will try to help the different parties reach a negotiated decision, without the need to set the tribunal machinery in motion. This service is impartial, confidential and free.

3. *How Independent Is the Complaints Procedure?*

a. ACAS is the statutory body set up under the **Employment Protection Act 1975** to promote industrial relations and help resolve industrial disputes of both a collective and individual nature. It is completely independent.

b. Industrial tribunals are independent judicial bodies. They consist of either a chairman (who is always a solicitor or barrister) and two lay members, or a chairman sitting alone, depending on the kind of case under consideration. Lay members are appointed by the President of the Board of Trade from lists of names solicited from representative organisations. Tribunals are almost always held in public, although reporting may be restricted in cases of alleged sexual harassment or misconduct.

4. *Compensation/Redress?*

a.   If a tribunal finds in your favour then your complaint will be settled accordingly: for example, you may be reinstated in your job if your complaint concerned unfair dismissal.

b.   Tribunals have the power to award financial compensation, which may include costs if the losing party has behaved unreasonably. You will be able to claim travelling expenses and loss of earnings.

c.   Tribunal decisions will be given in writing, in summary or extended form. You can ask for extended written reasons if these are not given, and will need to have them if you wish to appeal. You will also be told in writing how the amount of any compensation has been calculated.

5. *Any Appeal?*

a.   A tribunal may review its decision if various mistakes have been made, unforeseeable new evidence has become available, or the interests of justice require such a review. It will not review its decision merely because a party disagrees with the decision or now wishes to present previously available evidence. If you think you have grounds for a review you should write to the tribunal *within 14 days* of the date the decision is sent to you. Reviews are normally heard by the original tribunal.

b.   You have the right to appeal against the decision of an industrial tribunal only on a point of law. When you receive your copy of the tribunal's decision you will also receive information about how to make an appeal. Appeals are normally made to the Employment Appeal Tribunal, and applications must be received *within 42 days* of the tribunal decision being sent to you.

c.   Complaints about the way a case is being handled are dealt with progressively by the office manager at the office dealing with your case, the Area Customer Services Manager, and ultimately the Director of Operations at Central Office (the local office will give you the necessary address).

d. From August 1997 maladministration complaints which cannot be resolved by this internal complaints procedure may be referred to the Parliamentary Ombudsman
see **Government Departments**

6. *Other Options?*

see also **Discrimination**

Employment Agencies

Trade Unions 1 *and* **2**

Appointments

NB

a. New employment rights for people with disabilities came into effect in December 1996 under the Disability Discrimination Act. Ask your trade union, local job centre or employment tribunal office or call the national helpline for details
see **Discrimination**

b. There are strict time limits involved in taking a case to a tribunal, which are different for different types of case – be sure to note the relevant ones (these will be given in the appropriate booklet).

c. Many employment rights depend upon an employee having worked a specific period of continuous employment, varying according to the right, generally with the same employer. Also, for most of the rights, an employee must have worked at least 16 hours a week, or have a contract normally involving 16 hours' work a week. The rules for reckoning continuous employment are given in booklet PL 711: *Rules governing continuous employment and a week's pay*. Trainees on government training schemes do not count as employees.

d. Discrimination legislation is different in Northern Ireland
see **Discrimination**

e. Legal aid is not available for tribunal hearings, but some organisations may be prepared to offer representation services free of charge. A leaflet on the options available called *Legal aid: getting legal help* is free from Employment Services offices.

f. Either party may be ordered to pay a deposit of up to £150 as a condition of continuing with a tribunal if a pre-hearing review considers that party's case to have no reasonable chance of success.

Employment Agencies

1. *Who Can I Complain To?*

The nearest **Employment Agency Standards Office** (EASO):

Leeds

City House
Leeds LS1 4JH

Tel: 0113 283 6539
Fax: 0113 283 6547

Birmingham

Cumberland House
200 Broad Street
Birmingham B15 1PQ

Tel: 0121 608 9744
Fax: 0121 608 9749

Watford

Exchange House
60 Exchange Road
Watford WD1 7HH

Tel: 01923 210706
Fax: 01923 210622

2. *What Sort of Complaints Do They Deal With?*

The Employment Agency Standards Offices (EASOs) administer the Employment Agencies Act 1973 and regulations made under it, which set minimum standards of conduct for agencies. Some examples are:

- an agency must not charge you a fee for finding you work (except in certain cases, mainly in the entertainment and modelling industries)
- an agency which collects fees on your behalf must pay the money to you within 10 days of receiving it unless you have requested otherwise in advance in writing
- an agency employing you to do temporary work should pay you, whether or not it is paid by its client
- when you register for temporary work, an agency must give you written terms and conditions of work, including who is employing you, what sort of work you will be doing and the minimum amount you will be paid
- an agency which finds work for you abroad must give full written details of the job, travel arrangements and accommodation

3. *How Independent Is the Complaints Procedure?*

The EASOs are part of the Department of Trade and Industry.

4. *Compensation/Redress?*

An EASO cannot require agencies to pay compensation, but it can prosecute them in magistrates' courts for breaches of the Standards of Conduct. The courts have powers to order compensation payments in appropriate cases.

5. *Any Appeal?*

a. If you are unhappy with the way an investigation and/or prosecution has been dealt with you can complain to the manager of the EASO you have been dealing with, and further to Head Office if necessary. To do this, write to:

> **Operations Manager**
> **Employment Agency Standards Office**
> **Department of Trade and Industry**
> **1 Victoria Street**
> **London SW1H 0ET**
>
> **Tel: 0171 215 5980**
> **Fax: 0171 215 2636**

If you are still unhappy after this, and think the EASO is guilty of 'maladministration', you can ask your MP to refer your case to the Parliamentary Ombudsman

see Government Departments

b. If you think you have grounds for judicial appeal against a magistrate's decision, you should take legal advice

see Where to get help

6. *Other Options?*

For how to complain about an employer   see **Employment**

Environment 1 (Local Government)

This section describes the kinds of environmental problems which are the responsibility of local authorities (LAs). Most other environmental problems come under the remit of one of the government Agencies   see **Environment 2**

1. *Who Can I Complain To?*

The address and phone number of **your local authority (council)** can be found in the phone book. Some LAs list the departments to approach according to the nature of your complaint, others operate a 'one-stop shop' which will deal with all complaints.

In England and Wales:

- **London** and **metropolitan councils** are responsible for all local environmental services
- **District councils** provide environmental health, waste collection, planning, housing and leisure services
- **County councils** and Welsh **county borough councils** provide education, consumer protection, planning, and leisure services
- some responsibilities overlap between **district** and **county councils**
- **Town, parish** or **community councils** get involved with very local issues such as footpaths and planning applications

In Scotland

The unitary **councils** and the **islands' councils** have taken over all LA environmental responsibilities.

In Northern Ireland

The unitary **district councils** have full responsibility for environmental health issues.

2. *What Sort of Complaints Do They Deal With?*

a. *Air pollution*

  i. LAs have overall responsibility for regulating air quality in their areas. The Agencies will however be able to direct LAs to take steps to achieve air quality standards and objectives, according to the government's national air quality strategy.
  ii. LAs are involved in regulating industrial air pollution from small industrial processes only; larger industrial pollution issues and licences are dealt with by the Agencies.
  iii. Complaints about smoke from people's homes and property are dealt with by LA Environmental Health Officers (EHOs) (see section i on page 141 below).
  iv. Complaints about excessive exhaust fumes from vehicles

should be made to the local Department of Transport Vehicle Inspectorate (the number will be in the phone book, and may also be listed under 'smoky vehicle hot-line'). New LA powers to curb polluting vehicles are under consideration at the time of writing.

b.   *Beaches*

i. You can complain to your LA about the following problems:

- litter (including dog mess) between May and September (see also section h)
- oil pollution and any dangerous items, such as drums of chemicals or explosives, that may be washed ashore
- nuisance: for example, if you feel that dogs are a nuisance on a particular beach the LA can, if it agrees with you, ban dogs from a beach (see also section d).

ii. If you live in an area where the coast is subject to erosion, your LA may provide coast protection works. You are *not*, however, entitled to compensation if your property suffers damage as a result of coastal erosion.

iii. To complain about the quality of bathing water
see **Environment 2**

c.   *Common land*

i. You have a right to know which open spaces in your area are designated as public common land.

ii. If common land is *owned* by a body, e.g. a rail operator, the LA or the Crown, that body is responsible for its upkeep. If the LA is the owner it can designate common land as a litter control area, in which case you can apply for a litter abatement order if appropriate (see section h).

iii. If common land has no legal owner it can be difficult to make sure it is kept tidy or to solve any problems.

d.   *Dog nuisance*

i. LAs must clear dog mess from streets, roads and parks

except where there is heath or woodland or where there are grazing animals, and may make by-laws to force owners to clear up after their dogs.

ii. If you think a particular dog is a danger you should contact the police. If you feel a dog is more of a nuisance, contact the LA. They have the power to make by-laws to make owners keep dogs on leads, or to ban dogs from certain areas, e.g. children's playgrounds.

iii. LAs have a duty to collect stray dogs. If your dog is picked up as a stray you must reclaim it within seven days (you will be charged for the costs of holding your dog, plus up to £25 extra). If you do not claim your dog, the LA may give it a new home and the new owners will have a legal right to keep it. Unclaimed dogs may also be put down.

e. *Drainage*

i. You are responsible for all drains leading from your property until they connect to a public sewer; your LA will have a map showing where the public sewer starts. If a neighbour refuses to unblock their drains you can complain to the LA and they will take action. You can also do this if your landlord fails to clear drains.

ii. Your 'sewerage undertaker' – usually your water company – is responsible for maintaining the public sewer

see **Water 1**

iii. Flood defence is the responsibility of the appropriate environmental Agency   *see* **Environment 2**

f. *Drinking water*

i. LAs have a duty to monitor the quality of drinking water, and if you are worried about your own supply you can ask the LA to test it, but both supply and drinking water quality are now the responsibility of the water company. The Drinking Water Inspectorate is responsible for monitoring how LAs fulfil their duties

see **Water 1 and 2**

ii. If you get water from a private source such as a well or spring, your LA has a responsibility to test its quality. The LA can also make a supplier improve a supply.

iii. Lead pipes can be a risk to health. If you have lead

plumbing bringing the water into your house and are on a low income, your LA may give you a grant for the replacement of those pipes.

g. *Licensing*

All-night cafes, nightclubs and some sports stadia need a licence from the LA to do business, as do one-off open-air concerts and street-traders in some areas. You have the right to object to any licensed business at the time of original licence application or at annual renewal, and can also complain if you believe that the terms of a licence are being contravened.

h. *Litter*

  i. You can complain to your LA if it fails to clear litter within the target times set down by the litter laws. For example, a very heavily littered town centre should be cleared within one hour, a moderately littered public area within three hours, etc. Targets are longer in residential areas and the countryside; details of all of them can be found in the *Litter Code of Practice* (price £5), available from HMSO and other bookshops, or by ringing **0171 873 9090**.

  If the rubbish is still not cleared after five days' written notice, you may apply to the local magistrates for a 'litter abatement order'. If the council still fails to comply it may be fined by the magistrate, and fined for each additional day that the litter remains uncleared.
 ii. The LA can also:

- insist that some privately owned places (such as car parks, shopping centres and land outside sports stadia) are kept clear of litter, by turning the land into a 'litter control area'
- issue 'street litter control notices' to shop owners to ensure they keep the pavement near their shop clear of litter
- collect any abandoned shopping or luggage trolleys

in their area and charge a fee for returning them to their owners

- appoint litter wardens or allow other staff to issue 'fixed penalty tickets' to anyone who drops litter and refuses to pick it up.

ii. To complain about waste regulation (e.g. industrial waste, waste disposal sites, etc.) *see* **Environment 2**

i. *Noise, smoke, smells and other nuisances*

i. You can complain to an Environmental Health Officer (EHO) of your LA if you think your health or enjoyment of your home or property is being spoilt by a problem such as:

- noise from buildings or land and certain street noise which may include: barking dogs; hi-fis; parties; car or house alarms; machinery or equipment
- smoke coming from any buildings or land
- dust, steam or smells coming from factories, shops or offices
- fumes or gases coming from private homes
- buildings or areas of land which are left in a dangerous state or are a risk to people's health
- animals which are being kept in an unsuitable way

The problem of noise pollution nearly always comes under the remit of local authority Environmental Health Officers and *not* the police.

ii. If the EHO decides that you are suffering a 'statutory nuisance' they will usually try to sort out the complaint informally. If this does not work, the LA can issue the offending party with an 'abatement notice' which may require the nuisance to stop immediately and/or prohibit or restrict its occurrence.

If the noise continues EHOs can seize offending noise-making equipment if they feel this is necessary; the offender may also be taken to court and fined up to £5,000. The issuing of an abatement notice and/or the confiscation of the offending noise-making equipment can theoretically be performed within one hour.

iii. If the council is having difficulty dealing with your complaint, e.g. because the nuisance only happens occasionally, you may go to the Magistrates' Court yourself to seek the abatement of a nuisance.

iv. The last resort is to take private legal action against the offender (this is not the same as approaching a Magistrates' Court). You should be aware that private legal actions can be very expensive.

Note: Disputes with neighbours are often best resolved by mediation. For a list of neutral mediation schemes around the country contact **Mediation UK** (Tel: **01272 241 1234**).

see also **Noise**

j.   *Obstructions in the road*

i. You can complain to your LA if you think that a builder's skip, scaffolding, street stall or other object is causing a danger or a nuisance.

ii. If a car is causing an obstruction, is illegally parked or has been abandoned, the LA (and the police) can remove it. If a vehicle is merely causing an inconvenience, there is probably little that can be done.

k.   *Pest control*

i. You are responsible for dealing with any pests which you find on your own property. Many LAs provide pest control services, but these may not be free.

ii. If you have reason to believe there are pests in a neighbouring property and the owner refuses to deal with the problem, you can complain to your LA. The LA can inspect the property and clear up the problem itself, and charge the owner for this.

iii. Your LA must keep pests under control on its own property.

l.   *Planning*

i. *Air*: You have rights to know about and comment on

all applications for licences, see the public register of applications made by companies and the authorisations made by your council, and to comment on all applications (normally *within 28 days* of them being advertised in your local paper). The LA must consider your comments before they decide on the authorisation. Under the planning system, you also have a right to comment on where new factories or buildings are located.

ii. *Rights of way*: You can ask your LA to create new rights of way. The council can alter, restrict or even close rights of way, but only after consulting the public. The council must advertise any proposed changes in local newspapers and notices on the site.

iii. Planning procedures and appeals are dealt with in a separate entry   *see* **Planning**

m. *Recycling*

You have a right to see your LA Recycling Plan, comment on it and make suggestions. There are financial incentives for some kinds of recycling.

n. *Rights of way*

You have a right to inspect an up-to-date map showing the rights of way in your area. A right of way allows you to cross land, but it does not include the right to picnic or play games there. LAs must maintain and signpost all rights of way and must clear obstructions if requested. They may charge any costs to the landowner and if necessary can take the owner to court.

o. *Roads and pavements*

i. LAs have a duty to maintain all local roads and pavements properly. You should tell the appropriate LA if you think that defective or icy pavements or roads may cause an accident. The LA can also take action to put up and improve road signs.

ii. Trunk roads are the responsibility of the **Highways Agency** (Tel: **0171 928 3666**), although LAs may carry out day-to-day maintenance of stretches passing through their areas.

iii. If you have been injured because the council has failed to maintain a road or pavement properly, you may be able to claim compensation. You may also be able to claim if there was damage to something you own, like a car

see **Where to get help**

iv. You can complain to your LA about problems arising from utilities' street works if the utility company is being uncooperative, for example:

- if they make it hard to get to your property
- about nuisance such as noise; your LA can make the company do the work in ways which minimise any nuisance
- if the works are dangerous, either when they are in progress or when they have been finished
- if a road or path is not put back to its original condition
- if you are worried about cable or other utility companies damaging the roots of trees in the road (see also section r).

see also **Electricity**

Gas

Telecommunications

Water 1

Broadcasting 2

p. *Rubbish collection and illegal dumping*

i. The LA has a duty to collect everyday household rubbish. It can charge you for this service if you live in a particularly isolated or inaccessible place. The LA should tell you how often they will collect and what to do if a collection is missed.

ii. The LA must also collect:

- other rubbish from your home, e.g. old sofas,

fridges and waste from gardens. A charge may be
made for this

- rubbish from offices and shops if they are asked to do
  so, but they must charge for these services unless
  there is a good reason to do it free

iii. You can also complain to your LA:

- if you think a business is not fulfilling its legal obligations to: keep its rubbish safely and securely; dispose
  of it to someone legally authorised to take it; and
  make a record of what the waste was and who
  collected it
- about 'fly tipping' of illegally dumped rubbish (see
  section h).

q. *Traffic management and parking*

i. You should complain to the LA about any local traffic
and parking problems. They can introduce permanent,
temporary and/or peak hour controls. They can also
carry out 'traffic calming' measures, for instance by
installing road humps to slow down traffic.

ii. LAs have a duty to publicise, and you have a right to
comment on, any proposed traffic management or parking controls   *see* **Planning**

r. *Tree preservation*

i. You should tell your LA if you think trees or woodlands
of special value are being put at risk, or should for any
reason be protected by a tree preservation order. The LA
has a duty to publicise, and you have a right to comment
on, any proposed tree preservation. LAs have extra powers to protect trees in conservation areas.

ii. If you own a protected tree you must usually apply to the
LA for permission if you want to carry out work on it. If
you don't you can be fined up to £20,000. If the LA refuses
your application (or grants it with conditions) you can
appeal to the Secretary of State for the Environment or the
Secretary of State for Wales. For the addresses of these
government departments   *see* **Environment 2**

iii. If a tree on your land is dangerous you can ask your council to make it safe (they may charge for this). You can also ask them to take action on dangerous trees which affect your property.

s. *Waste regulation*

i. The council is responsible for licensing waste disposal sites such as landfill sites. They will only give licences to site operators who can control pollution. Any new disposal site needs planning permission. You can see the terms of local waste disposal site licenses at your council offices.

ii. The site operator is responsible for any pollution from waste sites. If you are concerned about the safety of any waste site, tell your council. They will investigate if necessary. They can also change the terms of the licence.

t. *Wildlife areas*

You have a right to see the Local Land Charges Register kept by your council, which gives details of Sites of Special Scientific Interest (SSSIs) and other details of wildlife sites. LAs must take account of SSSIs when considering development proposals, and you can draw attention to the possible impact on nature conservation when you comment on LA draft development plans and on individual development proposals   *see* **Planning**

u. *Access to environmental information*

All arms of government are expected to comply with the (voluntary) Code of Practice on Access to Government Information. LAs are additionally obliged under the terms of the Environmental Regulations 1992 to provide reasonable public access to all environmental information, such as sampling and survey results and reports as well as registers of authorisations, consents and licences, applications for any of these, and any enforcement actions taken. For more details
                                                    see **Information 1**

NB

The information in this entry is largely taken from a Department of the Environment leaflet *Your Council and the Environment*, which is available by ringing **0171 276 8854**.

Environment 2 (Government Agencies)

This section describes the kinds of environmental problems which are the responsibility of government environmental Agencies. Most other environmental problems will come under the remit of the local authority   *see* **Environment 1**

1. *Who Can I Complain To?*

In England and Wales

Contact your local **Area** or **Regional Office** of the **Environment Agency** – details will be in the phone book. Head Office and national contact details are as follows:

> **Environment Agency (EA)**
> **Head Office**
> **Rivers House**
> **Waterside Drive**
> **Aztec West**
> **Almondsbury**
> **Bristol BS12 4UD**
>
> Tel: **01454 624400**
> Fax: **01454 624409**
> General enquiries hotline (local rate call): **0645 333 111**
> Internet World Wide Web address: **www.environment-agency.gov.uk**
> e-mail address: **enquiries@environment-agency.gov.uk**

To report environmental problems only, call:

24-hour emergency hotline (freephone): **0800 80 70 60**

In Scotland

Contact the nearest office of the **Scottish Environment Protection Agency** or its Head Office at:

Scottish Environmental Protection Agency (SEPA)
Erskine Court
The Castle Business Park
Stirling FK9 4TR

Tel: 01786 457700

Note: For who to complain to in Northern Ireland *see* Other Options?, *below.*

2. *What Sort of Complaints Do They Deal With?*

a. *Flood defence*

The Agencies are responsible for flood protection, forecasting and warning. If you live in a designated flood risk area where a forecasting facility exists you should be given at least 2 hours' warning, 'where lead times allow'.

b. *Water resources*

The Agencies are responsible for water resource monitoring, conservation and redistribution. They do *not*, however, handle any complaints about water supply.
For who to complain to   *see* **Water 1 and 2**

c. *Pollution control*

Most industrial and agricultural pollution is now regulated by the Agencies. The main exception is that in England and Wales overall *air quality* is still regulated by local authorities (LAs), although the EA will have reserve powers to direct

LAs to take steps to achieve air quality standards and objectives, according to the government's national air quality strategy   *see* **Environment 1**

In Scotland, SEPA is now responsible for both large- and small-scale pollution control, removing this function from local authorities. However, in response to concerns about the transfer of local authority powers to SEPA, the Environment Act requires that Scottish LAs should still be consulted about environmental licences.

In general, anybody discharging pollutants must be licensed to do so by the appropriate Agency and keep within the terms of the agreement. The Agencies are responsible for the following specific kinds of pollution control:

i. *Integrated Pollution Control*

Large-scale industrial processes, for example oil refineries, power stations and chemical plants, are controlled through so-called 'Integrated Pollution Control (IPC) authorisations'. These are licences setting out exactly what, how much and how a particular plant may discharge or dispose of polluting waste products. They are assessed by identifying the 'best available techniques not entailing excessive costs' (BATNEEC) and the 'best practicable environmental option' (BPEO) to determine the preferred disposal route, to land, air or water, which minimises environmental pollution as a whole.

If you have reason to believe an industrial plant is exceeding its IPC authorisation (if, for example, you think fumes from a nearby factory have dramatically increased) you should complain immediately to the appropriate Agency on their emergency hotline.

ii. *Water*

The Agencies are responsible for water quality and pollution control of so-called 'controlled waters', which include surface water (rivers, canals, lakes), groundwaters (underground water, the 'water table') and tidal waters out to the three-mile limit, including the water off bathing beaches.

You should contact the appropriate Agency if you are worried about pollution in any of the above inland or tidal waters.

Complaints about drinking and domestic water quality should be referred to your water company

see **Water 1**

Pollution of the sea beyond the three-mile limit is the responsibility of the **Ministry of Agriculture, Fisheries and Food** (MAFF) – the address is given in the *Appendix* at the end of this entry.

After the year 2000 the Agencies will also be able to control water pollution from abandoned mines.

iii. *Radioactive substances*

The Agencies regulate the disposal of radioactive material, *including* that from licensed nuclear installations, and regulate the accumulation, keeping and use of radioactive materials, *except* from licensed nuclear installations.

They liaise with **HM Nuclear Installations Inspectorate**, which has responsibility for the safety of nuclear plants.

If you live in a radon area, e.g. Cornwall, and are worried about natural radiation levels in your home you can contact your LA or the **National Radiological Protection Board** (Freephone **0800 614529**).

You should contact the appropriate Agency immediately if you are concerned about radioactive contamination of the environment from any source.

iv. *Waste regulation*

The Agencies are responsible for the control and regulation of household, industrial and commercial waste ('controlled waste') and the licensing of all waste sites – e.g. waste transfer sites, public skips, landfill sites. Particularly hazardous wastes such as asbestos, acids and solvents are regulated by 'cradle to grave' consignment notes.

Waste site operators are responsible for all monitoring, such as checking for gas emissions or toxic leaching, but if you are worried about pollution coming from a waste site you should contact the nearest office of the appropriate Agency.

LAs are responsible for identifying 'special sites' in their area and for notifying the appropriate Agency. The Agency will then serve a notice on the LA specifying what needs to be done to improve the site.

New provisions for 'producer responsibility' are likely to be introduced in 1997 and will set targets for the re-use or recycling of packaging waste. The Agencies will be responsible for registering companies and auditing their operations.

d. *Fisheries*

The Agencies are responsible for maintaining, improving and developing fisheries in controlled waters. Their role includes issuing over one million fishing licences, improving fish habitats and stocks and advising fishery owners.

e. *Navigation*

The Agencies are responsible for managing and improving over 800km of inland waterways and several estuaries, to keep them fit for navigational purposes.

f. *Recreation and access to water and land*

The Agencies manage over 1,000 sites for recreational use, and have a general duty to promote recreational use of water and land.

Most complaints about facilities and the condition of the countryside should be directed to the LA, **English Nature** or (for comments about policy only) the **Countryside Commission**; the LA of the site in question will be able to tell you who is responsible.

g. *Conservation*

The Agencies have a duty to contribute to the conservation of nature, landscape and architectural heritage. They must strive to conserve and enhance flora, fauna and other environmental features when carrying out their pollution control functions, and have a specific duty to promote the conservation of flora and fauna dependent on the aquatic environment.

h. *Information*

All arms of government are expected to comply with the (voluntary) **Code of Practice on Access to Government Information**. The environmental Agencies are additionally obliged under the terms of the **Environmental Regulations 1992** to provide reasonable public access to all environmental information, such as sampling and survey results and reports as well as registers of authorisations, consents and licences, applications for any of these, and any enforcement actions taken. For more details   *see* **Information 1**

i. If your complaint is about the service provided by Agency staff, you should write initially to the Complaints Contact at your local office.

3. *How Independent Is the Complaints Procedure?*

a. The environmental Agencies are non-departmental public bodies (NDPBs, also known as quangos). The EA and the SEPA were created by the **Environment Act 1995** in a move towards greater integration of environmental protection and conservation. The EA combines the regulation of land, air and water through a merger of the National Rivers Authority (NRA), Her Majesty's Inspectorate of Pollution (HMIP), the Waste Regulation Authorities (WRAs) and several units from the Department of the Environment. The EA has a board of up to 15 members appointed by the Department of the Environment, the Ministry of Agriculture, Fisheries and Food (MAFF) and the Welsh Office.

b. Similarly, SEPA combines the activities of the seven River Purification Boards in Scotland and their counterparts in the islands councils, HMIP for Scotland and the waste and air pollution functions of the 56 district and islands councils. SEPA has a board of up to 12 members, appointed by the Secretary of State for Scotland.

Both bodies have a statutory commitment to the principles of sustainable development, and are operationally independent of other government departments such as Trade and Industry, MAFF, etc.

4. *Compensation/Redress?*

a. Anyone who reports an environmental problem or makes a complaint is kept up to date with the investigation and informed within 15 working days of its outcome.

b. Remedies to environmental problems will obviously depend on the problem, but the Agencies have wide powers: for example, dischargers found guilty of breaching the terms of their licence, or anyone suspected of polluting without consent, can be prosecuted and, if found guilty, fined or imprisoned.

c. Both local councils and the Agencies have powers to force landowners to remove illegally deposited waste, and also have powers to clean up themselves if the occupier of the land or perpetrator cannot be identified.

d. LAs have a duty to clear up after environmental disasters, floods, etc., but neither they nor the Agencies have powers to pay compensation to individuals or businesses not covered by insurance (but see *Other Options?*, below).

e. Requests for information under the Open Government Code should be answered within 20 days. Answers to requests under the Environmental Information Regulations should take no longer than 2 months.

5. *Any Appeal?*

a. If you feel an Agency's investigation of a complaint about bad service is unsatisfactory, or you wish to seek a higher review, you can write to the **Director General of the Environment Protection Group** at the **Department of Environment** (see the *Appendix* below for contact details).

b. If a complaint about maladministration is still unresolved after you have exhausted the internal complaints procedure you can refer your case to:

- the Local Government Ombudsman (flood defence issues only) *see* **Local Government**

   or

- (via your MP) the Parliamentary Ombudsman (all other duties and activities) *see* **Government Departments**

c. You have a statutory right of appeal (usually to the relevant Secretary of State) against various kinds of decision by an environmental Agency: for example against a refusal to issue a licence to pollute or to carry out works in, over or under a watercourse. Ask the Agency concerned for details in your case.

6. *Other Options?*

- In *Northern Ireland* the body with equivalent responsibilities to the EA and SEPA is the new **Environment and Heritage Service**, a 'next steps' (arm's-length) agency of the Department of Environment (NI), staffed by civil servants. Legislation on air quality, similar to that which already applies in Great Britain, is being put into place at the time of writing; full implementation of similar legislation on waste and contaminated land is expected to take two or three years. The contact details, depending on the environmental problem in question, are:

Environmental protection and natural heritage

Calvert House
23 Castle Place
Belfast BT1 1FY

Tel: 01232 254754

Water pollution incidents – emergency hotline

Tel: 01232 757414

Countryside and wildlife

**Commonwealth House
Castle Street
Belfast BT1 1GU**

Tel: 01232 251477

Built heritage

**5–33 Hill Street
Belfast BT1 2LA**

Tel: 01232 235000

General e-mail address:

EHS@nics.gov.uk

'Next steps' agencies are accountable in matters of maladministration to the **Parliamentary Ombudsman** (the Northern Ireland Ombudsman, in this case), and should have similar internal complaints procedures to government departments. There are (or will be) similar rights of appeal against certain decisions of the agency.

see **Government Departments**

The unitary district councils still have day-to-day responsibility for environmental health issues (clean air, smoke, food safety, noise, etc.); but overall responsibility for environmental health has now been moved to the Department of Health (NI).

see also **Environment 1**

Planning

Noise

Appointments

- Owners of industrial plants, oil shipping companies, major agrochemical users, etc. are expected to be insured against accidental pollution damage and environmental disasters, so if you can prove that damage to your health or property has been caused by something released into the environment by them (for example, if you can prove that a substance released into the local water supply has had a measurable effect on your health, or if your beachside cafe has been ruined by an oil slick) you should be able to claim compensation from their insurers. If they are not properly insured, or if you are not happy with the amount you receive, you may be able to sue a polluter in the courts.
- Although you have no right to compensation from the LA or government for 'natural' disasters such as floods, if you can prove that a preventable flood happened as a result of *negligence* by a particular person or business or the appropriate environmental Agency, you may be able to sue for damages.
- If you are considering legal action you should get advice
  see **Where to get help**
- The major environmental campaigning groups (e.g. Friends of the Earth, Greenpeace, CPRE, etc.) are often a good source of advice in the complex area of environmental rights and responsibilities.

NB

The environmental Agencies are responsible for enforcing over twenty-five EC Directives, and are affected by another seventy. Those enforced by the Agencies *include*:

Air quality

- The *Large Combustion Plants Directive* sets emission limits for sulphur dioxide (SO_2) and oxides of nitrogen (NO) and demands a programme of improvements by the year 2003 which will result in 60 per cent and 30 per cent reductions in SO_2 and NO over a 1980 baseline.
- The *Sulphur Dioxide and Suspended Particulates*, *Nitrogen Dioxide*, *Ozone* and *Lead Directives* prescribe sampling and analysis methodologies and set limits and guideline values for atmospheric concentrations of the substances in question.

Water quality

- The *Bathing Waters Directive* sets limits on indicator bacteria concentrations at designated beaches.
- The *Shellfish Waters Directive* protects shellfish in marine waters.
- The *Dangerous Substances Directive* sets limits for the concentration of trace metals and trace organic substances in fresh and marine waters.
- The *Nitrates Directive* is intended to control the pollution of controlled waters by the excess use of fertilisers on agricultural land, etc.

Waste

- The *Amendment to the Framework Directive on Waste* reinforces the need for waste minimisation, for disposal to be locally provided, and for adequate process control.
- The *Hazardous Waste Directive* insists that the disposal of such waste must be identified and recorded and separated from other waste. Hazardous wastes are defined by a lengthy list including substances (e.g. pigments, resins, biocides, etc.), constituents (e.g. cadmium, phenols, ether, etc.), and properties (e.g. flammable, toxic, mutagenic, etc.).
- The *Waste Shipments Regulation* requires Member States to ratify all transfrontier shipments of waste. The Regulation also restricts the countries from which or to which waste can be transported.

Appendix

Department of the Environment (DoE)
2 Marsham Street
London SW1P 3EB

Tel: 0171 276 3000

The Welsh Office
Environment Division
Cathays Park
Cardiff CF1 3NQ

Tel: 01222 825111

Ministry of Agriculture Fisheries and Food (MAFF)
Whitehall Place
London SW1A 2HH

Helpline no (local rate calls): **0645 335577**

The Scottish Office
Environment Department
St Andrew's House
Edinburgh EH1 3DG

Tel: 0131 556 8400

Estate Agents 1

1. *Who Can I Complain To?*

The Compliance Officer
The National Association of Estate Agents (NAEA)
Arbon House
21 Jury Street
Warwick CV34 4EH

Tel: 01926 496800
Fax: 01926 400953

2. *What Sort of Complaints Do They Deal With?*

a. Complaints by individual clients about the professional services of estate agents who are members of the Association.
Complaints can relate to any aspect of the buying, selling,
letting or renting of property. Some 60 per cent of estate

agents are NAEA members, including both small independent businesses and branches of major chains.

b. The NAEA Rules of Professional Conduct are in addition to your legal rights. See section 6, below, for a description of the specific protection afforded by the Estate Agents Act 1979 and the Property Misdescriptions Act 1991.

3. *How Independent Is the Complaints Procedure?*

The NAEA is a professional body, funded by membership subscriptions, with a self-regulatory role.

4. *Compensation/Redress?*

The Association has no power to award compensation, although in some cases it may recommend that a member company should reimburse its fees.

If it is found that a member has failed to comply with the Rules of Conduct, they may be fined up to £1,000, and can be disqualified from membership of the Association.

5. *Any Appeal?*

If your complaint is about a corporate estate agent, you can refer it to the Ombudsman   *see* **Estate Agents 2**

Otherwise there is no appeal (but see *NB*, below)

6. *Other Options?*

a. If your estate agent is a member of:

- The Royal Institution of Chartered Surveyors
  see **Surveyors**
- The Incorporated Society of Valuers and Auctioneers
  see **Valuers & Auctioneers**

If they are not a member of any professional body they will still be subject to the law – see below.

b. Estate agents are covered by the general laws relating to consumers' rights *see* **Goods & Services**

c. In addition to this, the **Estate Agents Act 1979** makes it compulsory for anyone engaged in estate agency work to:

- disclose any personal interests they or their associates have in a property with which they are dealing
- tell clients in advance which fees will have to be paid and how much they will be
- take care of and account properly for deposits held on trust for a client
- pay interest on deposits of more than £500, if this amounts to more than £10

The Act also prescribes that:

- the taking of pre-contract deposits is forbidden in Scotland
- bankrupts are not allowed to be estate agents, although they may work for one
- anyone classed by the Director General of Fair Trading as 'unfit' can be banned from taking part in estate agency work

d. In 1993 the **Property Misdescriptions Act 1991** came into force. Under this Act it is a criminal offence to 'deliberately misdescribe' (i.e. to mislead with regard to the facts about) a property in either written or verbal communication with a prospective client.

If you think your estate agent has broken any of these legal requirements you should complain to a local Trading Standards Officer, and may also be able to claim compensation through the courts *see* **Where to get help**

NB

At the time of writing there were plans to extend the remit and the associated Code of Practice of the Ombudsman for Corporate Estate Agents to cover all estate agents. For more information about the Ombudsman's procedures *see* **Estate Agents 2**

Estate Agents 2

1. *Who Can I Complain To?*

The Ombudsman for Corporate Estate Agents (OCEA)

PO Box 1114	*or*	Beckett House
Salisbury		4 Bridge Street
Wiltshire SP1 1YQ		Salisbury SP1 2LX

Tel: 01722 333306
Fax: 01722 332296

2. *What Sort of Complaints Do They Deal With?*

a.   The OCEA scheme covers most of the stock-market-quoted estate agency offices, i.e. large residential estate agency chains owned by banks, building societies and insurance companies. There are currently 14 Member Agencies of the OCEA Scheme with a combined network of some 2,000 outlets. Small, non-corporate estate agencies are outside the Scheme.

b.   The Ombudsman will investigate all complaints about the residential (not commercial) side of the corporate estate agency business which cannot be resolved by the company itself. Any complaint about maladministration (including inefficiency or undue delay), unfair treatment, or infringement of your legal rights or of the OCEA code of practice, that has cost you money or inconvenience, will be investigated.

c.   The Ombudsman *cannot* investigate a complaint if:

- it concerns something you knew about for 12 months or more *before* you complained to the estate agent
- you are currently pursuing compensation by other means (e.g. through the courts)
- it is about a survey
- you intend to claim compensation of more than £100,000

d. You can complain to the Ombudsman whether or not you actually bought or sold your home through a corporate estate agent – i.e. both potential and actual buyers are covered by the scheme.

e. You must complain to the OCEA within *six months* of the final decision on your complaint from the estate agency concerned.

f. The OCEA Code of Practice is in addition to your legal rights. For more information on the specific protection afforded by the **Estate Agents Act 1979** and the **Property Misdescriptions Act 1991**   *see* **Estate Agents 1**

3. *How Independent Is the Complaints Procedure?*

The OCEA is a voluntary, private sector scheme which operates independently of the corporate estate agencies. The Ombudsman himself is responsible to an independent council.

4. *Compensation/Redress?*

If the decision is in your favour, the Ombudsman can grant compensation of up to £100,000.

5. *Any Appeal?*

a. The Ombudsman's decision is in all cases binding on the Member Agency concerned.

b. If you accept the Ombudsman's decision (and any associated compensation) in full and final settlement of your complaint, you are legally bound by it.

c. If you choose not to accept the decision of the Ombudsman, you retain the right to claim compensation through the courts   *see* **Where to get help**

6. *Other Options?*

a. If your estate agent is a member of:

- The National Association of Estate Agents
  see **Estate Agents 1**
- The Royal Institution of Chartered Surveyors
  see **Surveyors**
- The Incorporated Society of Valuers and Auctioneers
  see **Valuers & Auctioneers**

b. If your estate agent is not a member of any of these professional associations, and not covered by the OCEA, your only option is legal action   *see* **Where to get help**

c. For more information on the law covering Estate Agents
    see **Estate Agents 1**

Goods & Services

European Union

1. *Who Can I Complain To?*

You should complain in writing (in any of the eleven languages of the Member States) directly to:

The European Ombudsman
1, avenue du President Robert Schuman
BP 403
F-67001 Strasbourg CEDEX
FRANCE

Tel: 0033 88 17 23 13/83
Fax: 0033 88 17 90 62

An information booklet, including a standard form for complaints, is available from:

The European Commission
8 Storey's Gate
London SW1P 3AT

Tel: 0171 973 1992
Fax: 0171 973 1900

2. *What Sort of Complaints Do They Deal With?*

a. Complaints about 'maladministration' on the part of European Union institutions or bodies. Generally speaking, 'maladministration' means poor or failed administration, through the improper application of the rules, for example:

- administrative irregularities
- administrative omissions
- abuse of power
- negligence
- illegal procedures
- malfunction or incompetence
- avoidable delay
- lack or refusal of information

b. You can complain to the European Ombudsman if you are

- a citizen of the European Union
- a non-Union national residing in the Union *or*
- representing a business, association or collective body with registered offices in the Union

c. The main institutions and bodies covered by the Ombudsman are:

- the European Parliament
- the Council of Europe
- the European Commission
- the European Court of Justice (administrative functions only)
- the European Court of Auditors
- the Economic and Social Committee
- the Committee of the Regions

- the European Monetary Institute (future European Central Bank)
- the European Investment Bank

All 'decentralised bodies' (i.e. European Union bodies with offices in Member Countries) are also covered.

d. The Ombudsman *cannot* investigate complaints:

- made more than *two years* after the date on which the relevant facts became known
- which are or have been the subject of legal proceedings
- about national or local administrations, even when the complaint refers to the implementation of Union law

e. If your complaint is accepted for investigation, you will be kept informed of its progress. Where appropriate, a complaint can be treated as confidential.

3. *How Independent Is the Complaints Procedure?*

The Ombudsman is appointed by the European Parliament but is completely independent in the performance of his duties. He has a statutory duty to act in the general interest of the Union and the citizens of the Union.

4. *Compensation/Redress?*

a. In the first instance the Ombudsman will seek an amicable solution which puts right the maladministration and satisfies the complainant.

b. If this attempt at conciliation fails, he will inform the institution(s) concerned and may make draft recommendations to resolve the case. The institution must answer within 3 months, at the end of which the Ombudsman may send a report to the European Parliament (and to the institution concerned) including firm recommendations, so that the Parliament can draw any necessary political conclusions (for more about the powers of the European Parliament, see below).

c. You will be informed of the outcome of the Ombudsman's investigation.

d. If the European Ombudsman cannot deal with your complaint he may be able to pass it on to the appropriate body (e.g. the Parliamentary or Local Government Ombudsman). And if, in the course of enquiries, the Ombudsman learns of facts which might relate to criminal law, he will notify the relevant national authorities.

5. *Any Appeal?*

No.

6. *Other Options?*

The other main way to complain or make your views known about European issues is to **petition the European Parliament**. All citizens of, and groups based in, the European Union have the right to do this on matters falling within the scope of the EU's activities. Petitions may relate to matters of general concern such as the protection of architectural, cultural or ecological heritage, as well as individual complaints on such matters as recognition of entitlement to social security benefits or a pension. The EU's main principles and objectives are:

- free movement of persons, goods, services and capital
- non-discrimination on the basis of nationality
- equal treatment for men and women
- fiscal harmonisation
- development of research and technology
- the right to education, training and health services
- environmental protection

For more information about how to petition the European Parliament contact:

European Parliament
2 Queen Anne's Gate
London SW1H 9AA

Tel: 0171 222 0411

Petitions may be addressed directly to:

The President of the European Parliament
L–2929 LUXEMBOURG

see also **Local Government**

Government Departments

NB

The following bodies also play a role in monitoring Union administration:

- *The European Parliament*'s role is to exercise political control over Community administration, using both traditional parliamentary mechanisms (questions, censure), and the avenues of committees of inquiry and the follow-up to petitions (see above).
- The *Commission*'s role is to ensure that Union law is applied by the Member States and by the institutions, and to refer cases of infringement to the Court of Justice.
- The *Court of Justice*'s role is to rule, in its judgments, on the proper application and interpretation of Union law.
- The *Court of Auditors*' role is to examine the accounts of all revenue and expenditure of the Union, and to check the soundness of financial management.

Examinations

1. *Who Can I Complain To?*

Independent Appeals Authority for Schools Examinations (IAASE)
Newcombe House
45 Notting Hill Gate
London W11 3JB

Tel: 0171 229 1234
Fax: 0171 221 2141

Note: Appeals to the IAASE must be made by the examination centre that entered the candidate for an exam, i.e. by the headteacher or principal of the college. Individuals (students or parents) cannot appeal directly to the IAASE, unless the candidate has been privately entered.

2. *What Sort of Complaints Do They Deal With?*

a. The IAASE exists to ensure that candidates, parents, schools and colleges who make use of the school examination system can have confidence that the grades awarded are as fair and accurate as possible. The Authority will hear appeals against results awarded in GCSE, and GCE A and AS level examinations. A list of the examining bodies covered is given in the *Appendix* at the end of this entry.

b. The IAASE will hear an appeal only when the internal complaints and appeal procedures of the examining body have been exhausted (although see next point). (The addresses of the relevant examining and accrediting bodies are listed in the *Appendix* at the end of this entry.) It can then investigate the full range of processes involved in, and leading to, the award of grades, including:

- the setting of papers
- marking and moderation
- the grade award

- enquires-upon-results and appeals *and*
- the administrative arrangements supporting these processes

c. A headteacher, college principal or private candidate wishing to appeal to the IAASE should notify it of their likely intention of doing so *before December 14* of the year of the examination (*May 14* following autumn or winter examinations), *even though the examining body's appeals procedures may not have been completed.* Only in exceptional circumstances will the Authority hear appeals affecting the previous summer's examination after *June 30.*

d. Applications to appeal to the IAASE should be made on the official application form and be accompanied by a £50 deposit. The Authority's Chairman will then decide whether an appeal should go ahead, and will inform the parties concerned of her decision within 14 working days. If leave to appeal is refused at this stage, the deposit will be returned.

e. If leave to appeal is granted, all parties will be given *10 working days* to provide more details of their side of the case in writing. These papers will then be circulated at least 7 working days before the hearing.

f. At the hearing both sides will

- have a chance to present their case and call witnesses
- be questioned by the panel
- have a chance to put questions to the other party *via* the panel chairman
- be asked to sum up

There will not normally be more than three representatives or witnesses in each party.

g. Observers from the School Curriculum and Assessment Authority, SCAA (in Wales the Assessment and Curriculum Authority for Wales, ACAC) and the inspection body OFSTED (in Wales the OHMCI) may also be present, and may be invited to give expert evidence at any time.

h. The decision to refuse or allow the appeal will be sent to both parties within 3 working days of the hearing. The reasons for that decision will be sent out within 15 working days of the first letter, to both parties and to all other interested official bodies.

3. *How Independent Is the Complaints Procedure?*

The IAASE is an independent body set up by government. Hearings are conducted by the Authority Chairman or Deputy Chairman plus two panel members, one drawn from the list of nominees of the examining bodies and one drawn from the list of nominees of the professional teacher and headteacher associations.

SCAA and ACAC are the statutory accrediting authorities for GCSE and GCE A and AS levels, with particular responsibility for approving GCSE syllabuses.

4. *Compensation/Redress?*

a. If the IAASE panel decides to allow an appeal, the examining body will be asked to reconsider the case. The Authority may make directions about what needs to be reconsidered, and the means of doing so. When appropriate, the Authority may offer broader recommendations to examining bodies and centres, to SCAA (ACAC) and to the Department of Education in Northern Ireland.

b. The outcome of any reconsideration must normally be conveyed in writing by the examining body to both the appellant and the IAASE within four working weeks. If the Authority is dissatisfied with the outcome, it may pursue the matter with the examining body, and ultimately report the matter to SCAA (or ACAC). SCAA (or ACAC) will investigate in such cases, and has more (statutory) leverage to force an examining body to comply.

c. The Authority is *not* empowered to re-mark candidates'

work, nor can it compel the examining bodies to raise grades.

d. Travelling and subsistence expenses will be reimbursed by the IAASE. If your appeal is allowed, the £50 deposit will also be returned.

5. *Any Appeal?*

a. Not within the system. You cannot, for example, appeal the Chairman's decision to refuse an application for an appeal hearing.

b. If you are unhappy with the way the IAASE has handled your case you can ask your MP to refer your case to the Parliamentary Ombudsman *see* **Government Departments**

6. *Other Options?*

• If you are unhappy about the *quality* of a particular qualification, you can complain to the relevant awarding body or accrediting body. The addresses are listed in the *Appendix* below.

see also **Further Education**

Local Government

NB

• Non-GCSE qualifications (GNVQs and NVQs) have no analogous appeals procedure: the complaints procedure ends with the NCVQ. There are proposals under consideration at the time of writing to merge SCAA and ACAC with the NCVQ, and to extend the remit of the NIAASE to cover all Further Education examinations.

Appendix

GCE A Level, AS and GCSE Awarding Bodies

The Associated Examining Board
Stag Hill House
Guildford
Surrey GU2 5XJ

Tel: 01483 506506

Northern Examinations and Assessment Board
Devas Street
Manchester M15 6EX

Tel: 0161 953 1180

Oxford & Cambridge Schools Examination Board
   (Cambridge Office)
Purbeck House
Purbeck Road
Cambridge CB2 2PU

Tel: 01223 411211

Oxford & Cambridge Schools Examination Board
   (Oxford Office)
Elsfield Way
Oxford OX2 8EP

Tel: 01865 54421

University of Cambridge Local Examinations Syndicate
Syndicate Buildings
1 Hills Road
Cambridge CB1 2EU

Tel: 01223 61111

University of London Examinations and Assessment
  Council
Stewart House
32 Russell Square
London WC1B 5DN

Tel: 0171 331 4000

University of Oxford Delegacy of Local Examinations
Ewert House
Ewert Place
Summertown
Oxford OX2 7BZ

Tel: 01865 54291

Joint Council for the GCSE
6th Floor
Netherton House
23–29 Marsh Street
Bristol BS1 4BP

Tel: 01272 214379

Vocational Awarding Bodies

Business & Technology Education Council
Central House
Upper Woburn Place
London WC1H 0HH

Tel: 0171 413 8400

RSA Examinations Board
Progress House
Westwood Way
Coventry CV4 8HS

Tel: 01203 470033

City & Guilds of London Institute
76 Portland Place
London W1N 4AA

Tel: 0171 278 2468

London Chamber of Commerce and Industry
    Examinations Board
Marlowe House
Station Road
Sidcup
Kent DA15 7BJ

Tel: 0181 302 0267

There are too many bodies involved in awarding NVQs to list here. Ask your college or LEA who you can complain to about these.

Accrediting Bodies for GCSEs and GCE A and AS levels

School Curriculum and Assessment Authority (SCAA)
Newcombe House
45 Notting Hill Gate
London W11 3JB

Tel: 0171 229 1234

Assessment and Curriculum Authority for Wales (ACAC)
Castle Buildings
Womanby Street
Cardiff CF1 9SX

Tel: 01222 375400

Accrediting Body for GNVQs and NVQs

National Council for Vocational Qualifications (NCVQ)
222 Euston Road
London NW1 2BZ

Tel: 0171 387 9898

F

Financial Services (General)

Introduction

The world of financial services regulation is complex: this general section is intended as a guide to which of the individual entries may be relevant to your needs.

The **Financial Services Act 1986** instituted the current regulatory structure. The Securities and Investments Board (SIB) is the top tier in a two-tier regulatory system. Underneath SIB is the second tier of so-called frontline regulators, consisting of the Self-Regulating Organisations (SROs), Recognised Professional Bodies (RPBs) and Recognised Investment Exchanges (RIEs). SROs and RPBs handle complaints by members of the public.

There are a number of Ombudsman schemes covering the financial services sector. In addition to this regulatory structure there are also some non-statutory bodies involved in specialised dispute resolution, e.g. OPAS (Pensions), PIAS (Insurance), as well as a range of 'rescue funds' set up by the various parts of the industry as a financial safety net for customers whose service providers go bust.

Some regulatory remedies may be legally binding and preclude further action through the courts (you will be told this at the time). The Financial Services Act specifically allows you to seek compensation through the courts if you have suffered loss resulting from a breach of a regulator's rules by a member company, and it is always worth bearing in mind that legal action may be the most appropriate, and sometimes the only, way of pursuing a complaint about financial services. If you are considering legal action, we recommend you to seek independent legal advice.

1. The Securities and Investments Board (SIB)

SIB's main responsibility is to make sure that companies and individuals providing investment services maintain a high standard of honesty, competence and solvency. SIB supervises the frontline regulators and delegates responsibility for authorisation and day-to-day regulation to specialist SROs and RPBs. A few investment firms are still directly regulated by SIB.

SIB maintains a computerised database of registered firms called the Central Register, which can be accessed by writing to, phoning, or visiting SIB (see below). The Central Register can tell you whether the firm you are dealing with is registered at all, and/or which frontline regulator should be approached with a specific complaint. If a firm or individual is carrying out investment business without authorisation, SIB has powers of criminal prosecution which can result in two years' imprisonment and/or an unlimited fine. Unauthorised firms may be wound up, and unfit individuals can be disqualified from carrying on investment business.

SIB publishes several guides to the financial services sector for the general public, and can give general advice by phone. SIB is overseen by the Treasury but is not a government department, and is wholly funded by the investment industry.

Securities and Investment Board (SIB)
Gavrelle House
2–14 Bunhill Row
London EC1Y 8RA

Tel: 0171 638 1240
Register enquiries: 0171 929 3652

2. **Self-Regulating Organisations (SROs)**

Investment Management Regulatory Organisation (IMRO)
IMRO regulates fund managers, authorised unit trust managers and venture capital companies, but has now stopped handling complaints against IMRO members. From 1 May 1995, complaints made against members of IMRO should go straight from the complaints department of the individual member firm to the Investment Ombudsman   *see* **Investment 3**

Financial Intermediaries, Managers and Brokers Regulatory Organisation (FIMBRA)
FIMBRA's members include financial advisers and other members of the financial profession who advise members of the public on investments and execute deals on their behalf. It has

now largely been replaced by the Personal Investment Authority (PIA) as it is expected to be derecognised in the near future. Any complaints about FIMBRA members should therefore be directed to the PIA   *see* **Investment 1**

Life Assurance and Unit Trust Regulatory Organisation (LAUTRO)
LAUTRO used to authorise life insurance and unit trust companies and friendly societies which market life insurance, endowment policies, investment bonds, unit trusts, permanent health insurance and pensions. It has also now largely been replaced by the Personal Investment Authority (PIA) as it is expected to be derecognised in the near future. Any complaints about LAUTRO members should therefore be directed to the PIA   *see* **Investment 1**

Personal Investment Authority (PIA)
Since July 1994 PIA has substantially taken over the regulation of firms which carry out investment business with private investors, and is now the main SRO for the retail financial market. Most of its members were previously regulated by LAUTRO and FIMBRA   *see* **Investment 1**

Securities and Futures Authority (SFA)
The SFA is responsible for regulating firms in the securities and futures sector, and was formed by the merger of the Securities Association with the Association of Futures Brokers and Dealers in April 1991   *see* **Investment 2**

3.   Recognised Professional Bodies (RPBs)
RPBs regulate investment business when it is carried out by professionals operating outside the sphere of their normal business, such as by accountants or lawyers. These firms must be certified to give advice about financial services by a Professional Body recognised by the SIB. The firms will then be listed in the SIB Central Register. The most important RPBs are:

Chartered Association of Certified Accountants (ACCA)
                    see **Accountants 1**

Institute of Chartered Accountants in England and Wales (ICAEW)   *see* **Accountants 2**

Institute of Chartered Accountants in Ireland (ICAI)
                    see **Accountants 2**

Institute of Chartered Accountants of Scotland (ICAS)
see **Accountants 2**

Insurance Brokers Registration Council (IBRC)   *see* **Insurance 1**

Law Society   *see* **Where to get help**

Law Society of Northern Ireland   *see* **Where to get help**

Law Society of Scotland   *see* **Where to get help**

4.   'Rescue Funds'

There are several 'rescue funds' set up to compensate investors suffering financial loss as a result of their authorised financial service provider going bust. If you do business with a firm that is *not* authorised by the SIB or one of the frontline regulators, and it goes bust, you probably won't get any compensation.

The **Investors Compensation Scheme** (ICS) was set up by SIB as the rescue fund for customers of failed investment firms that were authorised by an SRO or the SIB   *see* **Investment 4**

RPBs have their own compensation arrangements, so for the:

Certified Accountants Financial Services Compensation Scheme
see **Accountants 1**

Chartered Accountants Investment Business Compensation Scheme   *see* **Accountants 2**

Deposit Protection Scheme   *see* **Banks**

Building Societies Investor Protection Fund
see **Building Societies**

5.   Ombudsmen

There are also several Ombudsmen who have a role in the financial services sector:

Banking Ombudsman   *see* **Banking**

Building Societies Ombudsman   *see* **Building Societies**

Insurance Ombudsman Bureau   *see* **Insurance 2**

Investment Ombudsman   *see* **Investment 3**

Personal Investment Authority Ombudsman Bureau
see **Investment 1**

Pensions Ombudsman   *see* **Pensions**

NB

The Unit Trust Ombudsman has now merged with the Investment Ombudsman.

6.   Further advice
For more advice relating to:

Pensions   *see* **Pensions**

Insurance   *see* **Insurance 3**

Legal action   *see* **Where to get help**

General complaints tips   *see* **Introduction**

Funerals

1. *Who Can I Complain To?*

The Funeral Ombudsman
31 Southampton Row
London WC1B 5HJ

Tel: 0171 430 1112
Fax: 0171 430 1012

2. *What Sort of Complaints Do They Deal With?*

a.   Complaints about funeral companies which are members of the Funeral Ombudsman Scheme (FOS). This includes all companies that are members of either the Funeral Standards Council (FSC) or the Funeral Planning Council (FPC). The FOS therefore covers some funeral arrangements which are planned and paid for in advance as well as some funerals arranged at the time of death.

b. Any complaint should first be addressed to the funeral director or planning company concerned, who should respond within 21 days. If, after this, you are still unhappy and wish to refer your complaint to the Funeral Ombudsman, you should do so within *six months* of receiving the final offer of settlement from the company, or of receiving notification of your right to complain to the Ombudsman, whichever is later, but normally only as long as this date falls within *two years* of the event giving rise to the complaint. This time limit can, however, be waived where there are extenuating circumstances or it is not reasonably practicable for a complaint to have been made earlier.

c. The Ombudsman can consider complaints about, for example:

*   failure to provide services to the standard promised
*   charging more than was originally agreed
*   carrying out a funeral unprofessionally, inefficiently or with unnecessary delay
*   any deviation from the FOS Code of Practice

d. The FOS Code of Practice, drafted in consultation with the Office of Fair Trading, offers specific assurances and protection *in addition to your legal rights* in such areas as: conduct and training of staff; advertising and marketing; information and choice; prices, estimates and invoices. Members must, for example, offer customers a simple, basic funeral before providing a written quotation for any funeral, and display and make available fully itemised price lists. Copies of the Code of Practice are available from member companies.

e. The Ombudsman *cannot* consider complaints if:

*   the events in question happened before 4 April 1994 (when the Ombudsman Scheme came into effect)
*   the dispute is, or has previously been, the subject of legal proceedings
*   the funeral company you have been dealing with is not a member of the Scheme

3. *How Independent Is the Complaints Procedure?*

The Funeral Ombudsman Scheme is a voluntary, private sector scheme which operates independently of the funeral companies. It has been granted membership of the British and Irish Ombudsman Association, which has strict independence criteria.

The Ombudsman is appointed by and responsible to the Council of the Funeral Ombudsman, which is made up of a majority of independent consumer representatives, together with representatives from the FSC and FPC.

4. *Compensation/Redress?*

The Ombudsman will try to help you reach an informal settlement with the company concerned. If this is impossible, and the Ombudsman finds in your favour, he can award compensation of up to £50,000, including up to £5,000 for aggravation, distress, inconvenience and expenses where appropriate.

5. *Any Appeal?*

No, but if you are unhappy with the Ombudsman's decision you can still pursue a claim for compensation through the courts
see **Where to get help**

6. *Other Options?*

a.   If the company you have been dealing with is not a member of the Scheme, they may be a member of either the National Association of Funeral Directors (NAFD) or the Society of Allied and Independent Funeral Directors (SAIFD). Both of these trade associations operate their own two-stage self-regulatory complaints procedure, after which you have the option of going to independent arbitration (administered by the Chartered Institute of Arbitrators). This may save you time and money, and you may be awarded compensation, but arbitration is not free, and if you accept the decision of the arbitrator, you no longer have the option of going to court.

For more information on the NAFD Consumer Redress Scheme contact:

National Association of Funeral Directors
618 Warwick Road
Solihull
West Midlands B91 1AA

Tel: **0121 711 1343**
Fax: **0121 711 1351**

For more information on how to complain to the SAIFD Standards Committee contact:

Society of Allied and Independent Funeral Directors
Crowndale House
1 Ferdinand Place
London NW1 8EE

Tel: **0171 267 6777**
Fax: **0171 267 1147**

b. If the company you have been dealing with is not a member of the FOS, or of another trade association, or if you decide not to accept arbitration under the NAFD or SAIFD schemes, your only option is legal action *see* **Where to get help**

c. The two trade bodies set up to regulate pre-paid funerals, the FPC (linked to the FSC) and the National Association of Pre-Paid Funeral Plans NAPFP (linked to the NAFD) have their own Codes of Practice stating that funds must be controlled by independent trustees. You may, therefore, be protected if your complaint relates to a pre-planned funeral arranged with a member of either of these associations – ask the company you are dealing with about this. There are currently no laws to protect funds paid into these plans.

d. If your complaint relates to a life insurance scheme designed to cover funeral costs, you may be able to complain to the Insurance Ombudsman Bureau *see* **Insurance 2**

Further Education

1. *Who Can I Complain To?*

The right person to complain to in the first instance depends on the specific complaint – see below.

2. *What Sort of Complaints Do They Deal With?*

a. *Colleges* – you should complain directly to the **college authorities** if you are unhappy about any of the following:

- teaching standards
- administration
- facilities (e.g. availability of necessary library books, catering arrangements)
- equal opportunities policy, including sex and race discrimination and disabled access
- availability and accuracy of information

All colleges should have mechanisms in place for dealing with formal complaints and should provide an initial response to your query within 10 working days.

b. *Availability of courses* – if you want to take a particular course, but you have discovered that it is not available at a college within a reasonable travelling distance, you should complain to the **Funding Council** (addresses are given in the *Appendix*, below), or to the **LEA** (in your local phone book) in the case of some general educational and leisure courses that do not lead to formal qualifications.

c. *Course content* – if you are unhappy about the quality of a particular course, you can complain to **your college** and if still unhappy to the **Funding Council** (see *Appendix*, below).

d. *LEAs* – if you think your LEA has treated you unfairly (e.g. has been slow in processing your grant or has made serious administrative errors) you should complain to a **council official** or to **your local councillor** (in your local phone book).

e.   *Qualifications and exams*   *see* **Examinations**

3. *How Independent Is the Complaints Procedure?*

a.   All complaints procedures are internal except for the Local Government Ombudsman, who is independent (see *Any Appeal?*, below).

b.   GCSE and GCE examinations are subject to an independent appeals procedure   *see* **Examinations**

4. *Compensation/Redress?*

a.   If your complaint is found to be justified then matters should be put right to your satisfaction.

b.   If you have complained to the Local Government Ombudsman and they find in your favour they may recommend, for example, that your LEA pays you compensation.

5. *Any Appeal?*

a.   If you are unhappy about the *way* an LEA handled your complaint you can refer the matter to the Local Government Ombudsman   *see* **Local Government**

b.   If you believe that a Funding Council or LEA is not fulfilling its legal responsibilities, or is behaving unreasonably, you can always write to the Secretary of State for Education and Employment.

6. *Other Options?*

see also **Examinations**

Higher Education

Local Government

Discrimination

NB

- At the time of writing the government was planning to introduce a right of appeal to an outside authority for students who feel they have been unfairly treated by their campus student union.
- For the addresses of all the GCE A Level, AS and GCSE Awarding Bodies and Vocational Awarding Bodies, and associated Accrediting Bodies   *see* **Examinations**
- For the addresses of the offices of the Department for Education and Employment   *see* **Schools 1**
- For more information see the Further Education Funding Council leaflet, *Complaints about colleges of further education and sixth form colleges*, available from the addresses below.

Appendix

Funding Bodies

Further Education
  Funding Council for
  England
Sheriffs Orchard
Greyfriars Road
Coventry CV1 3PJ

Tel: 01203 530300

Further Education
  Funding Council for
  Wales
Lambourne House
Cardiff Business Park
Cardiff CF4 5GL

Tel: 01222 530300

G

Garages

1. Who Can I Complain To?

a. *Used car sales, servicing and repairs in England, Wales and Northern Ireland*

> National Conciliation Service
> Retail Motor Industry Federation (RMI)
> 2nd Floor
> Cheshunt House
> 32 North Street
> Rugby CV21 2AH
>
> Tel: 01788 576465
> Fax: 01788 547361

b. *Used car sales, servicing and repairs in Scotland*

> Customer Complaints Service
> Scottish Motor Trade Association Ltd (SMTA)
> 3 Palmerston Place
> Edinburgh EH12 5AF
>
> Tel: 0131 225 3643
> Fax: 0131 220 0446

c. *New cars only (UK)*

> **Consumer Affairs Officer**
> **Society of Motor Manufacturers and Traders (SMMT)**
> **Forbes House**
> **Halkin Street**
> **London SW1X 7DS**
>
> **Tel: 0171 235 7000**
> **Fax: 0171 235 7112**

Note: For who to complain to about vehicle body repairs or motorcycle garages (including motorcycle sales and repairs by RMIF members) see the end of this entry.

2. *What Sort of Complaints Do They Deal With?*

a. Complaints about the quality of goods or services provided by garages which are members of the above trade associations. (The RMI is an umbrella organisation incorporating several smaller trade associations.)

b. Members of these associations are covered by the Code of Practice for the Motor Industry, which has sections covering:

- new car sales
- car manufacturers' warranties (guarantees)
- used car sales
- replacement parts, accessories and petrol
- repairs and servicing
- advertising
- handling and monitoring of complaints

Copies of the Code are available from member garages or the addresses above.

c. The appropriate body will investigate all complaints that cannot be resolved with the garage concerned, or by the individual manufacturer if a new car dealer cannot help under a warranty, as long as they are not and have not been the subject of legal proceedings, and are not being pursued by a third party such as a Motoring Organisation.

d. The investigating body will first attempt to resolve the matter by (free) conciliation. Conciliation is almost always conducted via correspondence, although it may involve a vehicle examination by an independent engineer. If conciliation is not possible, you will be offered arbitration.

e. Arbitration procedures are broadly similar to those followed by the Chartered Institute of Arbitrators, with registration fees ranging from about £45 to about £90 per party, according to the amount claimed.

3. *How Independent Is the Complaints Procedure?*

Conciliation will be administered by the body concerned but is always impartial.

Arbitration is administered by an Independent Panel of Arbitrators where the chairman is appointed by the associations in consultation with the Director General of Fair Trading (DGFT), or under comparable arrangements also approved by the DGFT.

4. *Compensation/Redress?*

Conciliation may result in a mutually acceptable offer of compensation and/or redress.

Arbitrators can award compensation, which may include an amount for inconvenience and distress. He or she also has discretion to refund the registration fee to the successful party.

5. *Any Appeal?*

If an acceptable solution is arrived at through conciliation both parties can agree to make it legally binding.

If you decide to go to arbitration the results are normally legally binding.

6. *Other Options?*

a. If your complaint is about *vehicle body repair work* carried out by a garage which is a member of the Vehicle Builders and Repairers Association (VBRA), and you are still unhappy after having complained to the garage concerned, contact:

> **The Vehicle Builders and Repairers Association Limited**
> **Belmont House**
> **Gildersome**
> **Leeds LS27 7TW**
>
> Tel: 0113 253 8333
> Fax: 0113 238 0496

The VBRA operates a highly regarded Code of Practice, with conciliation and arbitration procedures similar to those described above.

b. An analogous Code of Practice for the Motorcycle Industry is administered by the RMI for garages which are members of the Motorcycle Retailers Association (itself a member trade association of the RMI), and by the Motorcycle Industry Association for motorcycle manufacturers. Members of other RMI trade associations who are only registered as car dealers but who sell the occasional motorbike will also be covered by this Code.

> i. If your complaint is about a *motorcycle garage* which is covered by this Scheme, and you are still unhappy after having complained directly to the garage concerned, you can write directly to the **National Conciliation Service** at the address given in section 1 a, above, or contact:
>
> > **The Motorcycle Retailers Association (MRA)**
> > **201 Great Portland Street**
> > **London W1N 6AB**
> >
> > Tel: 0171 580 9122
> > Fax: 0171 580 6376
>
> ii. If your complaint is about a *motorcycle manufacturer* which is a member of the Motorcycle Industry Association, and you are still unhappy after having complained

directly to the garage concerned, or the garage cannot help you under the warranty, contact:

Motorcycle Industry Association
Starley House
Eaton Road
Coventry CV1 2FH

Tel: **01203 227427**

iii. Arbitration procedures for both kinds of complaint are similar to those described above.
iv. An associated scheme is the Code of Conduct operated by *motorcycle rider training schools* which are members of the **Motorcycle Rider Training Association** (MRTA). Complaints about MRTA members should be sent to them at the address given for the MRA, above.

- If the garage you have been using is not a member of any of the associations listed, or you decide not to accept arbitration, you may still be able to claim compensation through the courts
  see **Where to get help**
- For more information on your rights as a consumer
  see **Goods & Services**

Gas

1. *Who Can I Complain To?*

Complaints can be made in writing, over the phone or in person to your regional **Gas Consumers Council**. The address and phone number is listed in the phone book under Gas, and shown on the back of your gas bill. Alternatively contact:

Gas Consumers Council
Head Office
Abford House
15 Wilton Road
London SW1V 1LT

Tel: 0645 060 708
Fax: 0171 630 9934
Minicom: 0345 581401

2. *What Sort of Complaints Do They Deal With?*

a. The GCC will look into any complaint regarding

- gas supply
- gas appliances
- gas installation
- servicing and repairs
- payment of bills, including debt and disconnection
- safety

or anything else to do with gas.

b. If you have not already complained to the supplier, installer, manufacturer, retailer, landlord, local authority or housing association or other organisation or person concerned, the GCC can help you do so. If you have already done so, the GCC will take up the matter on your behalf with managers and executives of the relevant Gas supplier or any other gas appliance or service company.

c. It will investigate all complaints relating to gas supply whether you are a customer (or wish to be a customer) of British Gas or of any other company in the gas business.

d. The GCC has a special interest in consumers of pension age or with a disability, and can arrange to visit you at home if this is necessary.

3. *How Independent Is the Complaints Procedure?*

The Gas Consumers Council is a watchdog body set up by Parliament to ensure that gas consumers get a fair deal from the gas companies. Its members are chosen to represent the regional interests of gas consumers, and are appointed by the President of the Board of Trade. It is completely independent from OFGAS, the government and all gas companies.

4. *Compensation/Redress?*

a. The Council has no statutory powers to force anyone to comply with its recommendations but manages to get satisfactory solutions in the vast majority of cases, with acceptable compromises being reached in about half of the remaining minority.

b. If the GCC cannot solve your problem it will:

- suggest other ways in which you might pursue it *and/or*
- refer the matter to the Director General of OFGAS for further action and possible enforcement *and/or*
- get advice about legal help

5. *Any Appeal?*

No, but if you are unhappy with the way GCC staff have dealt with your complaint, you can ask for your case to be reviewed by a manager.

6. *Other Options?*

a. The Director General of OFGAS has statutory powers relating to the price of gas and the maintenance of gas supply, among other things. He can, for example, order a gas company to reconnect you if you have been cut off following the burglary of your gas meter or in circumstances of genuine financial hardship. The GCC is under an obligation to inform OFGAS on receipt of any complaint which falls within OFGAS's powers, but you can also complain directly to OFGAS. Their address is:

OFGAS
Office of Gas Supply
105 Victoria Street
London SW1E 6QT

Tel: 0171 828 0898

b. Depending on your complaint you may be able to take a gas supplier, installer, appliance manufacturer or retailer, etc. to court to claim compensation *see* **Where to get help**

see also **Gas Installers**

Goods & Services

Gas Installers

1. *Who Can I Complain To?*

The Council for Registered Gas Installers (CORGI)
1 Elmwood
Chineham Business Park
Crockford Lane
Basingstoke
Hampshire RG24 8WG

Tel: 01256 372200
Fax: 01256 708144

2. *What Sort of Complaints Do They Deal With?*

a. Complaints about gas safety regarding all (registered and non-registered) gas installers, that cannot be resolved to your satisfaction by the installer themselves. These might include complaints about such things as the location of flues, ventilation, appliance location, etc.

b. CORGI *only* handles complaints about gas safety standards, it *cannot* investigate complaints about, for example, over-charging or damage to carpets from boiler leaks.

c. If the gas installer you have used is a member of CORGI, an Inspector will visit you and carry out a thorough examination of the gas appliance in question, with the help of the installer who did the work. You do not have to allow the installer you have a grievance with back into your property to assist the CORGI Inspector, but unless you do, the Inspector might be limited to making a visual inspection of the installation.

3. *How Independent Is the Complaints Procedure?*

CORGI is the body approved by the Health and Safety Executive (HSE), under the **Gas Safety (Installation and Use) Regulations**, to maintain a register of competent gas installation businesses in the United Kingdom. The Council is made up of representatives of relevant trade, training, professional and employee organisations, as well as of a few consumer and other bodies. It is financed by registration fees, but is operationally independent.

4. *Compensation/Redress?*

a. If the Inspector finds that the Gas Safety Regulations or British Standard specifications have not been followed, the installer, if registered, will be instructed to correct the faults identified within a set period (free of charge). The installer may also be advised that further training for himself or his operatives is necessary. In extreme cases, the HSE may prosecute registered installers for a dangerous gas installation.

b. If the installer is not registered, the Inspector will advise you which courses of action are available to you. Information about non-registered gas installers is forwarded to the HSE for enforcement action, as it is against the law for any business to carry out gas work without being registered with CORGI. Trading Standards Officers may also prosecute under the Trade Descriptions Act if an installer claimed to be CORGI registered and was then found not to be.

c. Your only option for compensation or redress, if you have used an unregistered installer (or if your complaint is about something other than safety), may be to go to court.

d. CORGI itself cannot make repairs, or contact registered installers on your behalf, nor can it act as an 'expert witness' in civil actions.

5. *Any Appeal?*

a. If you refuse to allow the original installer to correct the faults, CORGI cannot take any further action.

b. If you are unhappy with the Inspector's decision about the safety or otherwise of your installation, you can ask CORGI to review its findings. If you are still dissatisfied after this review, you will be advised to obtain a second opinion (for which you will have to pay). If the consultant's opinion is different from that of the CORGI Inspector, CORGI will review its findings for a second time in the light of the consultant's report.

c. Ultimately, you may wish to refer a complaint to the Health and Safety Executive (HSE), which is responsible for approving CORGI. They can be contacted at:

**Health and Safety Executive (HSE) Information Centre
Broad Lane
Sheffield S3 7HQ**

Tel: 0114 289 2345

6. *Other Options?*

- For advice on going to court　　　　*see* **Where to get help**
- For general information on consumers' rights
　　　　　　　　　　　　　　　　　　see **Goods & Services**

NB

- Under the **Gas Safety (Installation and Use) Regulations (Amendment) 1996,** landlords are obliged to have annual safety checks carried out on appliances in premises they let, and the checks must be carried out by CORGI-registered installers. If you are a tenant and you suspect your landlord is not using a registered installer, or you are concerned that an installer has carried out an inadequate safety check, you can complain to CORGI yourself. If you think your landlord is not carrying out annual checks (he or she must be able to show you a record of past tests on request), or you are otherwise concerned about the safety of your gas installation, you should contact your local Environmental Health Department, or the HSE direct.
- CORGI can provide details of consultants able to give second opinions. You may wish to arrange an inspection of your own for legal purposes.

Goods & Services

The sale of goods and the law

a. Under the **Sale of Goods Act 1979** and the **Sale and Supply of Goods Act 1994** buyers (including mail order buyers) are protected in three main ways:

- Goods must be of a 'satisfactory quality', i.e. they should be fit for their purpose; safe; free from minor defects; and of acceptable appearance, finish and durability (appropriate to their price)
- As well as being fit for their normal purpose, goods must be fit for any particular purpose that the buyer has made known to the seller
- Goods must conform with their description

If these conditions are not met, and the defect is serious, you are entitled to ask the seller (*not* the manufacturer unless bought directly from them) for a full *cash refund*.

b. You lose this right to return defective goods if you have 'accepted' them in the legal sense: for example, if you have told the seller that you have accepted them, or you have held on to the goods for some time after their defective nature became apparent.

c. You can also claim compensation for any loss suffered directly as a result of the defect. This is a limited right covering any loss which may fairly and reasonably be considered as arising naturally from the defect. Compensation cannot be sought for loss whose cause is only remotely connected with the defective goods.

d. Under the **Consumer Protection Act 1987,** which covers any goods purchased *after 1 March 1988,* individuals have an additional right to sue producers, importers, or retailers of 'own-brand' products if they have been 'injured' by defective goods. 'Injury' is taken to mean either death, personal injury, or damage to private property valued above £275. Liability is unlimited, and claims may be made for *10 years* after the product was originally supplied. A 'defective' product is one where the safety of the product is not such as persons generally are entitled to expect. In deciding whether a product is defective, a court will take into account all the relevant circumstances including:

- The manner in which the product is marketed
- Any instructions or warnings which are given with it
- What might reasonably be expected to be done with it
- The level of knowledge about the product at the time of its supply

e. You may also be able to sue if the seller's description of the goods turns out to be incorrect or misleading under the **Misrepresentation Act 1967.** 'Misrepresentation' is classified for the purposes of the Act in three different ways:

- *Fraudulent*: when somebody deliberately makes an untrue statement, knowing it to be untrue
- *Negligent*: when someone makes a statement but has no reasonable grounds for believing it to be true, and it turns out to be untrue

- *Innocent*: when the person making the statement has reasonable grounds for believing it to be true, and it turns out to be untrue.

Compensation will depend on the seriousness of the misrepresentation and is most likely if this is classified as 'fraudulent'.

1. *Goods – Who Can I Complain To?*

a. If you think you have grounds for complaint about something you have bought, you should:

- Go back to the shop (or where you bought it from) as soon as you can, with a receipt or other proof of purchase if at all possible (sometimes a witness is enough)
- Explain to the shop manager what the problem is and what you want done
- Set the shop a reasonable deadline for the situation to be remedied

b. If this does not work, complain in writing to Customer Services or the Chairman (at Head Office if the shop is a chain).

c. If you are still not satisfied you may wish to take advice on whether to pursue the matter in law, or take the matter to conciliation or arbitration. Advice can be obtained from:

i. Your local **Trading Standards (or Consumer Protection) Department** (TSD) – this is the department of your local council with responsibility for the enforcement of trading standards as set down by four main Acts of Parliament:

- The **Trade Descriptions Act 1968** – traders must describe the goods and services they sell accurately.
- The **Weights & Measures Act 1958** – traders must not sell short measures, and must use accurate weighing equipment.
- The **Consumer Protection Act 1987** – this empowers TSDs, by means of a suspension notice, to prevent a trader selling unsafe goods. They can prosecute traders who do this and can also confiscate their goods. TSDs

can also prosecute traders who give out misleading information on their prices.

- The **Consumer Credit Act 1974** – under this Act, TSDs help the Office of Fair Trading to ensure that applicants for consumer credit licences are fit to have them.

If you think your complaint may fall under any of the above Acts you should report the trader concerned to the TSD. The mere threat of a visit by a Trading Standards Officer may result in the trader making suitable amends. If you also have a claim under civil law (e.g. for breach of contract or misrepresentation), the trader's conviction in the Magistrates' Court for a trading standards offence could be useful evidence in your claim.

The contact details for TSDs in England, Scotland and Wales are in the phone book under the name of the regional council. In Northern Ireland the details will be listed under 'Government – Department of Economic Development, Trading Standards Branch'.

ii. **Trade Associations** – the supplier of the goods or services you are complaining about may belong to a trade association. If this is the case, it is worth enquiring if the association operates a code of practice including a mechanism for complaints. Some also offer low-cost conciliation and/or arbitration schemes.

iii. The **Environmental Health Department** of your local council – deals with health matters such as unfit food and drink, dirty shops and restaurants, and, in Northern Ireland, consumer safety matters.

iv. Your local **Citizens Advice Bureau** – can help with a wide variety of problems, including pursuing a matter in the courts, or the relative merits of arbitration and conciliation schemes.

v. **Utilities and public transport** have their own complaints procedures and regulatory bodies – for example

see **Gas**

Electricity

Transport 1 *to* **7**

vi. In *Northern Ireland* only there are two extra bodies:

- The **General Consumer Council of Northern Ireland** promotes and safeguards consumer interests, carries out research, investigates matters of concern and publishes information. The Council can investigate complaints about electricity and transport if you are unable to resolve the problem with the company concerned, and may also consider other complaints as a matter of last resort. The address is:

    General Consumer Council of Northern Ireland
    Elizabeth House
    116 Holywood Road
    Belfast BT4 1NY

    Tel: 01232 672488

- Free help and advice is also available from:

    The Consumer Advice Centre
    6 Callender Street
    Belfast BT1 5BN

    Tel: 01232 328260

d. For more addresses and ideas about who may be able to help   *see* **Where to get help**

2. *Services – Who Can I Complain To?*

Generally, the procedure for complaining about a service you have bought is the same as that for complaining about goods. When you buy a service – from, for example, a drycleaner, travel agent, shoe repairer, hairdresser or builder – there are several additional standards which you are entitled to expect to be met:

- The service should be provided with reasonable care and skill, and to a proper standard of workmanship
- The service should be provided within a reasonable time, e.g. a shop should not take three months to repair a television
- You should not pay an unreasonable amount for a service

Problem Areas

a. You have the same rights when buying *second-hand goods* but you must bear in mind that second-hand quality is unlikely to be the same as new. You can still claim your money back or the cost of repair if the goods are faulty, unless the fault is a matter of the wear and tear to be expected with second-hand goods, or it was obvious or pointed out to you before you paid.

b. You may have fewer rights if you buy at *auction*
see **Auctioneers**

c. You have fewer rights when buying from a *private seller*, for example through an advert in the local paper. Goods only have to be 'as described': your rights will depend upon what you are told by the seller, and will be difficult to enforce unless you have a witness, or have got a description in writing. Traders pretending to be private sellers are acting illegally and should be reported to the local TDS.

d. If you sign an agreement at home or agree to buy something costing more than £35 from a *doorstep seller* who calls uninvited, you will have *7 days* to cancel the deal (there are some exceptions to this: for example perishable goods and home extensions). If you agreed to the seller visiting your home you may not have the right to cancel. If the salesperson is a member of the Direct Selling Association you will be more protected
see **Mail Order**

Some trade associations (for example the Glass and Glazing Federation – *see* **Double Glazing**) also allow customers of member companies to cancel even if a sales call has been invited: in general you should cancel in writing as soon as possible and then ask about any protection schemes.

e. For information on how to stop *direct sales via mail and telephone*
see **Direct Mail**

Telecommunications

f. You have the same statutory rights when you buy through

mail order, but there are extra risks involved. For more information   *see* **Mail Order**

Credit

Under the **Consumer Credit Act 1974** consumers have additional rights when buying goods on credit, including:

- the right to cancel a credit agreement in certain circumstances
- the right to repay a loan early
- the right to limited liability in the event of the loss of a credit card
- the right to claim compensation for faulty goods or services purchased with a credit card (at a price of over £100) directly from the credit card company as well as from the retailer

You should, however, be very careful about withholding payments if you have a credit agreement. If you stop paying it could affect your credit rating and so your chance of getting credit in the future.

see also **Credit Reference Agencies**

Going to Court

If all else fails you can go to court to sue for the return of your money and/or for compensation. Before doing this, you should take legal advice. If the sum you are claiming is not more than £3,000 (not more than £750 in Scotland) you can use the 'small claims procedure' of the County Court (Sheriff Court in Scotland). There will be a modest court fee, but even if you lose (unless the court thinks your claim was wholly unreasonable) you will not have to pay your opponent's legal costs. For claims between £750 and £1,500 in Scotland a slightly different procedure called 'summary cause procedure' is used, again in the Sheriff Court.

For more information   *see* **Where to get help**

NB

- To be sent free booklets on any aspect of your rights as a consumer, and/or for guidance on where practical help may be obtained call the **Office of Fair Trading Consumer Information Line** on: **0345 224499** (local call rate).

- For more information on specific goods and services see appropriate entry, for example:

see **Drycleaning & Laundry**

Garages

Builders

Holidays 1 *to* **3**

Government Departments

1. *Who Can I Complain To?*

England, Scotland and Wales

> **Office of the Parliamentary Ombudsman**
> **Church House**
> **Great Smith Street**
> **London SW1P 3BW**
>
> **Tel: 0171 276 2130/3000**

Northern Ireland

in writing to:	*or* in person to:
The Ombudsman **Freepost** **Belfast BT1 6BR**	**Northern Ireland** **Ombudsman** **33 Wellington Place** **Belfast BT1 6HN**
Fax: 01232 234912	

or telephone:
Freephone: 0800 282036

Note: The Parliamentary Ombudsman's address should be used for queries only, as he can only investigate complaints which have been referred by an MP. The NI Ombudsman has a wider remit (see NB, *below) and can investigate complaints about non-governmental listed bodies, sent to him directly by members of the public, but he still needs an MP's referral to look into complaints about government departments. Your local MP can be contacted at the constituency office, or at:*

House of Commons
London SW1A 0AA

Tel: 0171 219 3000

2. *What Sort of Complaints Do They Deal With?*

a. Complaints from members of the public about the way they have been treated by government departments and various other public sector bodies (these bodies are listed in booklets available free from the Ombudsman's office, and known as 'listed bodies'). The service is free and confidential. The Ombudsman can investigate complaints about:

i. *Maladministration*
   This can occur when a government department or listed body does something in the wrong way, does something which should not be done, or fails to do something which ought to be done. Some examples are:

   - avoidable delay
   - bias or unfairness
   - failure to give appropriate advice when asked
   - discourtesy or harassment
   - failure to follow proper procedures
   - failure to take account of representations
   - mistakes in the handling of claims
   - broken promises

   The maladministration should have affected you personally, or the specific interests of the business, society or group making the complaint.
ii. *Refusal of access to official information*
   For this function of the Ombudsman   *see* **Information 1**

b. The Ombudsman *cannot* investigate complaints about:

- government policy or the content of legislation
- investigation of crime or the protection of national security
- the commencement or conduct of court proceedings
- contractual or commercial dealings of government departments or other listed bodies *except matters concerning the compulsory purchase of land or its subsequent disposal*
- public service personnel matters
- any body not listed in the Ombudsman's remit

c. He will *not normally* investigate:

- anything for which there are other ways of obtaining a remedy, e.g. where there is a right of appeal to an independent tribunal, or a right of recourse to the courts
- complaints about events which took place *more than 12 months* before you first contacted your MP

Although he may exceptionally decide to do so.

d. It is up to your MP to decide whether to pass your complaint on to the Ombudsman or not (but see *NB*, below). He or she may first try to get the government department or listed body to put the matter right.

e. When the Ombudsman receives a complaint, he will usually decide within three to four weeks whether or not to investigate it. He will then write to the MP giving reasons for his decision, and will send the MP an extra copy to pass on to you.

3. *How Independent Is the Complaints Procedure?*

The Office of the Parliamentary Ombudsman (officially known as the Parliamentary Commissioner for Administration) was created by Act of Parliament in 1967 and is completely independent of government. The Ombudsman reports to a Select Committee of MPs, which holds hearings on a selection of cases.

The Northern Ireland Ombudsman is officially known as the Northern Ireland Commissioner for Administration and the

Commissioner for Complaints. He is also completely independent of government.

4. *Compensation/Redress?*

a. If the Ombudsman finds a complaint which he has investigated to be justified, he will recommend that the department or listed body concerned takes appropriate steps to remedy any resulting injustice. This may include a financial remedy.

b. The Ombudsmen do not have the power to order their recommendations to be carried out, but they generally are. They will also recommend in appropriate cases that steps be taken – such as improving procedures or revising guidance – to prevent similar problems from arising again.

c. The Ombudsmen have no power to *stop* a department taking action – only courts have this power.

5. *Any Appeal?*

a. No, the Ombudsman's decision is final. He also has complete discretion to decide whether to investigate a particular case or not.

b. An investigation may only be reopened if new material evidence comes to light.

6. *Other Options?*

see also **Information 1**

Local Government

NB

- The remit of the Ombudsman in Northern Ireland is a combination of the remits of the Local Government Ombudsman and the Parliamentary Ombudsman in

England, Scotland and Wales: i.e. he investigates complaints from members of the public about the way they have been treated by government departments, listed public sector bodies *and* local government, in Northern Ireland. In the interests of clarity his other functions are described in the separate entry for the Local Government Ombudsman. *see* **Local Government**

- Although some MPs will only refer complaints from their own constituents this is not a requirement of the Ombudsman. So if your own MP refuses to refer your case, or you think he or she might not be sympathetic, you can ask another.
- Many investigations take six months or longer, particularly in complex cases.

H

Health (Mental)

1. Who Can I Complain To?

England and Wales

   i. **Chief Executive**
      Mental Health Act Commission
      Maid Marion House
      56 Hounds Gate
      Nottingham NG1 6BG

      Tel: 0115 943 7100

  ii. **A Mental Health Review Tribunal.** Head office contact:

      Department of Health
      Mental Health Division
      Wellington House
      133–155 Waterloo Road
      London SE1 8UG

      Tel: 0171 972 2000

Scotland

  i. and **The Secretary of the Commission**
   ii. **Mental Welfare Commission for Scotland**
      25 Drumsheugh Gardens
      Edinburgh EH3 7RB

      Tel: 0131 225 7034
      Fax: 0131 226 4027

Northern Ireland

   i. **The Northern Ireland Ombudsman** *see* **Health Service 2**

  ii. **The Secretary**
      Mental Health Review Tribunal for Northern Ireland
      Room 112B
      Dundonald House
      Upper Newtownards Road
      Belfast BT4 3SF

      Tel: **01232 485550**

2. *What Sort of Complaints Do They Deal With?*

There are two kinds of complaints associated with mental health treatment: complaints about the *care and treatment* of people with a mental disorder; and complaints about *detention* under the relevant mental health legislation. All complaints of the first kind about the standard of care, treatment decisions, conditions, staff behaviour, etc. in NHS facilities are now initially handled by the unified NHS complaints procedures   *see* **Health Service 1**
   After this, there are significant differences in different parts of the country:

a. In *England and Wales*, if you have already gone through this procedure and are still unhappy, *and the complaint relates to the treatment of a patient detained under the Mental Health Act*, there is another stage before the Health Service Ombudsman (*see* **Health Service 2**), which is to complain to the Mental Health Act Commission.

    The MHA Commission can *only* look into your complaint if:

    ● you are, or were, a detained patient and your complaint is about something which happened while you were detained in hospital under the Mental Health Act
    ● you wish to complain about the way somebody used their powers or carried out their duties (for example, in authorising a particular treatment) under the Act in respect of a detained patient

The MHA Commission *cannot* help if your complaint:

- is, or is likely to be, the subject of legal proceedings
- is simply that you are being detained against your will
- concerns professional negligence

If the MHA Commission agrees there should be a further investigation, a member of the Commission with appropriate experience will be appointed to carry it out.

b. In *Scotland*, the Mental Welfare Commission for Scotland can investigate any complaint about the care and treatment of *anyone with a mental disorder* – defined as mental illness and mental handicap, and including dementia – whether or not they have been detained in hospital, and whether or not they are being cared for by the NHS. As with the MHA Commission, if the complaint does relate to NHS treatment you should have already exhausted the primary complaints procedure – you should then complain to the Commission *before* approaching the Health Ombudsman.

The MW Commission will look into any case where it appears to them that there may have been:

- ill-treatment
- deficiency in care or treatment
- loss or damage to a person's property as a result of their mental disorder

c. If you want to complain to either Commission, on your own or someone else's behalf, you should normally do so *within 12 months* of the event in question. Third parties may complain directly to either Commission, but their concerns will also usually be referred to the hospital managers first.

d. The second kind of complaint – where you have been detained in hospital (i.e. 'sectioned') under the relevant mental health legislation and want this decision reviewed – is handled in *England, Wales* and *Northern Ireland* by the Mental Health Tribunals. In *Scotland* the Mental Health Commission can convene an 'Office Committee', which meets in court form, to review such decisions. Applications to a Tribunal or the Scottish Commission may be made either by the patient or by his or her nearest relative.

Mental Health Tribunals and Office Committees meet in private at the hospital concerned. The patient will be given the opportunity to address the Tribunal and to call an independent psychiatrist as witness, and the patient's nearest relative will also be asked to attend. The patient can also be represented by a legal professional, medical practitioner or anyone else acceptable to the Tribunal, and this authorised representative cannot be excluded from any part of the hearing.

3. *How Independent Is the Complaints Procedure?*

a. The Mental Health Act Commission is a statutory body set up to protect the rights and interests of all patients detained under the **Mental Health Act 1983**. The MHA Commission is completely independent of all staff and managers of hospitals and mental nursing homes.

b. The Mental Welfare Commission for Scotland was set up under the **Mental Health (Scotland) Act 1984** to protect people who may, by reason of mental disorders, be incapable of adequately protecting themselves or their interests. The MW Commission is completely independent of all mental health care providers and management.

c. Both Commissioners are appointed by the relevant Secretaries of State. Complaints about the actions, conduct, etc. of a member of a Commission will be investigated by a different member.

d. The Mental Health Review Tribunals are independent judicial bodies. Review Tribunals and the Office Committee of the Scottish Commission are chaired by legal professionals and have both medical and lay representation.

4. *Compensation/Redress?*

a. If the Mental Health Act Commission decides that a detained patient has not been cared for properly according to the law it will take steps to put things right and to make sure the problem does not happen again.

b. If the Mental Welfare Commission for Scotland decides that any mentally disordered person in need of care has been treated badly or inadequately, or had his or her property damaged, it will take steps to put things right in liaison with local health authorities, NHS Trusts, Social Services Departments, private health care providers and registration authorities, etc. as appropriate.

c. If a Mental Health Review Tribunal or the Office Committee of the Scottish Commission finds in a patient's favour he or she will be released from detention.

d. Neither the Commissions nor the Tribunals have the power to award compensation.

e. If either a Commission or a Tribunal thinks an offence may have been committed they will notify the police.

5. *Any Appeal?*

a. If you wish to complain about the actions or performance of a particular member of a Commission (for example, the member investigating your case) you can ask another member of the Commission to look into the matter.

b. If you are unhappy with a Commission's decision you can refer your complaint to the Health Service Ombudsman. If you decide to contact the Ombudsman you should do so *within 12 months* of your first complaint   *see* **Health Service 2**

c. There is no appeal against a decision of a Review Tribunal or Office Committee, although you have the right to seek judicial review on a point of law (you should get legal advice if you are considering this). You do, however, have the right to apply again for a review whenever the detention order comes up for renewal, or earlier if the situation changes before then.

6. *Other Options?*

a. You have the right to go to court to claim damages for professional negligence, injury, assault, etc. If you are considering legal action you should get advice
see Where to get help

b. For more about the NHS complaints procedure
see Health Service 1 and 2

c. To complain about private healthcare   see **Health Service 3**

d. To complain about a medical professional
see Health Professions 1 to 4

e. Most private mental health therapists – from psychoanalysts and psychotherapists to counsellors and the huge range of humanistic, holistic and alternative therapy practitioners – are completely unregulated, although there are various associated professional bodies, some of whom operate to respectable codes of practice. If you have a complaint about a private therapist you should ask them if they are a member of any such body (it is of course a good idea to check this out *before* you start any course of treatment); if they are not, you *may* be able to claim compensation for inadequate service through the courts. You should be aware that 'incompetence' charges in such cases are almost impossible to prove, and even assault charges are problematic as therapy is usually conducted in private   see **Goods & Services**

Where to get help

NB

a. To contact a Mental Health Commission when you are in hospital, you can:

- ask the hospital staff to make an appointment with a member when the Commission next visits the hospital
- write to the Commission at the address given – letters to

the Commission are private and may not be stopped or opened by hospital staff

- telephone the Commission, or ask someone to call for you, if the matter is urgent

b. Since the introduction of the new NHS complaints procedures in April 1996 the Mental Health Commission for *Northern Ireland* is no longer responsible for investigating complaints, although if a patient complains to a member of the Commission during a hospital visit the Commission will still try to help. Letters of complaint addressed to the Commission are now passed on to the appropriate stage of the NHS complaints procedure – either back to the hospital managers, or on to the Northern Ireland Ombudsman (who acts as the Health Service Ombudsman for Northern Ireland). You may still wish to copy a serious complaint to the Commission – their address is:

The Secretary
Mental Health Commission for Northern Ireland
Elizabeth House
118 Holywood Road
Belfast BT4 1NY

Tel: 01232 651157
Fax: 01232 471180

Health Professions 1 (Doctors)

1. *Who Can I Complain To?*

Conduct, Performance, Health and Standards Division
The General Medical Council
178–202 Great Portland Street
London W1N 6JE

Tel: 0171 580 7642
Fax: 0171 915 3642

2. *What Sort of Complaints Do They Deal With?*

a. Allegations of 'serious professional misconduct' by a medical practitioner, i.e. behaviour so serious that it could justify restricting or removing the doctor's registration in the Medical Register. These can include complaints about:

- neglect of professional responsibilities to patients
- indecent or violent behaviour towards patients
- breaches of professional confidence
- dishonesty

b. You can also complain to the GMC about doctors who may be unfit to practise because of health problems – and see *NB*, below, for another category of unfitness to be recognised in 1997.

c. The GMC *cannot* usually review medical reports by doctors, nor can it usually investigate complaints about a doctor's clinical judgement.

d. Complaints about NHS treatment may be referred to the NHS complaints procedure – see *Other Options?*, below.

e. Disciplinary hearings are conducted as adversarial proceedings, with a criminal standard of proof required to convict a doctor of serious professional misconduct. New mechanisms are to be introduced for allegations of professional incompetence – see *NB*, below.

3. *How Independent Is the Complaints Procedure?*

The GMC was set up by statute to safeguard the medical interests of patients; the *Medical Act 1983* sets out its current powers and responsibilities. The majority of the Council is made up of doctors, with 25 per cent lay members appointed by the Privy Council including MPs from the three major parties.

The GMC cannot dismiss a complaint without the approval of at least one of the lay members.

4. *Compensation/Redress?*

The GMC has the power to attach conditions to, suspend or remove a doctor's registration. Conditions might include, for example, restricting a GP to working in multi-partner practices to ensure adequate peer support, and have in the past included instructions to seek postgraduate training from a nearby medical school. The situation regarding medical competence is being formalised under new legislation coming into force in 1997 – see *NB*, below. The GMC has no power to award compensation.

Doctors who are not registered with the GMC cannot practise medicine in the UK.

5. *Any Appeal?*

No. If the GMC decides that there is insufficient evidence to take any disciplinary action against a doctor, or if some disciplinary action is taken but the doctor is not found guilty of serious professional misconduct, that is the end of the matter.

You may still be able to claim compensation for professional negligence through the courts.

6. *Other Options?*

- For how to complain about NHS services
                                see **Health Service 1** *and* **2**
- For how to complain about other health professionals
                                see **Health Professions 2** *to* **4**
- For more information on taking legal action
                                see **Where to get help**

NB

- From September 1997, under the **Medical (Professional Performance) Act 1995,** you will also be able to complain about doctors who may be unfit to practise because of seriously deficient knowledge, skills or attitudes. If such a complaint is confirmed – and unless the doctor agrees to voluntary removal from the register – the doctor will be asked to undergo retraining and, as already happens with cases of incapacitating ill health, will be subject to indefinite suspension until the problem is judged to be solved. The Act establishes two new kinds of statutory committee with specialist representation to investigate such complaints, backed up by rigorous examination procedures which will also be used to determine if and when a doctor who has undergone a period of retraining can be accepted back into full registration.

Health Professions 2
(Nurses, Midwives & Health Visitors)

1. *Who Can I Complain To?*

Director of Professional Conduct
United Kingdom Central Council for Nursing,
   Midwifery and Health Visiting (UKCC)
23 Portland Place
London W1N 4JT

Tel: 0171 637 7181
Fax: 0171 436 2924

2. *What Sort of Complaints Do They Deal With?*

a. Complaints about 'professional misconduct', defined as 'conduct unworthy of a registered nurse, midwife or health visitor', and sufficiently serious to warrant disciplinary action. Examples include:

- failure to protect or promote the interest of patients
- verbal or physical abuse of a patient
- theft from a patient
- failure to keep essential records
- falsifying records
- reckless and wilfully unskilful practice

- concealing untoward incidents
- failure to act knowing that a colleague or subordinate is improperly treating or abusing patients
- abuse of patients by improperly withholding prescribed drugs, or administering unprescribed drugs or an excess of prescribed drugs
- drug-related offences
- sexual abuse of patients
- breach of confidentiality

The Council's expectations of all practitioners are set out in its Code of Professional Conduct, copies of which are available from the address above.

b. Anyone can allege misconduct; you do not have to be the patient or in any way personally affected. You can also complain to the UKCC if you know of a court judgment against a registered nurse, etc. and you believe the offences of which the practitioner has been found guilty call into question their fitness to practise.

c. You can also complain to the UKCC if you think a practitioner is so ill that they are unfit to practise. The definition of serious illness can include alcohol and drug dependency and mental illness. As with misconduct, anyone can express concern about a practitioner's ill health.

d. The UKCC *cannot* deal with complaints about clinical (as opposed to professional) incompetence, unless the matter is so serious as to amount to 'misconduct'. Complaints of this nature about a nurse, midwife or health visitor should be made to the individual's employer, who may be able to deal with the problem by retraining or down-grading the practitioner concerned.

e. Complaints about NHS treatment may be referred to the NHS complaints procedure – see *Other Options?*, below.

f. Allegations of misconduct will be investigated by the Preliminary Proceedings Committee. If there appears to be a case to answer they will then be referred to the Professional Conduct Committee. PCC hearings are conducted as public adversarial proceedings, with a criminal standard of proof required to convict a practitioner of professional misconduct.

g. Allegations of serious ill health are subject to a medical examiner's report and may be referred to the Health Committee for further consideration.

3. *How Independent Is the Complaints Procedure?*

The UKCC is the statutory body responsible for regulating nursing, midwifery and health visiting through the UK. The means of regulation include setting standards for entry to the professions, standards for education, and for conduct. Only practitioners registered with the UKCC are permitted to practise.

The Council consists of 40 members elected from the register and 20 members appointed by the Secretary of State for Health, including representatives of relevant consumer organisations. All Committees have at least one lay member in three.

4. *Compensation/Redress?*

a. Depending on the seriousness of the charges, practitioners found guilty of professional misconduct may be officially warned, or have their registration (i.e. their right to practise) restricted, suspended or removed.

b. Practitioners found to be too ill to practise, and who do not wish to accept voluntary de-registration (i.e. retirement on health grounds) will either be suspended until they are judged to have recovered or removed from the register.

c. The UKCC has no powers to award compensation.

5. *Any Appeal?*

a. No, although in exceptional circumstances you may be able to seek judicial review of a UKCC decision or procedure on a point of law.

b. If you are unhappy with the outcome of a UKCC investigation you retain the right to claim compensation for professional negligence through the courts.

6. *Other Options?*

● For how to complain about NHS services
                              see **Health Service 1** *and* **2**
● For how to complain about other health professionals
                      see **Health Professions 1, 3** *and* **4**
● For more information on taking legal action
                                    see **Where to get help**

Health Professions 3 (Dentists)

1. *Who Can I Complain To?*

General Dental Council (GDC)
37 Wimpole Street
London W1M 8DQ

Tel: 0171 486 2171
Fax: 0171 224 3294

2. *What Sort of Complaints Do They Deal With?*

a. Allegations of 'serious professional misconduct' by registered dentists and enrolled dental auxiliaries (dental hygienists and dental therapists). You may be asked to make a statutory declaration (in front of a solicitor, etc.) or other legal affidavit. Examples of serious professional misconduct include:

   ● failure to satisfactorily carry out necessary treatment
   ● failure to employ a proper degree of skill and attention

- failure to follow the Council's published guidance in relation to the administration of general anaesthesia or sedation, etc.

b. You can also complain to the GDC if you think a practitioner is so ill that they are unfit to practise. The definition of serious illness can include alcohol and drug dependency and mental illness.

c. Complaints about NHS dental treatment should initially be made to the practice concerned, and go through the NHS complaints procedures. If the Health Service authorities' findings indicate that the dentist may have been guilty of serious professional misconduct the case will be reported officially to the GDC.

d. If a matter is referred to the Professional Conduct Committee, the facts alleged in the charge have to be proved to the criminal level of proof, i.e. beyond reasonable doubt. A public hearing will be held, and you may be called upon as a witness.

e. The police have a duty to report the criminal conviction of any dentist to the GDC. The Council will then decide whether the conviction constitutes professional misconduct (without re-trying the case).

f. The Council will also prosecute in cases of illegal dental practice by unregistered persons, such as dental technicians.

3. *How Independent Is the Complaints Procedure?*

The GDC is the statutory registration and regulatory authority for dentists, as defined by the **Dentists Act 1984**. It is funded by professional registration fees. The Council consists of forty registered dentists, one dental auxiliary, and six lay members appointed by the government on a territorial basis. Two lay members serve on the Professional Conduct Committee and two on the Health Committee.

4. *Compensation/Redress?*

a. If a dental practitioner is found guilty of serious professional misconduct, or if their criminal conviction is judged to amount to it, their name may be erased from the Dentists Register or they may have their registration suspended. They will then be unable to practise in the UK.

b. If the Council's Health Committee finds that a dentist's fitness to practise is seriously impaired, it may impose conditions on the dentist's registration or suspend it until the dentist is judged to have recovered.

c. The GDC has no power to award compensation.

5. *Any Appeal?*

a. No (not for the complainant). Investigations will only be reopened if new evidence becomes available.

b. You retain the right to claim damages for professional negligence (or under consumer law) through the courts.

6. *Other Options?*

*   For more information on taking legal action
                                    see **Where to get help**
*   To complain about NHS services
                                see **Health Service 1** *and* **2**
*   For information about medical and other health-related professions   *see* **Health Professions 1, 2, 4** *and* **5**
*   To complain about private health care services
                                        see **Health Service 3**

NB

At the time of writing the government was consulting on legislation to establish a complaints scheme for non-NHS dental patients.

Health Professions 4 (Opticians)

1. *Who Can I Complain To?*

To complain about an optician's *conduct*, contact:

General Optical Council (GOC)
41 Harley Street
London W1N 2DJ

Tel: 0171 580 3898
Fax: 0171 436 3525

To complain about the quality of an optician's *goods or services*, contact:

Optical Consumer Complaints Service (OCCS)
PO Box 4685
London SE1 6ZB

Tel: 0171 261 1017

2. *What Sort of Complaints Do They Deal With?*

a. The GOC has a statutory duty to investigate allegations of misconduct by any:

- registered optometrist (ophthalmic optician) or registered dispensing optician
- company carrying on the business of an optometrist or dispensing optician

It has *no* power to investigate complaints about the standards of goods or services.

b. The OCCS can look into, and try to mediate with regard to, complaints about the standard or quality of the goods or services supplied by a registered optician or company carrying on the business of an optician. If you want to complain to the OCCS you should do so *within one year* of the supply of the spectacles or contact lenses in question.

3. *How Independent Is the Complaints Procedure?*

a. The GOC is the statutory body set up under the **Opticians Act 1989** to regulate the optical professions. It is independent and has associated statutory powers and duties, including disciplinary powers.

b. The OCCS was set up by the optical professions in 1989 to handle the large proportion of complaints which, since the Act, fall outside the remit of the NHS complaint procedures. It is financed by the profession but has an Independent Committee of Management with a lay majority and a lay chairman. It has no statutory powers.

4. *Compensation/Redress?*

a. An optician or company found guilty of a disciplinary offence by the GOC may have a disciplinary order made against them. The order may impose a fine and/or a suspension or the erasure of registration. Opticians under suspension or who have been removed from the register can no longer practise. The GOC has no power to award compensation.

b. Similarly, where a complaint is found to be justified, the OCCS will seek to obtain redress or compensation up to a maximum of the full cost of the spectacles or contact lenses in question, but has no power to force a member to comply with any recommendations. The OCCS does not get involved with claims for associated costs or damages.

5. *Any Appeal?*

a. No, although in exceptional circumstances you may be able to seek judicial review of a GOC decision or procedure on a point of law.

b. If you are unhappy with the outcome of a GOC investigation you retain the right to claim compensation for professional negligence through the courts.

c. If you are unhappy with the outcome of an OCCS intervention you may ask to have your complaint referred to the Chairman of the Committee of Management. If you remain unhappy after this, you can still take an optician or company to court under consumer law.

6. *Other Options?*

- For more information on taking legal action
  see **Where to get help**
- For more information on your rights as a consumer
  see **Goods & Services**
- For how to complain about NHS services
  see **Health Service 1** *and* **2**
- For information about other health-related professions
  see **Health Professions 1, 2 , 3** *and* **5**

Health Professions 5
(Professions Supplementary to Medicine)

1. *Who Can I Complain To?*

The Council for Professions Supplementary to Medicine (CPSM)
Park House
184 Kennington Park Road
London SE11 4BU

Tel: 0171 582 0866
Fax: 0171 820 9684

2. *What Sort of Complaints Do They Deal With?*

a. Complaints about 'infamous conduct' by registered:

- chiropodists
- dieticians
- medical laboratory scientific officers
- occupational therapists
- orthoptists
- physiotherapists
- radiographers

b. Allegations of 'infamous conduct' can be made by members of the public via Statutory Declaration (i.e. in the presence of a solicitor), or by a senior line manager of the NHS or social services acting in a public capacity.

c. Properly made complaints are first assessed by a solicitor to ensure that they fall within the remit of the **Professions Supplementary to Medicine (PSM) Act 1960**. If they do, they are referred to the Investigating Committee of the CPSM which decides whether there is a case to answer, often calling for further evidence. If there is a case to answer, the complaint then goes before the Disciplinary Committee, which sits as a judicial body under the direction of a legal assessor.

d. The person making the complaint is normally expected to act as a witness in any hearing of the Disciplinary Committee. Either or both sides may arrange for legal representation, although legal aid is not available for such cases.

3. *How Independent Is the Complaints Procedure?*

The procedure is self-regulatory. The Council and the seven Boards were established by the PSM Act in 1960, the structure as a whole operating under the aegis of the Privy Council. Each profession is regulated by a Board, the majority of whose members are elected directly from and by the profession. The

Investigating Committee and the Disciplinary Committee are statutorily independent of the Council, each consisting of between five and seven elected Board members.

4. *Compensation/Redress?*

No, but if a practitioner is found guilty of 'infamous conduct' he will be removed from the register. This stops him practising in the NHS and for local authorities but does not prevent him continuing in private practice.

5. *Any Appeal?*

a.   Not under the Act, although proceedings can be subject to judicial review on a point of law.

b.   Your rights to claim compensation for professional negligence, and/or under consumer law (against a private practitioner), are unaffected by the above procedure.

6. *Other Options?*

● For more information on taking legal action
see **Where to get help**
● For more information on your rights as a consumer
see **Goods & Services**
● To complain about other health-related professions
see **Health Professions 1** *to* **4**
● To complain about NHS services   *see* **Health Service 1** *and* **2**
● To complain about private health care services
see **Health Service 3**

NB

● Complaints about poor or unsatisfactory treatment are unlikely to meet the definition of 'infamous conduct'. Each case is, however, assessed on its merits.
● The PSM Act is under revision at the time of writing.

Health Service 1 (NHS General)

1. *Who Can I Complain To?*

Starting in 1996, the NHS has a new complaints procedure covering all parts of the service. It has a number of stages to it:

Stage 1

> Try to sort out the problem where it has occurred, with the people concerned. This is called *Local Resolution*. If you need to, you should contact the **complaints manager at the NHS Trust concerned,** or, in the case of family practitioners, the **complaints manager at the health authority.** All trusts and GP, dentist, pharmacist and optician services must have their own complaints systems. Trusts are obliged to give replies to written complaints to the chief executive, normally within four weeks. Your complaint should have been made *within six months* of the event or *six months* from the time that you realised there was cause for the complaint, as long as this is *not more than twelve months* from the event itself (unless there are special reasons).

Stage 2

> When you are not satisfied with the outcome of the Local Resolution procedure. You can then ask the trust or the health authority to refer your complaint for *Independent Review.* You should do this *within four weeks* of the date of the Local Resolution outcome; the letter telling you about this outcome will also tell you who to contact to request an Independent Review.
>
> The request will be considered by someone known as a **convenor** (a member of the trust or health authority), who also consults an independent lay person. The convenor then decides whether there should be an Independent Review – this is not an automatic right. You should be informed within four weeks of making a request whether an Independent Review has been agreed and what it will cover.

If there is an Independent Review, it will be conducted by a panel of three people (with an independent lay chair) and will undertake an investigation and take whatever special advice it needs. It will produce a report and the chief executive will also write about any consequent action.

2. *What Sort of Complaints Do They Deal With?*

This complaints system is designed to cover all parts of the NHS and all kinds of complaints through a common procedure. However, some matters are excluded – e.g. complaints about private treatment, disciplinary matters which are the concern of the professional bodies, and cases where legal action is being taken.

3. *How Independent Is the Complaints Procedure?*

a. The initial Local Resolution procedure is wholly internal, and the convenor who decides on Independent Reviews is a non-executive member of the trust or health authority board.

b. The Independent Review stage has a special panel with an independent lay chair.

c. If the case reaches the **Health Service Ombudsman** (see below) this is wholly independent.

4. *Compensation/Redress?*

If your complaint is upheld, you should be told what action is being taken as a result. You should receive a full explanation and apology, but also information about improvements that are being made to prevent similar problems in future. In some cases there may be a reference to one of the professional bodies, for possible disciplinary action. There is unlikely to be financial redress.

5. *Any Appeal?*

Yes, to the **Health Service Ombudsman**. You can take your case to the Health Service Ombudsman if you are still unhappy after the Independent Review stage; if you want to challenge a convenor's decision not to set up an Independent Review panel; or if you have complaints about how the complaints procedure is being run. However, the Ombudsman (not you) decides whether to take up a case.

The only other options are the courts and the professional bodies covering the various professions that work in the NHS.

6. *Other Options?*

- The professional bodies (e.g. for doctors, dentists, etc.)
  see **Health Professions 1** *to* **4**
- Health Service Ombudsman   *see* **Health Service 2**
- **Community Health Councils** (CHCs) are independent bodies and are a good source of advice and help on NHS complaints. Your local CHC will be in the phone book (under 'Community').
- If you are considering legal action, **Action for Victims of Medical Accidents** (AVMA) may be able to offer useful advice:

  AVMA
  Bank Chamber
  1 London Road Hill
  London SE23 3TP

  Tel: 0181 219 2793

- Further information on the NHS complaints system can be obtained by phoning the Health Information Service (**0800 665 544**) or Health Line (**0800 555 777**).

NB

In *Northern Ireland*, the complaints system is somewhat different and the health boards – which cover Health and Social Services – set up the Independent Review panels.

Health Service 2
(NHS Ombudsman)

1. *Who Can I Complain To?*

Health Service Ombudsman for England
Millbank Tower
Millbank
London SW1P 4QP

Tel: 0171 217 4051

Health Service Ombudsman for Scotland
Ground Floor
1 Atholl Place
Edinburgh EH3 8HP

Tel: 0131 225 7465

Health Service Ombudsman for Wales
Fourth Floor
Pearl Assurance House
Greyfriars Road
Cardiff CF1 3AG

Tel: 0222 394621

Northern Ireland Ombudsman
33 Wellington Place
Belfast BT1 6HN

Freephone: 0800 282036

2. *What Sort of Complaints Do They Deal With?*

a. The Health Service Ombudsmen investigate complaints about the NHS. You must first have used the local NHS complaints system before taking your case to the Ombudsman.

see **Health Service 1**

You should say why you are dissatisfied with the outcome of the local complaints system (e.g. it took too long; you did not get an adequate response; you were unreasonably refused independent panel review).

b.   The Ombudsman investigates complaints about:

- poor service
- failure to provide a service to which you are entitled
- maladministration (e.g. delay, discourtesy, faulty procedures, inadequate explanations, poor complaint handling)
- poor care and treatment
- failure to provide information under the Code of Practice on Openness in the NHS

c.   The Ombudsman does *not* investigate:

- where legal action is involved or damages sought
- personnel issues
- commercial or contractual matters
- where decisions have been poorly made
- non-NHS services
- if it is a social services matter

d.   You (or someone acting on your behalf) should normally complain *within a year* of the events complained about.

e.   The Ombudsman decides whether or not to investigate a particular complaint. If he decides not to investigate he will tell you why.

3. *How Independent Is the Complaints Procedure?*

The Ombudsman is completely independent of the NHS.

4. *Compensation/Redress?*

When he has completed his investigation, the Ombudsman will send you his report. It will also be sent to the bodies complained about. If your complaint is found to be justified, the Ombuds-man will seek an appropriate remedy for you. This may be an apology, or getting a decision changed, or repayment of unneces-sary costs (but not damages). The Ombudsman may also recom-mend changes to be made so that similar problems do not occur again – and ask for reports on how this has been done.

5. *Any Appeal?*

No, the Ombudsman's decision on a complaint is final (unless, in exceptional cases, new information comes to light and an inves-tigation may be re-opened).

6. *Other Options?*

- For details of the NHS local complaints system
  see **Health Service 1**
- To complain about individual health professionals
  see **Health Professions 1** *to* **4**
- For independent advice and help on making complaints, contact your local **Community Health Council** (under 'Community' in the phone book).

NB

The Ombudsman's services are free.

Health Service 3 (Independent Sector)

1. *Who Can I Complain To?*

Stage 1

The **Director of Nursing Services** and/or the overall **Direc-tor** of the healthcare facility (e.g. the private hospital) concerned.

Stage 2

The **corporate owners, charity board** or other controlling body.

Stage 3

The **Health Authority** (HA) with which the facility is registered and/or the **Local Authority** (LA) if the facility is a residential care home.

At any stage (if the facility is a member)

Independent Healthcare Association (IHA)
22 Little Russell Street
London WC1A 2HT

Tel: 0171 430 0537
Fax: 0171 242 2681

2. *What Sort of Complaints Do They Deal With?*

a. Complaints about the standards of service and amenities in independent health care facilities, for example private and charitable hospitals, psychiatric hospitals, nursing homes and mental nursing homes. Complaints might relate to:

- quality and cleanliness of facilities
- treatment by staff
- staffing levels
- unnecessary delays
- clinical decisions

b. Minor complaints can usually be dealt with informally and on the spot. More serious complaints and complaints which cannot be resolved informally can be referred to the Director of Nursing Services and/or the facility (e.g. the hospital) director.

c. If you feel your complaint has not been adequately investigated by the relevant director, you may be able to complain to whoever owns and/or controls the facility: this could be the board of directors of a private health care company, the board of a charity, or some other superior authority.

d.   If you are still unhappy after exhausting the internal complaints procedure you can complain to the registration authority, which will be the HA or LA.

e.   If the health care facility concerned is a member of a quality assurance scheme, for example ISO 9000 or the King's Fund, you may wish to complain to them. Ask the facility concerned if you are unsure if they are accredited by one of these schemes.

f.   Approximately 85 per cent of independent health care beds are maintained by members of the IHA. The IHA does not operate a formal complaints procedure, but will try to act as an honest broker between patient and management where communication has broken down.

g.   All medical doctors, including consultants in independent health care facilities, are regulated by the General Medical Council (GMC). If you have a serious complaint about a consultant which cannot be resolved informally, or via his or her medical protection society (mutual medical insurance scheme), you should certainly inform the hospital director, but you should also take your complaint to the GMC   *see* **Health Professions 1**

h.   Complaints about nurses can be made *both* to the facility management (their employer) and the nursing profession's regulatory body, the UKCC   *see* **Health Professions 2**

i.   Financial disputes, for example over charges relating to hospital and/or consultant fees and shortfalls arising from medical insurance cover, will almost always be referred back to your insurer, as financial cover is a contract between patient and insurer. If you are paying for your care or treatment personally and do not have insurance you will almost always be advised to buy a package to avoid unexpected extra costs.

3. *How Independent Is the Complaints Procedure?*

a.   *Stage 1* and *Stage 2* are internal.

b. HAs and LAs (*Stage 3*) are independent of the facilities, but will only investigate individual complaints as these relate to the statutory requirements of registration.

c. The IHA is the trade association of non-public sector health care providers and is funded by subscription. It is developing a Code of Practice, which may tie in to the quality assurance schemes.

d. Quality assurance schemes are independent accreditation schemes policed by specialist assessors. The ISO 9000 scheme employs criteria set by the British Standards Institute and is used by NHS facilities as well as by the independent sector.

4. *Compensation/Redress?*

a. Complaints about staff may result in them being disciplined or dismissed. Complaints about doctors may result in a private hospital refusing to do business with them. Independent health care providers may also offer financial compensation, discounts or alternative benefits.

b. If a private health care facility is found to be failing to meet the general standards laid down by the **Registered Homes Act 1984** (for example, that the facility is fit for its purpose, safe, and properly run) the LA will require it to come up to standard, and can ultimately remove it from the register and close it down. If a private nursing home accommodating NHS as well as non-NHS patients is failing to meet the stringent medical standards required by all HAs it will have to put things right immediately or be closed down.

c. If the IHA has become involved where a facility and/or a consultant is clearly at fault, it will recommend that this should be acknowledged in writing to the patient, together with an appropriate proposal for compensation or rectification. However, the IHA has no power to impose its recommendations on members. Facilities can in theory ultimately be expelled from the IHA, and disciplinary procedures are likely to be strengthened once a Code of Practice is in place.

d. If a quality assurance assessor finds a facility to be falling short of its quality criteria it will review the facility's accreditation. If a facility is expelled from an assurance scheme this does not stop it doing business, although it may indirectly mean that it is no longer allowed to accommodate NHS patients, as similar standards are required by HAs.

5. *Any Appeal?*

There is no appeal against any of the procedures described; you may, however, be able to take a health care provider to court for damages under civil law. If you are considering this you should take legal advice   *see* **Where to get help**

6. *Other Options?*

● Some NHS-funded treatment and residential care is now contracted out to private facilities. If your care is NHS-funded, wherever it has been carried out, you can make use of the NHS complaints procedure
                                        see **Health Service 1** *and* **2**
● For more information about residential and nursing homes
                                        see **Social Services 3**
● To express concerns about the way a charity is being run
                                        see **Charities**
● To complain about health professionals
                                        see **Health Professions 1** *to* **5**
● For how to complain about medical insurance
                                        see **Insurance 3**
● For more information on taking legal action
                                        see **Where to get help**
● For more about your legal rights as a consumer
                                        see **Goods & Services**

NB

● It is expected that within about two years almost all independent health care facilities will be covered by a quality assurance scheme.

Higher Education

1. *Who Can I Complain To?*

In the first instance you should complain to the university, college or other body responsible for delivering the service. They will also be able to supply you with details of other formal complaints mechanisms open to you.

2. *What Sort of Complaints Do They Deal With?*

Your first step regarding any complaint should always be to try and sort it out in an informal manner with the university, college or body responsible for delivering the service. They should respond to you within 10 working days. The rest of this section deals with more formal complaints procedures.

a.   *Universities and colleges:*

All universities and colleges should operate their own internal complaints mechanisms.

For serious complaints which cannot be resolved through the internal mechanisms, some universities or colleges provide for someone outside the institution, normally a senior judge, to review the case. Your university or college will provide you with details of this.

If your complaint is specifically about *misleading information* in a prospectus, and you are not satisfied with the outcome of the internal complaints system, you should contact the **Higher Education Quality Council** – see *Appendix* below.

b.   *LEA* (e.g. grants):

If you think *your LEA has treated you unfairly* (e.g. has been slow in processing your grant or has made serious administrative errors) you should complain to your **council officials** or your **local councillor**. You may also write to the **Local Government Ombudsman**.

c. *Student loans:*

If you have a grievance about the performance of the **Student Loans Company**, you can ask the company's independent assessor to investigate – see below for the address.

d. *Student Union:*

You will be able to appeal to an outside authority under the government's proposed reforms. Ask your college or union for more information about this.

3. *How Independent Is the Complaints Procedure?*

The Higher Education Quality Council, the Local Government Ombudsman and the Student Loans Company's assessor are independent.

All other complaints mechanisms are internal.

4. *Compensation/Redress?*

If your complaint is found to be justified then matters will usually be put right to your satisfaction. If the Local Government Ombudsman finds in your favour then they may recommend, for example, that your LEA pays you compensation.

5. *Any Appeal?*

The various appeals mechanisms are described above. As a last resort you can always write to the Secretary of State if you believe that the body in question is not fulfilling its legal responsibilities or is behaving unreasonably.

6. *Other Options?*

see also **Local Government**
Government Departments
Trade Unions 1
Further Education

Appendix

Useful addresses:

The Higher Education Quality Council
344–354 Gray's Inn Road
London WC1X 8BP

Tel: 0171 837 2223

Higher Education Funding Council
Northavon House
Coldharbour Lane
Bristol BS16 1QD

Tel: 01272 317317

Student Loans Company Ltd
100 Bothwell Street
Glasgow G2 7JD

Freephone: 0800 405010

Holidays 1
(Tour Operators)

1. *Who Can I Complain To?*

The Association of Independent Tour Operators (AITO)
133a St Margaret's Road
Twickenham
Middlesex TW1 1RG

Tel: 0181 744 9280
Fax: 0181 744 3187

2. *What Sort of Complaints Do They Deal With?*

a.   Complaints about tour operators which are members of AITO and which cannot be resolved by the company concerned. You should also contact AITO if you have bought a holiday from an AITO member company and the company ceases trading.

b.   AITO will initially try to resolve the problem informally. If you and the tour operator cannot agree on a solution then you can ask to use AITO's 'Independent Dispute Settlement Service'.

c.   If you decide to use the mediation service, you should normally apply *within 9 months* of returning from the holiday in question. There is a flat fee of £40 at the time of writing. Mediation is legally binding, and is not suitable for claims dealing solely, or largely, with physical injury or illness or with the consequences of injury or illness.

3. *How Independent Is the Complaints Procedure?*

AITO is a voluntary self-regulatory organisation.

The Independent Dispute Settlement Service is a legally binding mediation service run by an independent consultancy with wide experience of dealing with travel problems.

4. *Compensation/Redress?*

a.   If the mediator decides in your favour he or she can award compensation of up to £1,500 per individual, and up to £7,500 for any one booking. Compensation payments should be received within 14 days of the mediator's decision.

b.   Under AITO's bonding scheme (AITO Trust), if you have bought a holiday from an AITO member company and the company ceases trading, you are guaranteed either a full refund of the cost of the holiday (excluding any travel insurance premium paid) or that the holiday will continue as planned.

5. *Any Appeal?*

No – if you agree to mediation the mediator's decision is legally binding.

6. *Other Options?*

- If you decide not to accept mediation, or if your tour operator is not a member of AITO, you have the right to claim compensation through the courts. If you are considering legal action you should take advice

see **Where to get help**

see also **Holidays 2** *and* **3**

Holidays 2
(Travel Agents)

1. *Who Can I Complain To?*

Consumer Affairs Department
Association of British Travel Agents (ABTA)
55–57 Newman Street
London W1P 4AH

Information Bureau Tel: 0171 307 1907
Pre-departure section Tel: 0171 307 1963/4

2. *What Sort of Complaints Do They Deal With?*

a. Complaints about travel agents which are members of ABTA and which cannot be resolved by the agent concerned.

b. Pre-departure problems should be dealt with by your travel agent. If you need to talk to someone you can call the ABTA Information Bureau on the number given above: this line will advise on your query but cannot deal with it. If you are due to travel within 10 days, ABTA's pre-departure section will be able to help.

c. If your holiday has already taken place and you have a complaint against a member, you should contact the **tour operator** in the first instance. Your travel agent is responsible for ensuring that any queries are put to the tour operator and that the tour operator answers them.

d. If you are still unhappy after two letters have been exchanged, you will be given the option of going to independent arbitration. If you agree to arbitration you cannot then pursue a claim through the courts. Arbitration is not suitable for claims dealing solely, or largely, with physical injury or illness or the consequences of either of these, or with claims for more than the arbitrator's limit (see below).

e. If you decide to accept arbitration, you should normally apply *within 9 months* of returning from the holiday in question, and you will have to pay a registration fee.

3. *How Independent Is the Complaints Procedure?*

ABTA is a trade association operating a self-regulatory complaints procedure.

The ABTA arbitration scheme is administered by the independent Chartered Institute of Arbitrators.

4. *Compensation/Redress?*

Arbitrators have the power to award compensation of up to £1,500 per individual, and up to £7,500 for one booking. The successful party may also have their registration fee reimbursed.

5. *Any Appeal?*

Arbitrators' decisions are usually legally binding, although they are still subject to judicial review on points of law.

6. *Other Options?*

- If you decide not to accept arbitration, or if your travel agent is not a member of ABTA, you have the right to claim compensation through the courts. If you are considering legal action you should take advice   *see* **Where to get help**

- *see* also **Holidays 1** *and* **3**

Holidays 3 (British)

1. *Who Can I Complain To?*

England

> **English Tourist Board**
> **Thames Tower**
> **Black's Road**
> **Hammersmith**
> **London W6 9EL**
>
> **Tel: 0181 563 3367**
> **Fax: 0181 563 3350**

Scotland

> **Scottish Tourist Board**
> **23 Ravelston Terrace**
> **Edinburgh EH4 3EU**
>
> **Tel: 0131 332 2433**
> **Fax: 0131 332 9212**

Wales

> **Welsh Tourist Board**
> **Brunel House**
> **2 Fitzallan Road**
> **Cardiff CF2 1UY**
>
> **Tel: 01222 499909**
> **Fax: 01222 485031**

Northern Ireland

> **Northern Ireland Tourist**
>   **Board**
> **St Anne's Court**
> **59 North Street**
> **Belfast BT1 1NB**
>
> **Tel: 01232 231221**
> **Fax: 01232 240960**

Britain

British Tourist Authority (BTA)
(same address as the English Tourist Board, above)

Tel: 0181 846 9000
Fax: 0181 563 3002

2. *What Sort of Complaints Do They Deal With?*

a. The national Tourist Boards and the BTA will look into complaints about:

- any of the services they provide directly, such as information, booking, advice, etc.
- accommodation covered by any of the national grading and classification schemes
- holidays and any other tourist facilities or services in Britain, including unclassified accommodation, visitor attractions, public transport, restaurants, shops and suppliers, public facilities, litter and pollution, etc.

and which cannot be resolved by the company or proprietor concerned.

b. All complaints about classified accommodation will be investigated by the Quality Assurance Department of the relevant Board. Complaints about accommodation which is not covered by a Board classification scheme are forwarded to the relevant Area Tourist Board.

c. You should also complain to the relevant Board if you are a proprietor or otherwise involved in the tourist industry and your business is misrepresented in any Tourist Board information or publication.

3. *How Independent Is the Complaints Procedure?*

The Tourist Boards and the British Tourist Authority are official bodies set up by Act of Parliament to develop and promote tourism in Britain. They are completely independent of the tourism industry, and are accountable to the Secretary of State for National Heritage and ultimately to Parliament.

4. *Compensation/Redress?*

a. You should receive a response from a Board within 15 days.

b. The Boards have no powers to make any proprietor or company do anything, or to award compensation in disputes over tourist accommodation or facilities.

c. If a Board agrees that classified accommodation is not up to its published standard it will ask the proprietor to put things right, may demote the property's classification, and has the ultimate sanction of dropping a property from its scheme.

d. The Boards have no statutory jurisdiction over the quality of holidays, tourist facilities, public transport, etc. and will usually pass such complaints on to the relevant public body or trade association. You will be told if a Board has passed your complaint on to another body, and should then pursue the matter with them.

e. If a Board has been at fault, for example if it has made a mistake in advertising or promotional copy, it may offer free entry into the appropriate publication by way of compensation. A Board will only pay compensation if it is legally directly liable for demonstrable loss.

5. *Any Appeal?*

a. If you are unhappy with the *way* a Board has handled a complaint about the quality of classified accommodation you can ask the Chief Inspector to look at your case again.

b. If you are unhappy with the *way* a Board has handled a complaint about its own service, you can write to its Chief Executive. If you are still unhappy after this (but only if your complaint is about a Tourist Board, *not* the BTA) you can ask your MP to refer your case to the Parliamentary Ombudsman   *see* **Government Departments**

6. *Other Options?*

● Depending on the nature of your complaint, you may be able to claim compensation through the courts for inadequate goods or services. If you are considering legal action you should take advice   *see* **Where to get help**

Goods & Services

● The BTA and the national Tourist Boards comply with the government's code of practice on access to information

see **Information 1**

see also **Holidays 1 and 2**

NB

● The BTA's main job is to promote tourism to Britain from overseas, from 40 offices abroad.

Housing 1 (General)

1. *Who Can I Complain To?*

a. Local authority landlords and housing associations should have their own internal complaints procedures. If complaints cannot be resolved internally, tenants or prospective tenants of these bodies can refer cases relating to maladministration to the appropriate Local Government Ombudsman or Housing Association Ombudsman   *see* **Local Government**

Housing Associations

If all else fails, some housing disputes may be resolved by taking the landlord to court (e.g. when they are in breach of their duty to repair).

b. Secure tenants of housing associations and most private sector tenants can refer complaints or disputes about their rent levels to the local rent officer or rent assessment committee of the local authority. The powers of these officers and committees vary in relation to the type of tenancy

see **Rent**

c. Private landlords do not usually have formal complaints procedures. Tenants who wish to pursue a complaint against a private landlord will generally have to do so through the courts.

d. The law protects people living in residential property against harassment and illegal eviction. It does this in two ways: by making harassment and illegal eviction a criminal offence, and by enabling someone who is harassed or illegally evicted to claim damages through the civil court. If you think you are being harassed or your landlord is trying to evict you illegally, you should get advice   *see* **Where to get help**

e. If your legal claim against a landlord is for less than £3,000 (£750 in Scotland, £1,000 in Northern Ireland) you will be able to use the relatively cheap and easy 'small claims procedure'. In Scotland there is also a slightly more complex and expensive procedure called the 'summary cause' procedure for claims between £750 and £1,500. Finally, at the time of writing the government was considering introducing an even simpler form of court proceedings called the 'housing action', although this may not come in for some time. For sources of legal advice

see **Where to get help**

f. Owner-occupiers may have complaints about housebuilders and building and repairing services. These are dealt with in separate entries. For example   *see* **Builders**

Double Glazing

Goods & Services

g. The importance and complexity of housing, especially for tenants, makes it advisable to get help and advice

see **Where to get help**

Housing 2 (Council)

1. *Who Can I Complain To?*

Stage 1

> Your local **Housing Office** (the address will be in the phone book)

Stage 2

> The **Complaints Officer of your Local Council** (the Housing Office can tell you who this is)

Stage 3

> Your **Local Councillor** (the Housing Office can tell you where you can go to see your councillor, or you can write to him or her at the Town Hall or Civic Centre)

Stage 4a (maladministration complaints)

> The **Local Government Ombudsman**
> *see* **Local Government**

Stage 4b (urgent major repairs)

> The local **Magistrates' Court**

Note: The following details apply to council tenants. If you are a tenant of Scottish Homes, *a* new town development corporation *or the* Northern Ireland Housing Executive *see* NB, *below.*

2. *What Sort of Complaints Do They Deal With?*

a. Complaints about council homes and estates. If you are a council tenant you can complain to the council about, for example:

- problems with the structure and outside of your home
- the condition of basins, sinks, baths and toilets
- problems with your central heating, fixed fires or water heaters
- the condition of common areas including grassed areas
- problems with lifts
- vandalism and graffiti
- crime and problems with security
- drug-related problems
- violence and racial harassment
- the refusal of a grant application for improvements, etc.

You can complain about the behaviour of neighbours whether or not they are council tenants, although the council may have fewer powers to put things right if they are not (see below). Complaints about services which have already been contracted out should still be addressed to your local council (see also *NB*, below). Complaints relating to criminal offences will be referred to the police.

b. Noise complaints are dealt with separately   *see* **Noise**

c. You can also complain if you think your council is stopping you from exercising your rights as described in the Council Tenants' Charter. These include the rights to:

- live in your home for the rest of your life as long as you do what your tenancy agreement says
- buy your home at a discount
- pass on your home to someone in your family living with you when you die
- take in lodgers and sub-let part of your home
- carry out improvements to your home
- exchange your property for another one
- be given information about how your council runs the homes it owns (usually in an annual report to tenants)

d. Four new rights in *England and Wales only* are:

- the right to get certain urgent repairs done quickly and at no cost to you (under the 'right to repair' scheme)

- the right to financial compensation at the end of a tenancy for certain home improvements carried out at your expense (under the 'right to compensation' scheme)
- the right to be consulted about who should provide certain tenants' services, for example rent collection, cleaning, repairs and nuisance control (see *NB*, below)
- the right of tenants' organisations to take over the management of their homes (the 'right to manage')

If you want to claim compensation for improvements you should do so *within 14 days* of your tenancy coming to an end

e. You have a right to see personal housing files relating to you and held by public bodies. For more details on how to get hold of them, and how to complain if they are refused

see **Information 2**

f. Complaints proceed through the system as indicated above. A complaint should be made to the Housing Office in the first instance. If they cannot resolve it you should ask to go through the council's complaints procedure, at which stage you may be offered impartial mediation. If you are still unhappy after this you can refer the matter to your local councillor.

g. If your complaint is still unresolved after all this, and you want to complain about the *way* the council has handled your case, you can contact the Local Government Ombudsman. There are various conditions attached to doing this.

- For how to complain to the Ombudsman

see **Local Government**

h. If the state of repair of your home is very poor, and is affecting your well-being, you can, as a last resort, take your council to a magistrates' court under a very straightforward procedure called the 'statutory nuisance procedure'. You must give three weeks' notice in writing to give the council a chance to do the repairs first. To find out more about how to do this

see **Where to get help**

3. *How Independent Is the Complaints Procedure?*

a. The process is internal until you get to the level of taking your complaint to a councillor.

b. Mediation (as part of a council's complaints procedure) may be in-house or may be provided by an independent mediation organisation such as Mediation UK.

c. The Local Government Ombudsman is completely independent of local government.

d. The courts system is of course completely independent.

4. *Compensation/Redress?*

a. If the council finds your complaint to be justified it should put things right. For example, it may:

- clean a public area
- improve security
- carry out repairs, including repairs to any damage caused by contractors (e.g. builders)
- warn, issue injunctions against and ultimately evict a neighbour found guilty of nuisance offences or breaches of the council tenancy agreement

Councils also have the power to make by-laws to control certain problems, although these can be hard to enforce.

b. Problematic tenants may also be moved to another (sufficiently distant) council house, although only in Scotland can a council tenant be moved without their consent.

c. Some councils now include in their tenancy agreements an obligation to refrain from racial harassment. In a few cases of harassment the victims, rather than the perpetrators of the harassment, have been moved.

d. Neighbours found guilty of criminal offences may be liable to eviction if this breaks the terms of their tenancy agreement, for example if they are found guilty of using a council house for illegal or immoral purposes.

e.   Neighbours who have bought their council homes cannot be evicted, although they may be under an obligation to behave responsibly under the terms of a 'covenant' written into the sales contract by the council at the time of the sale. Owner-occupiers of nearby private houses cannot be evicted, but will be subject to the ordinary laws of nuisance

see **Environment 1**

Noise

f.   If a repair comes under the 'right to repair' scheme, the council will tell a contractor to do it within the time limit set down by law. You will be sent a copy of the repair notice showing the contact details of the contractor and the date and time agreed for the contractor to call. If the first contractor fails to carry out the repair in time, you can tell the council to call a second contractor in. The process then repeats itself, with the same time limits. If the second contractor doesn't do the repair in time, the council will then have to pay you compensation of £10 plus another £2 for every extra day you wait, up to a maximum of £50 for any one job. The time limit will depend on the type of repair: for example, the council has one day to mend a toilet that isn't flushing, 3 days to fix a broken banister and 7 days to mend a broken extractor fan in your kitchen or bathroom.

g.   If a home improvement comes under the 'right to compensation' scheme the amount will be based on how much you spent, but will take into account how old the improvements are and whether you got a grant towards them at the time, etc. You can be awarded up to £3,000 for any one improvement.

h.   If the Ombudsman finds your complaint to be justified, he or she can recommend various remedies, including financial compensation. For details of the powers of the Local Government Ombudsman   *see* **Local Government**

i.   If a magistrates' court rules in your favour under the 'statutory nuisance procedure', the council will be ordered to do the repairs, and will be fined. Your legal costs may also be refunded, and in some cases you may be awarded compensation. If you lose the case, you may have to pay the council's legal costs.

5. *Any Appeal?*

a.   You can always ask the council (and the Ombudsman) to reconsider your case if new evidence becomes available, if circumstances change significantly or if the problem happens again. In general there is *no* appeal against an Ombudsman's decision.

b.   If you disagree with the Ombudsman's decision, or if the Ombudsman decides he cannot consider your case, you also have the right to take your landlord (or a neighbour) to court. If you are considering legal action you should get advice.

c.   There is *no* legal right of appeal against a magistrate's decision under the 'statutory nuisance procedure', as 'nuisance' is currently a discretionary judgment.

6. *Other Options?*

- If you are considering legal action   *see* **Where to get help**

     see also **Discrimination**

     Environment 1

     Noise

- For how to complain about a Housing Association
     see **Housing Associations**
- For how to appeal against a Housing Benefit assessment
     see **Housing Benefit/Council Tax Benefit**
- To complain about rent   *see* **Rent**
- For more about your rights to official information
     see **Information 1**

NB

- The *new town development corporations* (which are being wound down now, with their housing stock transferring to councils) and *Scottish Homes* (in its role as a direct landlord) operate similar internal complaints procedures: contact them to find out who to complain to. It is still worth complaining to your councillor at *Stage 3* as these bodies have close relationships with local authorities. Unresolved complaints about any of these bodies can also be referred to the Local Government Ombudsman.
- In *Northern Ireland* all complaints about public sector housing should be made to the **Housing Executive,** which is the comprehensive authority for housing. The process and the kinds of complaints considered are similar to those described above, but you should complain in writing to:

Stage 1

The **District Manager** at your local office of the **Housing Executive** (in the phone book)

Stage 2

The **Regional Director** (the address will be given in the District Manager's reply to you)

Stage 3

The **Chief Executive** (the Regional Director will give you his name and address)

Stage 4

The **Northern Ireland Ombudsman**   *see* **Local Government**

For more information contact:

Housing Executive Information Services
2 Adelaide Street
Belfast BT2 8PB

Tel: 01232 318703
Fax: 01232 318715

Housing Policy in Northern Ireland is under comprehensive review at the time of writing, with major changes expected to be introduced. Contact the Executive for more information.

- New town development corporations, Scottish Homes and the Housing Executive produce their own Tenants Charters setting out your rights as a tenant. Contact them for a copy.
- Since 1 April 1996 in *England* and 1 October 1996 in *Wales*, most local authorities have been obliged to put many tenants' services out to so-called Compulsory Competitive Tendering (CCT), meaning that they cannot use their own staff to do something if someone else could provide the same services better or more efficiently. As part of this change, tenants must now be asked about how CCT services should be provided and who the new contractor should be, and councils must take their views into account. If and when services are contracted out, the council is responsible for making sure contractors keep to their contracts. The council must also take into account any complaints and comments made during a contracted period when the contract comes up for renewal.
- To find out more about any of your rights as a council tenant, including which repairs and improvements qualify under the new rights to repair and to compensation, and about where you can get advice about the right to manage, contact the council's housing department.

Housing Associations

1. Who Can I Complain To?

England

> **Housing Association Tenants Ombudsman Service**
>   (HATOS)
> **Palladium House**
> **1–4 Argyll Street**
> **London W1V 1AD**
>
> Tel: **0171 437 1422**
> Fax: **0171 437 1424**
> Local call rate number: **0345 125973**

Scotland

> **Housing Association Ombudsman for Scotland (HAOS)**
> **Drumsheugh Toll**
> **2 Belford Road**
> **Edinburgh EH4 3BL**
>
> Tel: **0131 220 0599**
> Fax: **0131 220 0577**

Note: For who to complain to about housing associations in Wales *and* Northern Ireland *see* Other Options ?, *below.*

2. What Sort of Complaints Do They Deal With?

a. HATOS deals with complaints against housing associations (HAs) registered with the **Housing Corporation;** HAOS with complaints against HAs and housing co-operatives registered with **Scottish Homes**, and against other landlords who have voluntarily agreed to participate in the scheme. Ask the relevant Ombudsman if you are not sure whether your landlord is covered.

b. At the time of writing you can complain to HATOS if you are a tenant or prospective tenant of a registered HA, or if you pay a registered HA to provide services for your home (see below for details of changes in the pipeline).

c. You can complain to HAOS if you have:

- a tenancy
- a shared ownership agreement *or*
- a housing management agreement

with a landlord in the scheme.

d. The Ombudsman can normally only investigate a complaint if you have already exhausted the internal complaints procedure of the HA itself. All HAs must have a formal complaints procedure, and they should be able to provide you with a copy of theirs; if you are refused a copy of it, or are told there isn't one, you should tell the Ombudsman. If, after you have embarked on the association's internal procedure, the Ombudsman thinks it is taking too long, or that the procedure is difficult or inadequate, he may decide to accept your complaint before you have been through every stage.

e. The Ombudsman will usually only look into complaints of personal injustice resulting from bad, inefficient or improper administration (known as 'maladministration'), i.e. if you think your HA has done something the wrong way, has done something it shouldn't have done, or has failed to do something it should have done, and this has affected you or your group personally. Examples of this include:

- failure to carry out repairs in reasonable time
- claiming you were in rent arrears when you were not
- charging you more than anybody else for the same service
- unreasonably refusing to give you a home or a transfer

f. The Ombudsman will *not* generally deal with:

- complaints made because you simply don't agree with what the association is doing

- complaints between you and your neighbours – although they *will* consider complaints about the *way* an association dealt with the quarrel
- problems that are about to go, or have already gone, to a court or tribunal, or that the Ombudsman thinks would be better dealt with that way
- problems that other bodies, such as other Ombudsmen, have the power to deal with (the HA Ombudsman will point you in the right direction)
- complaints about the level and amount of rents and service charges – a rent officer or rent assessment committee of your local council will generally consider these *see* **Rent**
  but the Ombudsman *will* consider complaints about *how* rents or service charges are set, failures to supply services, or the *way* charges are applied to an individual
- complaints from contractors, consultants, association employees or others who are paid by the association, about their professional or commercial relationship
- complaints from people who live near housing association property but do not receive a service from the association

However, if you can show that any of these problems involved maladministration by the HA then the Ombudsman may be able to help.

g. You have a right to see personal housing files relating to you and held by public bodies. For more details on how to get hold of them, and how to complain if they are refused *see* **Information 2**

h. Complaints about the way in which an HA is governed, fraud or other malpractice should be addressed to the regulatory authority, see *Other Options*?, below.

i. The Ombudsman will normally only look into a complaint if you raised it with the HA concerned *within 12 months* of you becoming aware of the problem, and if you have referred it to the Ombudsman *within 12 months* of you reaching the end of the HA's internal complaints procedure. You can complain by letter or on a special form which you can get from the Ombudsman, or you can ask to be interviewed (in which case you are allowed to have a friend with you). You can also get someone else to complain on your behalf, as long as you personally authorise them to do so.

j.   The Ombudsman will first try to resolve your complaint informally. If it cannot be resolved informally, he or she may suggest mediation or arbitration, or may carry out a formal investigation.

- In *mediation* an independent person will discuss the complaint with you and the association. This is a free service and can be arranged quickly. For mediation to proceed, both sides must agree to it.
- Under *arbitration* an independent person will consider the complaint in an informal legal manner. Again, both sides must agree to it, and the arbitrator's decision is final and legally binding on both sides.

k.   If both sides cannot agree to mediation or arbitration, or if mediation fails to produce an acceptable solution, the Ombudsman's staff will conduct a formal *investigation* to establish the facts. You will then receive a copy of the final report.

3. *How Independent Is the Complaints Procedure?*

a.   At the time of writing HATOS is still a department of the Housing Corporation, although committed to operating independently of the HAs. From 1 April 1997, under the **Housing Act 1996**, the Ombudsman will become statutorily independent of the Housing Corporation, and will be funded by its members. Its remit will also be extended to cover complaints from people other than tenants, and a greater variety of landlords.

b.   The HA Ombudsman for Scotland is completely independent of all Scottish HAs and its other member landlords and of Scottish Homes.

4. *Compensation/Redress?*

a. If the Ombudsman finds your complaint to be justified he will recommend what the HA should do to put things right. This could include carrying out repairs, a refund for overcharging, the reversal or amendment of a decision and/or an apology. He may also recommend that the HA pays you some compensation.

b. The Ombudsmen have no powers to enforce their recommendations, but they are nearly always accepted by the landlord concerned. If the Ombudsman is not satisfied with the landlord's response, the report on the findings can be published (usually in a local paper).

c. If a voluntary member refuses to accept an Ombudsman's recommendations they can be expelled from the scheme. (After 1 April 1997 the reformed HATOS will be able to accept private non-profit-making landlords as voluntary members, as HAOS does already.)

5. *Any Appeal?*

a. You can always ask your landlord (and the Ombudsman) to reconsider your case if new evidence becomes available, if circumstances change significantly or if the problem happens again. In general there is *no* appeal against an Ombudsman's decision.

b. If you disagree with the Ombudsman's decision, or if the Ombudsman decides he cannot consider your case, you still have the right to take your landlord (or a neighbour) to court. If you are considering legal action you should get advice   *see* **Where to get help**

c. If you have a complaint about the *way* HATOS has investigated your case you can write to the Secretary of HATOS and ask him to look at the way it was handled. If you are still unhappy you can write to the Ombudsman in person, and ultimately ask the Advisory Panel to review your case (this system may change – see below).

6. *Other Options?*

a.   *Wales*

There is no Housing Association Ombudsman for Wales at the time of writing, although a scheme will be set up under the Housing Act, to come into operation on or shortly after 1 April 1997. Unresolved complaints about HAs are currently handled directly by the regulatory authority, **Housing for Wales**. If you have exhausted your HA's internal complaints procedure you should write to:

> **Tenant Services Co-ordinator**
> **Housing for Wales (Tai Cymru)**
> **25–30 Lambourne Crescent**
> **Llanishen**
> **Cardiff CF4 5ZJ**
>
> Tel: 01222 747979
> Fax: 01222 741500

They will then investigate whether your HA has acted in accordance with:

- the law
- the Tenants' Guarantee
- its own policies and procedures
- Housing for Wales' performance standards

If you are still unhappy after this you can appeal to the **Director of Performance Audit**, and ultimately to the **Board of Housing for Wales**. If you are unhappy with the *way* Housing for Wales has investigated your complaint you may finally be able to refer your case (via an MP) to the Parliamentary Ombudsman

see Government Departments

b.   *Northern Ireland*

There are no publicly funded housing associations in Northern Ireland at the time of writing, although this is likely to

change in the near future. Contact the Housing Executive for more information. For the address   *see* **Housing 2**
   Unresolved complaints involving maladministration by public sector bodies, including government departments, in Northern Ireland can be referred to the Northern Ireland Ombudsman   *see* **Local Government**

Government Departments

c.   Complaints about the way in which a housing association is governed, fraud or other malpractice should be addressed to the regulatory authority (as, obviously, should complaints about the regulatory authority itself – for example a refusal to release official information on request), i.e.:

In England

> **The Housing Corporation**
> **149 Tottenham Court Road**
> **London W1P 0BN**
>
> **Tel: 0171 393 2000**

In Scotland

> **Scottish Homes**
> **Thistle House**
> **91 Haymarket Terrace**
> **Edinburgh EH12 5HE**
>
> **Tel: 0131 313 0044**
> **Fax: 0131 313 2680**

In Wales

> **Housing for Wales** – at the address above

The final stage in complaints of this kind is to refer your case (via an MP) to the Parliamentary Ombudsman
     see **Government Departments**

- From 1 April 1997 all social (i.e. publicly subsidised) landlords will have to join a recognised Ombudsman scheme, but private non-profit- (e.g. charitable) and profit-making HAs will not. If your complaint is about an HA which is not a member of any scheme, your only option may be to go to court   *see* **Where to get help**

see also **Discrimination**

Environment 1

Noise

- If you are a council tenant with a complaint
  see **Housing 2**
- For how to appeal against a Housing Benefit assessment
  see **Housing Benefit/Council Tax Benefit**
- To complain about rent   *see* **Rent**
- For more about your rights to official information
  see **Information 1**

NB

- The kinds of things you can complain to an HA about are similar to those which council tenants can complain about, although complaints about noise and some kinds of disrepair may be better made to local authority environmental health departments.
- More information on the standards of service you should be able to expect from your HA (equivalent to the Tenants' Charter for council tenants) should be available from them.

Housing Benefit/Council Tax Benefit

1. *Who Can I Complain To?*

Stage 1

The **council** or **new town development corporation** responsible for your Housing Benefit and/or Council Tax Benefit (HB/CTB) assessment (their address will be on your assessment letter)

Stage 2

A **Housing Benefit** or **Council Tax Benefit Review Board** (the council will set this up)

2. *What Sort of Complaints Do They Deal With?*

a. If you disagree with your HB/CTB assessment it is a good idea to ask the council for a 'statement of reasons' explaining the part of the assessment you are querying – this will tell you in detail how the amounts you ask about have been calculated. They should send you a statement of reasons within 14 days or as soon after this as possible.

b. After studying the statement of reasons you may decide to ask your council for a review of your benefit assessment. This should be done *within 6 weeks* of being told how much HB/CTB you will get, or of receiving the statement of reasons if you have asked for one of these. When you write you should say why you disagree with the assessment. The council will reconsider your case and write to you again within 14 days or as soon after this as possible.

c. If you still disagree with the assessment after the council has reviewed your case, you can write to it to ask for a further review. You must do this *within 4 weeks* of being told the outcome of the first review, and explain why you disagree with it. The council will then set an HB or CTB Review Board to hear your case.

d.   A hearing will be held within 6 months of your request, or as soon after this as possible. You and anyone else affected will be invited to take part, and you should be given 10 days' notice to appear. At the Review Board hearing you can be represented by someone else (with your authorisation) or take a friend, and you have the right to call witnesses. Everyone concerned will be sent a copy of the Board's decision within 7 days of the hearing or as soon as possible.

e.   If you are complaining about both your HB and CTB assessments, the Review Board can consider them together if everyone concerned agrees.

3. *How Independent Is the Complaints Procedure?*

a.   A council/new town development corporation review is internal.

b.   Review Boards are independent of the authorities that assess HB/CTB. They are made up of at least 3 local councillors or members of the new town board (unless all parties agree that 2 is enough), none of whom will have had any previous involvement in your case.

4. *Compensation/Redress?*

a.   If the council's first review finds in your favour then your HB/CTB assessment will be adjusted accordingly, from the date you were first given the wrong HB/CTB and not from the date of the review.

b.   If the Review Board's decision goes in your favour your HB/CTB assessment will be adjusted accordingly, from the date you were first given the wrong HB/CTB. You and any friend may also be paid travelling expenses for attending the hearing.

In both cases arrears can be backdated up to 52 weeks before the date of the council's review.

5. *Any Appeal?*

a. You can appeal a Review Board's decision on a point of law
    only (i.e. if you think the Board has misapplied the law
    relating to HB/CTB). If you are considering doing this you
    should get legal advice.

b. A Review Board's decision may be 'put aside' if important
    documents have only become available since the hearing, or
    if someone was unavoidably absent from it. If you think a
    decision should be put aside you should write to the Review
    Board *within 13 weeks* of receiving its decision. Everyone
    concerned may be asked to comment before any decision is
    put aside. You will then be able to ask for another Review
    Board hearing.

c. If you think you have suffered an injustice as a result of bad,
    inefficient or improper administration by your local author-
    ity you may be able to complain to the Local Government
    Ombudsman   *see* **Local Government**

6. *Other Options?*

- To complain about rent   *see* **Rent**
-                                      *see also* **Housing 1**
                                              Where to get help

NB

- Councils and new town development boards are to be given
  extended powers from 1 April 1997 to make *discretionary*
  payments above the 'maximum eligible rents', although the
  funds available from central government to do this have at
  the same time been more strictly capped. Review Boards also
  have the power to adjust or award discretionary payments,
  in exceptional cases.

- The maximum eligible rent for single people under 25 was restricted to the 'average cost of non-self-contained accommodation in the locality' (i.e. an average or below average priced bedsit or room in a shared house) in January 1996.
- The conditions and circumstances in which you can claim HB are complicated – if unsure ask your landlord or the council whether your accommodation is eligible. Housing Benefit is not available to help with mortgage repayments, although you may be able to get help from Income Support – again, ask the council.

I

Immigration 1
(Appeals)

1. *Who Can I Complain To?*

Stage 1

The relevant **Regional Immigration Adjudicator**. To find out the Adjudicator for your region, contact:

Chief Adjudicator's Secretary
Immigration Appellate Authorities
Thanet House
231/232 Strand
London WC2R 1DA

Tel: 0171 353 8060
Fax: 0171 583 0353

Stage 2

The **Immigration Appeal Tribunal** at the address above.

2. *What Sort of Complaints Do They Deal With?*

a. Appeals against immigration decisions made by the Home Office, the Immigration Service and British posts abroad, concerning:

- refusal of entry to the UK for long-term visits or permanent residence
- refusal of a visa extension to someone already in the UK

- deportation orders
- certain refusals to grant asylum (see below)

b. Appeals are heard first by an Immigration Appeal Adjudicator, who sits alone to determine a case. You must lodge an appeal *within 10 days* of receiving notification of the decision in question.

c. If you are still unhappy after the Adjudicator has reviewed your case you have a right to apply for leave to appeal *on a point of law only* to the Immigration Appeal Tribunal.

d. Appeals against deportation orders concerning 'conduct contrary to the public good' should be made directly to the Tribunal.

e. There is *no* right of appeal against an immigration decision if:

- application for permission to remain longer was made *after* previous permission ran out
- you have been refused entry clearance, or refused entry at a port when you did not have entry clearance, if you are: a visitor; a student coming for less than 6 months; or a prospective student
- the refusal of your application was 'mandatory under the immigration rules', i.e.:

    - you do not hold a relevant document, *or*
    - you do not satisfy a requirement as to age, nationality or citizenship, *or*
    - you are seeking entry, or an extension of stay, for a period longer than that permitted, *or*
    - you have not paid a required fee (relating to an application for leave to remain)

f. Two recent Acts of Parliament, the **Asylum and Immigration Appeals Act 1993** and the **Asylum and Immigration Act 1996**, have significantly altered the rights of asylum-seekers. The right to appeal of people refused asylum *on or after 26 July 1993* no longer depends on their immigration status, and there is now a two track system for asylum appeals, with an accelerated or 'fast track' procedure for claims designated as being:

- 'certified claims' (known as 'without foundation' before October 1996) – which are claims either where the Secretary of State believes they do not raise any issue as to the UK's obligations under the UN Convention on Refugees, or (since October 1996) where the asylum-seeker has failed to provide any explanation for missing documents, *or*
- 'otherwise frivolous or vexatious'

Accelerated appeals are heard by 'special adjudicators', the time limits are shorter (for example, a person whose claim is certified has *only 2 working days* to lodge an appeal), and there is *no* further right of appeal to the Appeals Tribunal.

g. Since *21 October 1996* (under the 1996 Act) the accelerated appeals procedure has been extended to any person claiming political asylum from a country allocated to the so-called 'white list' (a list of countries deemed 'safe', subject to Parliamentary approval and revision), and anyone claiming asylum in the UK, but whose first port of call after leaving their home country was a 'safe' third country (i.e. a country in the EU, the USA, Canada, Norway or Switzerland) now has to return to that third country before they can make an appeal.

h. You can be represented at any Immigration Appeal hearing by a lawyer, the Immigration Advisory Service, the Refugee Legal Centre or a lay adviser (for contact details of advice organisations, see *NB*, below).

3. *How Independent Is the Complaints Procedure?*

The IAA is run by the Lord Chancellor's Department, so is separate from and independent of the Home Office.

In addition, since the Asylum and Immigration Appeals Act 1993 removed the right to appeal from visitors or short-term and prospective students, such refusal decisions made abroad have been monitored by an Independent Monitor, who reports to the Foreign Secretary.

4. *Compensation/Redress?*

If the Adjudicator, the Tribunal or any higher court finds in your favour, the original immigration decision may be amended or reversed. If you have suffered financial loss as a result of having to appeal (for example, if your benefit was cut off at the same time as the first decision, under the new asylum laws) you may be awarded compensation or have any benefit backdated.

5. *Any Appeal?*

a. There is a further right to apply for leave to appeal against a decision of the Tribunal to the Court of Appeal, again on a point of law only.

b. If the Tribunal refuses leave to appeal there is *no* right to appeal to the Court of Appeal against this refusal, and in these circumstances an application for judicial review may be made to the High Court.

6. *Other Options?*

a. If you are unhappy with the *way* your case has been handled by IAA staff you should contact the Centre Manager at Thanet House (at the above address). If you are still unhappy after exhausting the IAA's internal complaints procedure you can write to the Lord Chancellor and/or ask your MP to refer your case to the Parliamentary Ombudsman
see **Government Departments**

b. To complain about aspects of immigration and asylum policy or legislation, write to the Home Secretary and/or your MP.
see also **Housing Benefit/Council Tax Benefit**
Social Security
Police

NB

- The Immigration Advisory Service is an independent charity providing free and confidential advice and legal representation. They can be contacted at:

  Immigration Advisory Service
  County House
  190 Great Dover Street
  London SE1 4YB

  Tel: 0171 357 6917
  Fax: 0171 378 0665
  e-mail: iasuk@gn.apc.org

- Free help and advice on asylum matters is available from:

  Refugee Legal Centre
  Sussex House
  Bermondsey Street
  London SE1 3XS

  Tel: 0171 827 9090
  Fax: 0171 378 1979

Immigration 2

1. *Who Do I Complain To?*

Immigration and Nationality Department (IND)
Complaints Unit
Room 812
Apollo House
36 Wellesley Road
Croydon CR9 3RR

Tel: 0181 760 8190
Fax: 0181 760 8226

2. *What Sort of Complaints Do They Deal With?*

a. Complaints about misconduct and inefficiency by IND staff, including interpreters and others acting on the Department's behalf. Complaints might include allegations of rudeness, discrimination, incompetence or avoidable delay.

b. If your complaint cannot be resolved by a manager on the spot, or if you are not satisfied with the manager's answer, you should contact the Complaints Unit. Complaints should be made in writing *within 3 months* of the matter first coming to your attention (although this time limit may be waived in certain circumstances). You should include:

- a short description of your complaint
- the names of the people you have dealt with so far
- your name and address
- your Home Office reference number (if you have one)
- copies of any relevant documents

c. The Unit *cannot* investigate complaints:

- relating to individual decisions
- about aspects of policy or legislation
- solely about administrative or operational matters
- about the refusal to disclose information
- which are considered to be frivolous, vexatious, malicious or trivial

d. You should receive a reply within 8 weeks.

3. *How Independent Is the Complaints Procedure?*

a. The procedure is internal, but investigations are carried out by a senior officer who should normally:

- be at least two grades above that of the member of staff complained about
- not be the line manager or a social acquaintance of the member of staff

- have had no operational involvement in the circumstances surrounding the complaint

b. The system is monitored by the independent Complaints Audit Committee, which reports to the Home Secretary.

4. *Compensation/Redress?*

a. If your complaint is upheld the Unit will explain what has gone wrong and make a full apology. You may also be reimbursed for any costs you have incurred as a direct result of an IND mistake.

b. Even where the complaint has not been upheld, the investigation may have revealed shortcomings in IND's procedures which they will take steps to put right.

5. *Any Appeal?*

If you are not satisfied with the outcome of the Complaints Unit investigation you can ask your MP to raise the matter with the Home Office Minister responsible for IND, or with the Parliamentary Ombudsman   *see* **Government Departments**

6. *Other Options?*

a. If you have a complaint relating to aspects of legislation or policy, administrative or operational matters, or the refusal to disclose information, you should write to:

The Immigration and Nationality Department
Lunar House
40 Wellesley Road
Croydon CR9 2BY

- For more about your rights to information
                              see **Information 1 and 2**
- To appeal an immigration or asylum decision
                              see **Immigration 1**

Information 1 (Official)

There are three kinds of right of access to official information:

a. Under the **Code of Practice on Access to Government Information** ('the *Code*') you have rights of access to government information (but not documents), although with important exclusions. You should ask the relevant government department or public body for the information you want: contact names and addresses are in a leaflet, *Open Government*, obtainable from:

> **Room 417b**
> **Office of Public Service**
> **70 Whitehall**
> **London SW1A 2AS**

b. Under the **Environmental Information Regulations 1992** ('the *Regulations*') you have a statutory right to see 'information which relates to the environment' held by bodies with 'public responsibilities for the environment', although there are some broad exemptions and the definition of which bodies are covered is rather vague. The Regulations have also been interpreted rather narrowly in the past as applying only to explicit, statutory environmental responsibilities, and to *regulatory* responsibilities only.

c. Under the **Local Government (Access to Information) Act 1985** you have a right to see only the meeting papers of local authorities. The Code does *not* extend to local government, although LAs have been issued with a 'guidance note' and a new position of 'monitoring officer' has been created. For more information   *see* **Local Government**

1. *Who Can I Complain To?*

Stage 1

If you have applied for information under the *Code* or the *Regulations* and your request is refused, or not answered properly, or the response has taken too long, or you have been charged too much, you should first ask the **department or body concerned** for an internal review. Details of this will be given with the original response to you.

Stage 2

a. If you applied under the *Code* and the information is still refused to you, or you have complaints about inadequate treatment, delay, or charges, you can then complain to the:

> **Office of the Parliamentary Ombudsman**
> **Church House**
> **Great Smith Street**
> **London SW1P 3BW**
>
> **Tel: 0171 276 2130**

But you have to complain *via* your MP (or another MP), asking him or her to refer the case to the Parliamentary Ombudsman. The MP will decide whether to refer the complaint. The Ombudsman decides whether to investigate the complaint. He will inform the MP, with a copy for you.

b. If you applied for information under the *Regulations* and it is refused, the only further options are to apply for judicial review or to take the public body to court for breach of statutory duty. If you applied to a government department or public body and wish to complain about inadequate treatment, delay, or charges, you can still complain to the Parliamentary Ombudsman, as above.

2. *What Sort of Complaints Do They Deal With?*

a. The Ombudsman can investigate such complaints as:

- delay in responding to requests for information
- charges for information that are thought to be excessive

- refusals of information when you believe you are entitled to have it
- incomplete and inadequate responses to information requests

But the Ombudsman *cannot* investigate where the information is in one of the many categories exempted from disclosure (such as national security, policy advice, commercial confidentiality), unless he believes there is a public interest in making it available. Also he *cannot* investigate where there is a legal remedy for the complaint – which is why he cannot get involved with refusals for information under the *Regulations*.

b. Judicial review is only available on a point of law. You can take a public body to court for breach of any statutory duty as laid down in the published legislation. You should take legal advice in both of these cases   *see* **Where to get help**

3. *How Independent Is the Complaints Procedure?*

a. The internal review stage is internal to the government department or public body.

b. The Ombudsman is completely independent of government as, of course, is the legal system.

4. *Compensation/Redress?*

a. If the Ombudsman decides that a complaint is justified, he will recommend an appropriate remedy. This could, for example, be the provision of the information that was requested or the reduction of the charges that were made. Government departments are not obliged to implement the Ombudsman's recommendations, but they invariably do.

The Ombudsman makes his report to the MP, with a copy for you.

b. If judicial review or a court hearing finds in your favour regarding the disclosure of environmental information under the *Regulations*, the information will be released.

5. *Any Appeal?*

a.   There is no appeal against a decision of the Ombudsman.

b.   There may be circumstances in which an appeal to a higher and/or European court is appropriate under the *Regulations* – see below for where to get advice on this.

6. *Other Options?*

- *see also* **Information 2**

    Environment 1 *and* **2**

    Government Departments

    Local Government
- If you are considering legal action you are advised to contact the Campaign for Freedom of Information at the address below and *see also* **Where to get help**
- The Health Service Ombudsman deals with complaints about the operation of the NHS Code of Practice on Openness *see* **Health Service 2**

NB

- Because the Ombudsman can only get involved where a request has been made under the *Code*, and because legal action can be prohibitively expensive, it is a good idea to apply for environmental information under *both* the *Regulations* and the *Code*.
- For more information and advice on all of these issues contact:

    The Campaign for Freedom of Information
    88 Old Street
    London EC1V

    Tel: 0171 253 2445
    Fax: 0171 608 1279

- The 1993 White Paper on Open Government promised to introduce a statutory right to health and safety information, although at the time of writing this was still not in the pipeline. The Labour and Liberal Democrat parties are, however, committed to introducing a comprehensive Freedom of Information Act, so this situation may change.

Information 2 (Personal)

You have a right to see five kinds of personal information held about you: computer records, credit reference records, some local authority housing and social work records and a specific kind of medical report. This entry will concentrate on computer records: for more about the other kinds see *NB*, below.

Under the **Data Protection Act 1984** you have the right to see personal information about yourself held on computer, and the right to get it corrected if it is wrong. The Act also gives you the right to complain if you don't like the way an organisation is collecting or using computer records about you.

Your rights apply to public sector organisations and private companies which keep information about individuals (children as well as adults) on computer. All such organisations (with some exemptions, see below) must be registered and must comply with the Act's eight Data Protection Principles of good practice.

1. *Who Can I Complain To?*

Stage 1

Complaints Department
Office of the Data Protection Registrar
Wycliffe House
Water Lane
Wilmslow
Cheshire SK9 5AF

Tel: 01625 545745
Fax: 01625 524510

2. *What Sort of Complaints Do They Deal With?*

a. The Data Protection Registrar will investigate complaints from individuals who consider there has been a breach of any provision of the **Data Protection Act 1984,** or of the Data Protection Principles contained in the Act. These Principles state that organisations holding personal computer files must:

    i. obtain and process the information fairly and lawfully
    ii. register the purposes for which they hold it
    iii. not use or disclose the information in a way contrary to those purposes
    iv. hold only information which is adequate, relevant and not excessive for the purposes
    v. hold only accurate information and, where necessary, keep it up-to-date
    vi. not hold the information any longer than necessary
    vii. when requested, give individuals copies of information about themselves, and where appropriate, correct or erase the information
    viii. take appropriate steps to keep the information safe

b. You can find out if an organisation is registered, and what general purposes the information held by them is being used for (but *not* whether or not a particular computer is holding information about you) by contacting the Registrar's office.

c. Organisations holding personal data on computer include:

- Department of Social Security
- Inland Revenue
- hospital and GP records
- housing departments
- electricity, gas, water and telephone companies
- credit card companies
- employers
- high street retailers
- mail order companies
- computer dating services

- schools and colleges
- any membership organisation, for example sports clubs, charities and pressure groups

d. Principle vii above refers to the so-called 'subject access right', which means you are entitled, on written request to a data user, to be supplied with a copy of any personal data held about you. You may save time if you call first to find out if there is a Data Protection Officer to whom requests should be addressed, and if there is an application form which can be sent to you. The data user may charge a fee of up to £10 for each register entry for supplying this information. If an organisation holds information for more than one purpose, and has registered each purpose separately, you may have to make separate applications – and pay separate fees – to get all the information you need.

You can then complain to the Registrar if:

- your request is not responded to within 40 days of the data user receiving any information reasonably required to identify you and locate the data
- the information you receive is factually incorrect, and the data user refuses to correct it
- you think an organisation is breaking any of the Principles

If you do complain you will be kept informed of the progress of your complaint by your individual case officer. A complaint may take some time to resolve, but you should never go more than eight weeks without hearing from your case officer.

e. The Act allows certain information on your record to be withheld. There is a long list of such *exemptions*, including information held for the purpose of:

- preventing or detecting crime
- catching or prosecuting offenders
- assessing or collecting tax or duty

although *only* if providing the information would hinder these purposes.

Legislation since the Act has also restricted your right to see: certain health and social work details (see below); data held by financial regulatory bodies; adoption and special needs records; and data identifying children born as a result of fertilisation/embryology treatment. Contact the Registrar if you are unsure if information is exempt.

The data user is *not* required to tell you whether information is being withheld under an exemption.

f. Data users must list in their register entry the bodies to whom they may want to disclose personal information: as long as a body is listed they are free to pass details on. They are also allowed and sometimes required to disclose personal information (that might normally only be accessible to the individual concerned) to state and other bodies if such disclosure is deemed necessary for prevention of crime or taxation purposes, or for reasons of national security, legal requirement or in an emergency. Data users do not have to tell you if your details have been passed on to anyone else.

3. *How Independent Is the Complaints Procedure?*

The Data Protection Registrar is a completely independent officer reporting directly to Parliament.

4. *Compensation/Redress?*

a. If it appears a criminal offence has been committed the Registrar (in Scotland the Procurator Fiscal) may decide to bring a prosecution in the Criminal Courts.

b. If there has been a breach of one of the eight Principles, the Registrar may serve an enforcement or de-registration notice on the data user in question. Failure to comply with an enforcement notice (for example, ordering withheld information to be released) is a criminal offence.

c.   The maximum penalty for an offence under the Data Protection Act is an unlimited fine. If a data user is de-registered, it can no longer legally undertake the activities which were previously covered by the de-registered entry. If all a data user's register entries are removed, for example, it commits a criminal offence if it continues to hold personal data.

d.   The Registrar has no power to award costs. You have the right to claim compensation through the courts (see *Other Options?*, below).

5. *Any Appeal?*

No.

6. *Other Options?*

● You are entitled to seek compensation through the courts if damage (not just distress) has been caused by the loss, unauthorised destruction or unauthorised disclosure of your personal data. If damage is proved, then the court may also order compensation for any associated distress. You may also seek compensation through the courts for damage caused by inaccurate data.

● If you are considering legal action for any reason you should get advice   *see* **Where to get help**

● *see also* **Information 1**

Security & Privacy 4

NB

a.   Under the **Consumer Credit Act 1974** you have a right to know whether a lender has consulted a credit reference agency, and if so which one. You also have a right to see the information which credit reference agencies hold on you at any time – you don't have to wait until you are refused credit. This subject is covered in a separate entry

see **Credit Reference Agencies**

b. Under the **Access to Personal Files Act 1987** you have the rights:

- To see your *housing records*, and the records of another member of the family living with you, held by local authorities or Housing Action Trusts. This right applies if you are a tenant, former tenant, have applied for council housing or have bought your council house, although there are certain exceptions to the kind of information the LA or Trust has to disclose.
- To see local authority *social work records* held about you. Again, there are exemptions of information which the LA does not have to disclose, and you will only be shown information about yourself, not other members of your family.

You also have the right to ask the authority to correct or remove inaccurate information or an opinion based on inaccurate or misleading information. To find out either of these kinds of information you should write to the local authority concerned. There may be a fee of up to £10.

If your request for access to your housing or social work records has been refused, or if you think information has been improperly withheld, you can ask for the decision to be reviewed by the local authority concerned. The review will be carried out either by a group of councillors not involved with the original decision or by a meeting of the full council. You will be able to give evidence orally or in writing.

If the LA still refuses to show you the information you have requested and you are unhappy about the *way* it has handled your case you can complain to the Local Government Ombudsman   *see* **Local Government**

If you are unhappy about the outcome but do not suspect maladministration you may be able to apply for judicial review on a point of law.

c. Although there is no general right to see *medical records* – unless they are on computer – there is a voluntary code of practice to encourage doctors to give such access to their patients. There is also a specific legal right to see medical reports on you which your doctor gives to an insurance company or employer, under the **Access to Medical Reports Act 1988.**

- If you want to see your ordinary medical or any other kind of records (for example records which are exempt simply because they are 'manual' rather than computer) it is always work asking.

Insurance 1 (Brokers)

1. *Who Can I Complain To?*

Insurance Brokers Registration Council
63 St Mary Axe
London EC3A 8ND

Tel: 0171 621 1061
Fax: 0171 621 0840

2. *What Sort of Complaints Do They Deal With?*

a. All complaints concerning inadequate professional service by registered insurance brokers. The IBRC is the regulatory body for insurance brokers, but it cannot handle complaints about unregistered intermediaries (and registration is currently voluntary). The Council's Code of Conduct should be available from registered brokers.

b. The Council is also a Recognised Professional Body (RPB) under the terms of the **Financial Services Act 1986**
see **Financial Services**
As such it is responsible for authorising some registered firms to give advice about financial services, and for investigating complaints relating to this authorised business.

c. Complaints should normally be made to the Council only after the internal complaints procedure of the firm has been exhausted. The Council expects registered brokers to reply to a complaint within four weeks. If the firm takes an unreasonably long time to deal with your complaint, or if you are not satisfied with the reply, you should write to the IBRC.

3. *How Independent Is the Complaints Procedure?*

The IBRC is operationally independent of the industry. The Council includes twelve elected brokers and five members appointed by the Secretary of State. The Investigating Committee normally sits with four members, one of whom must not be an insurance broker.

4. *Compensation/Redress?*

a. If an investigation reveals unprofessional conduct the matter is referred by Council to the Disciplinary Committee, which has the power to strike a firm off the register on disciplinary grounds. This does not in itself stop a broker from practising, but the results of investigations are published in a monthly schedule and reported in the trade press, and insurance companies may cancel their agencies with brokers who are reported to have fallen foul of the IBRC Code.

b. Although the Council will investigate complaints concerning negligence, you may have to go through the courts to claim compensation. The Council does, however, operate a Grants Fund to relieve or mitigate losses, usually in cases where members of the public are awarded damages by the courts but the firm is unable to pay.

5. *Any Appeal?*

No.

6. *Other Options?*

- If the firm you have been dealing with is *not* registered with the IBRC, it may be worth approaching the Association of British Insurers (ABI) to see whether the matter can be dealt with under their Code of Practice for non-registered intermediaries. The address is:

    Association of British Insurers
    51 Gresham Street
    London EC2V 7HQ

    Tel: 0171 600 3333

-

    see also **Insurance 2 and 3**

    Where to get help

Insurance 2
(Ombudsman)

1. *Who Can I Complain To?*

The Insurance Ombudsman Bureau
City Gate One
135 Park Street
London SE1 9EA

Tel: 0171 928 7600
Fax: 0171 928 8700

2. *What Sort of Complaints Do They Deal With?*

a. Complaints from individual policyholders concerning non-life insurance such as car, house, medical or travel insurance, as well as life insurance and pensions *not* covered by the Personal Investment Authority Ombudsman (*see* **Investment 1**) which has been issued or arranged by a member of the Scheme. The Ombudsman can also receive complaints from investors with unit trust management companies which are members of the Scheme.

b. The Ombudsman *cannot* investigate your complaint if:

- the matter is the subject of legal proceedings or arbitration
- the dispute is between you and someone else's insurer
- the policy or contract is in the name of a company, a partnership or a club rather than an individual
- the matter concerns a policy which relates to a commercial risk
- the complaint concerns your insurer's level of premiums or the decisions as to which risks to cover
- the complaint relates to how an insurer has worked out the bonuses, surrender values or returns on life policies

c. Before approaching the Ombudsman, you should refer your complaint to the senior management of your insurer and give them the opportunity to resolve it. If you are still not satisfied, you have *six months* from the date of the insurer's decision to refer your complaint to the Insurance Ombudsman.

3. *How Independent Is the Complaints Procedure?*

The Ombudsman scheme is self-regulatory but is operationally independent.

4. *Compensation/Redress?*

The Ombudsman can make awards for inconvenience as well as financial loss. If you accept the Ombudsman's decision, it is legally binding, and awards can be up to £100,000, or up to £20,000 a year in permanent health insurance cases.

5. *Any Appeal?*

If you decide not to accept the Ombudsman's decision, you still have the right to take the matter to court.

6. *Other Options?*

Other Ombudsman schemes:

Personal Investment Authority Ombudsman	*see* **Investment 1**
Pensions Ombudsman	*see* **Pensions**
Investment Ombudsman	*see* **Investment 3**
Banking Ombudsman	*see* **Banks**
Building Societies Ombudsman	*see* **Building Societies**
	see also **Insurance 1**
	Financial Services

NB

- Notable *non-members* of the Insurance Ombudsman Bureau include: Co-operative Insurance, BUPA and PPP. Complaints about some non-members will be covered by the Personal Insurance Arbitration Service   *see* **Insurance 3**
- Where an insurer has left the Insurance Ombudsman to join the recently established Personal Investment Authority (PIA), but has *not* opted into the voluntary scheme allowing the PIA Ombudsman to deal with complaints relating to maladministration, as well as to financial services, you may have to resort to legal action instead for maladministration complaints.
- If your insurer is not covered by an Ombudsman scheme or by the PIAS your only option is legal action. If you are considering legal action you should get advice

see **Where to get help**

Insurance 3

1. *Who Can I Complain To?*

Personal Insurance Arbitration Service (PIAS)
24 Angel Gate
City Road
London EC1V 2RS

Tel: 0171 837 4483
Fax: 0171 837 4185

2. *What Sort of Complaints Do They Deal With?*

a. Complaints about insurers who are members of the PIAS scheme, which is an alternative to the Insurance Ombudsman Bureau and the PIA voluntary schemes. Members include BUPA and Private Patient Plan. Complaints cannot be referred to the PIAS unless the firm's own complaints procedure has been exhausted first, and both sides have to agree to go to arbitration.

b. Complaints mostly concern contractual disputes over settlements offered in response to insurance claims.

c. The PIAS offers a 'documents only' arbitration service, i.e. you should not be required to appear as a witness at any hearing.

d. The PIAS service is not free; the fee payable will depend on the amount you are claiming.

e. If you agree to go to arbitration you cannot then take an insurer to court.

3. *How Independent Is the Complaints Procedure?*

PIAS arbitrators are fellows of the Chartered Institute of Arbitrators, and are completely independent of the insurance industry.

4. *Compensation/Redress?*

If the arbitrator finds your complaint to be justified your claim will be adjusted as appropriate, and you may be awarded compensation of up to £50,000. The arbitrator will also decide how the costs of arbitration itself, including his or her own fees, should be divided between the parties.

5. *Any Appeal?*

Arbitration decisions are normally legally binding on both sides.

6. *Other Options?*

a. If your insurer is a member of the Insurance Ombudsman scheme   *see* **Insurance 2**

b. Other related Ombudsman schemes:

Personal Investment Authority Ombudsman
see **Investment 1**

Pensions Ombudsman   *see* **Pensions**

Investment Ombudsman   *see* **Investment 3**

Banking Ombudsman   *see* **Banks**

Building Societies Ombudsman   *see* **Building Societies**

see also **Insurance 1**

Financial Services

c. If your insurer is not covered by an Ombudsman scheme or by the PIAS, or if you decide not to accept arbitration, your only option is legal action. If you are considering legal action you should get advice   *see* **Where to get help**

Investment 1

1. *Who Can I Complain To?*

**Personal Investment Authority Ombudsman Bureau
  (PIAOB)
3rd Floor
Centre Point
103 New Oxford Street
London WC1A 1QH**

Tel: 0171 240 3838

2. *What Sort of Complaints Do They Deal With?*

a. The PIAOB will look at complaints relating to investments sold by members of the Personal Investment Authority (PIA) or by companies that used to be members of FIMBRA or LAUTRO, and which cannot be resolved by the internal complaints procedures of the company concerned.

b. To find out if a company is a member of the PIA and/or was a member of FIMBRA or LAUTRO contact the company itself or the SIB Central Register (**0171 929 3652**). The Ombudsman will also be able to tell you if the firm you are complaining about (as well as the complaint itself) is covered by the scheme.

c. The sorts of investments covered by the PIAOB scheme include:

- life insurance policies (including endowment policies)
- personal pensions
- unit trusts
- personal equity plans (PEPs)
- guaranteed income bonds
- offshore funds (e.g. gilt funds, bond funds)
- advice on and arranging deals in shares
- management of a portfolio of investments
- broker funds

- advice on business expansion schemes (BES) and enterprise investment schemes
- advice on arranging deals and trading options

d.   The PIAOB *cannot* investigate complaints relating to:

- bank and building society deposits
- terms of mortgages and loans (unless related to an investment)
- falls in the value of an investment caused only by market movement

e.   Advice on risk-only insurance (such as term assurance) *may not* be covered – check with the Ombudsman's office.

f.   If the outcome of a firm's internal investigation is unsatisfactory, you have *six months* from the date of their final reply to refer the matter to the Ombudsman. If the firm takes *longer than two months* to complete its investigation you can refer the matter directly to the Ombudsman. The PIAOB can only deal with complaints received by the firm *after it became a member* of the PIA (or FIMBRA or LAUTRO), and normally only if the event which led to the complaint happened *on or after 29 April 1988.*

g.   Since April 1995 the Bureau has operated a voluntary extension of its jurisdiction to allow it to consider complaints against its members which relate to matters which do not come within the PIA's regulatory scope, for example: advice relating to long-term insurance policies not classed as investment policies, and permanent health insurance; administration; and events which occurred before 29 April 1988. Not all PIA members have agreed to such an extension, however, and complaints which fall into areas of extended jurisdiction will only be accepted if they are first made *after* a firm has joined the extended scheme. It is therefore always worth checking with the Ombudsman's office if you are not sure whether your complaint comes under his jurisdiction.

h.   In general, if you have delayed more than *six years* since the date of the event which led to the complaint, or more than *three years* since the date when you first realised, or should have realised, that the advice or service you received was unsatisfactory, you will have to have an exceptional reason for the Ombudsman to take on your case.

3. *How Independent Is the Complaints Procedure?*

The Ombudsman is completely independent of the PIA and its members. The PIAOB Council includes representatives from public interest groups and unions as well as from the industry.

4. *Compensation/Redress?*

a.   The maximum binding amount the Ombudsman can award is normally £50,000. He also has the authority to award up to £750 for distress or inconvenience. In permanent health insurance cases the limit is £20,000 per annum. He can also make a non-binding recommendation for payment of more than £50,000, but the firm cannot be forced to honour this.

b.   Under the extended voluntary jurisdiction the maximum binding amount the Ombudsman can award is £100,000, and there is no limit to the amount he can award for distress or inconvenience. The limit is still £20,000 per annum for permanent health insurance cases. He can also still make a non-binding, unenforceable recommendation for payment of more than £100,000.

c.   The Ombudsman may decide that other action should be taken: for example, that you should be given an apology by the firm.

5. *Any Appeal?*

a.   No.

b.   If you disagree with the Ombudsman's decision, you can still take your complaint to court. If you are considering doing so you should get legal advice.

6. *Other Options?*

- If the PIA Ombudsman Bureau cannot consider your case they should be able to point you in the right direction.
- Related Ombudsman schemes: *see* **Investment 3**

                                                              Insurance 2

                                                      Building Societies

                                                              Pensions

                                                              Banks

- For general advice on complaints about financial services
                                                      see **Financial Services**
- For where to get legal advice   *see* **Where to get help**

NB

- The PIA has produced a free *How to Complain* leaflet setting out the procedures for complaining against a PIA member, or its employees, or representatives for whom it is responsible. To obtain copies of this, contact:

  Personal Investment Authority
  PIA Consumer Help Desk
  1 Canada Square
  Canary Wharf
  London E14 5AZ

  Tel: 0171 538 8860

  The PIA itself does not handle complaints.

Investment 2

1. *Who Can I Complain To?*

The Complaints Bureau
The Securities and Futures Authority (SFA)
Cottons Centre
Cottons Lane
London SE1 2QB

Tel: 0171 378 9000
Fax: 0171 403 7569

2. *What Sort of Complaints Do They Deal With?*

a. The SFA will look into any complaint about the standard of service provided by one of its members as long as:

- it relates to SFA authorised business
- it is not already the subject of litigation or arbitration
- it is about something which happened on or after 29 April 1988 (when the **Financial Services Act 1986** came into force)

b. Before taking a complaint to the SFA, you should first exhaust the internal complaints procedure of the member firm you have been dealing with. If you are not satisfied with the firm's findings or with the way it has dealt with your complaint, you can then write to the Complaints Bureau of the SFA.

c. The Complaints Bureau will first try to conciliate between you and the firm in question. If this is not possible, and you are a private customer claiming no more than £50,000, you can then refer the matter to the Consumer Arbitration Scheme (CAS). You will be asked to make a payment of £50 for this service.

d. For claims falling outside the CAS, there is a separate Full Arbitration Scheme which the firm has to agree to if you decide to accept. If you agree to arbitration you cannot later take the firm to court.

e. If evidence is found suggesting that a firm has breached the SFA Rules the matter will be referred to a Disciplinary Tribunal.

3. *How Independent Is the Complaints Procedure?*

a. The SFA is the Self-Regulating Organisation for the securities and futures sector under the **Financial Services Act 1986**. It was formed by the merger of the Securities Association with the Association of Futures Brokers and Dealers in April 1991. The Board of the SFA is made up of senior practitioners from investment firms as well as approximately 25 per cent independent members representing the interests of the investor.

b. Arbitrators are completely independent.

c. The Commissioner is independent of the SFA and makes an annual report to the Securities and Investment Board, which is published.

4. *Compensation/Redress?*

a. Conciliation may result in a mutually acceptable solution.

b. If an arbitrator decides in your favour you may be awarded compensation, including costs.

c. If a firm or practitioner is found guilty of a breach of the SFA Rules they can be reprimanded, fined, suspended and ultimately removed from the SFA register. Unregistered firms and practitioners cannot legally continue to practise. Disciplinary Tribunals are also able to award compensation.

5. *Any Appeal?*

a. If you agree to arbitration the outcome is usually legally binding.

b. If you are unhappy with the way the SFA has handled your complaint, you may write to the independent **Complaints Commissioner** (at the same address, c/o the SFA **Tribunal Secretariat**). He will not consider the merits of the complaint itself, but will consider whether the SFA has handled it correctly, fairly and promptly, and may ask the SFA to look at it again.

6. *Other Options?*

●   If you decide not to go to arbitration you retain the right to pursue the matter through the courts. If you are considering legal action you should take advice   *see* **Where to get help**
●   *see also* **Financial Services**

Investment 3 (Ombudsman)

1. *Who Can I Complain To?*

The Office of the Investment Ombudsman
6 Frederick's Place
London EC2R 8BT

Tel: 0171 796 3065
Fax: 0171 796 4345

2. *What Sort of Complaints Do They Deal With?*

The Investment Ombudsman (formerly the Investment Referee) is able to examine complaints from customers of IMRO Members or of IMRO's Appointed Representatives. This will usually mean that the firm must have been providing some kind of investment management or related service for you.

Since the Unit Trust Ombudsman merged with the Investment Ombudsman, complaints about the management of a unit trust by an IMRO Member or against a trustee of a Unit Trust Scheme may also be referred to the Investment Ombudsman. Because of the legal structure of a unit trust, however, the Investment Ombudsman may require the trustee to take up the complaint on your behalf.

As usual, complaints should initially be directed to the firm in question, and only referred to the Ombudsman if the outcome is unsatisfactory. You may refer your complaint to the Investment Ombudsman if:

a. You believe that you have lost money or suffered distress and inconvenience because of what the IMRO Member has done or failed to do, and for which you think the IMRO Member is at fault. It should be noted that investments can go down in value through no fault of the investment manager, so the fact that a particular investment has performed badly is not usually regarded as sufficient grounds for complaint.

b. You have given the IMRO Member a reasonable opportunity (and in any event *no less than two months*) after you first complained, to satisfy you on the matter about which you are complaining.

c. Your complaint relates to something that happened *after 29 April 1988* (or after the date on which the Member became authorised under the **Financial Services Act 1986**, whichever is later).

d. You first knew or should have known about the problem *less than three years* ago, although the Ombudsman has limited discretion to accept complaints after this time limit.

e. Where you allege financial loss, your complaint does not involve more than £100,000, as this is the maximum financial award which can normally be made by the Ombudsman. Complaints involving higher amounts may only be considered with the consent of the Member.

3. *How Independent Is the Complaints Procedure?*

The Ombudsman is appointed by IMRO but is effectively independent of any influence or control by them.

IMRO itself is a Self-Regulating Organisation created under the **Financial Services Act 1986**.

4. *Compensation/Redress?*

a. If the Ombudsman takes up your case, he will try to establish the relevant issues by a process of 'investigation' on an informal basis, with a view to recommending a settlement to you and the IMRO Member which he considers to be fair and reasonable. If you and the Member accept the recommended settlement, that will be the end of the matter.

b. If you or the Member do not accept the recommended settlement, or the Ombudsman concludes that there is no reasonable prospect of an agreed settlement, he may offer to arrange for an 'adjudication' of the matter. This is a more formal process, and can only be provided in cases of alleged financial loss if you are also alleging that the IMRO Member has done something for which you would have a *legal* remedy. If you choose this option, both you and the Member will be bound by the Ombudsman's decision. Neither of you will be able to pursue the case in the courts at a later stage if you disagree with the Ombudsman's decision (but see d, below). The Adjudicator will be a different person from the person who first investigated your complaint with a view to reaching an agreed settlement.

c. Where no financial loss is claimed, the maximum the Investment Ombudsman can award, if he carries out an adjudication, is £750 in respect of any distress and inconvenience caused to you as a result of the Member's acts or omissions.

d. As already mentioned, £100,000 is the maximum financial award which can normally be made by the Ombudsman. The Adjudicator may anyway decide that you should be paid more than £100,000, but he can only *invite* – he cannot compel – the Member to pay the full amount. If the Member did not agree, you would have the choice of accepting £100,000 and waiving the balance, or (in this particular case only) refusing, in which case the Adjudicator would cancel his decision and you would be free to take alternative action against the Member, for example in the courts.

5. *Any Appeal?*

The Ombudsman's adjudication will normally be final and binding on you and the Member. However, the law does permit you or the Member to ask the High Court to hear an appeal (provided application is made within a very short time limit), but only on a point of law, and you should note that under normal practice leave to appeal is rarely given.

6. *Other Options?*

- If the IMRO Member is unable to pay the compensation awarded, you may be able to apply to the Investors Compensation Scheme   *see* **Investment 4**
- A number of financial companies come under the remit of the PIA Ombudsman with regard to their advice and sales activities, but under IMRO with regard to the management of investments   *see* **Investment 1**
- Legal action   *see* **Where to get help**

NB

IMRO Members have to cooperate with the Investment Ombudsman, and abide by the Adjudicator's decision if you decide to opt for adjudication. They also cannot avoid a reference to the Ombudsman by going straight to the courts if your complaint falls within the Ombudsman's jurisdiction.

The Ombudsman's Adjudicator *may* decide that on balance *you* should pay something to the IMRO Member, but he cannot compel you to do so. If you did not agree, the Adjudicator's award would be cancelled and both you and the Member would be free to pursue the matter elsewhere, for example through the courts.

Investment 4
(Compensation Scheme)

1. *Who Can I Complain To?*

Investors Compensation Scheme (ICS)
Gavrelle House
2–14 Bunhill Road
London EC1Y 8RA

Tel: 0171 628 8820

2. *What Sort of Complaints Do They Deal With?*

a. The ICS is a 'rescue fund' for customers of investment firms that have gone bust. In order to claim compensation the investment firm *must* have been regulated by one of the following watchdogs: FIMBRA, IMRO, LAUTRO, the PIA, the SFA, or the SIB.

b. The ICS can consider:

- Claims for money lost through an authorised firm's 'investment business' as defined by the **Financial Services Act 1986**. This includes managing in, dealing in and giving advice on 'investments'. 'Investments' are also legally defined by the Financial Services Act, and include: stocks and shares, unit trusts, personal pension plans and some long-term insurance policies.
- Complaints by individuals or small companies, but not large ones or financial firms. Investments held by 'nominee' companies on your behalf will be covered if an authorised firm has accepted responsibility for their losses.
- Claims for money lost as a result of bad advice to invest abroad, if the firm has been ordered by the relevant watchdog to pay you compensation, but does not have the money.

It *cannot* pay out compensation just because investments have fallen in value due to market fluctuations or inflation, or because investments have failed to achieve a 'guaranteed' return.

c.   There are two kinds of loss which ICS can cover, to which different dates apply:

- Claims for investments lost as a result of a firm becoming *insolvent* can be considered for any investments with an authorised firm which were made *from 18 December 1986* (when 'investment business' was defined in the Financial Services Act).
- Claims for money lost through *bad advice* or *management* can also be considered if the firm is no longer in business and the investment was made *after 28 August 1988* (when the ICS started up) or after the date the firm joined one of the investment watchdogs, whichever is the later date.

d.   Before claims can be considered, the ICS has to have declared the firm in question 'in default', i.e. unable to hand over the money or investments it owes to private investors. Once this happens, you should make your claim for compensation as soon as possible, and normally within *six months* of the default declaration.

3. *How Independent Is the Complaints Procedure?*

The ICS is a statutory, non-profit-making organisation that receives its funding from a levy on the investment industry and its customers.

The board of directors includes people who do not work in the industry and who represent the public interest.

4. *Compensation/Redress?*

If a claim is accepted the Scheme will pay the first £30,000 of the claim in full, and 90 per cent of the following £20,000. The Scheme can therefore pay a maximum of £48,000. If an investment is made jointly, then investors can expect up to £48,000 each.

If the process takes longer than six months, the ICS will usually add interest to any compensation they pay you.

5. *Any Appeal?*

If you are not happy about the compensation offered, you should write first to the manager responsible for your claim, and if necessary then to the Chief Executive.

If the Chief Executive cannot solve a problem to your satisfaction, the board of directors can investigate your case.

The final step is for the directors to ask the Independent Investigator to re-examine your case. The Independent Investigator will then present an official report to the board of directors.

6. *Other Options?*

- Recognised Professional Bodies (RPBs) have their own compensation arrangements   *see* **Financial Services**

- Banks' and building societies' accounts are covered by different financial watchdogs   *see* **Banks**
Building Societies

- Investments in coins, precious stones, antiques and so on are not covered by the ICS either.

NB

Investors with Lloyd's of London, known as Lloyd's 'Names', should complain directly to Lloyd's, which is its own regulator, with its own compensation scheme:

Lloyd's of London
1 Lime Street
London EC3M 7HA

Tel: **0171 623 7100**

L

Legal Profession
(Ombudsman)

1. *Who Can I Complain To?*

Office of the Legal Services Ombudsman
22 Oxford Court
Oxford Street
Manchester M2 3WQ

Tel: 0161 236 9532
Fax: 0161 236 2651

2. *What Sort of Complaints Do They Deal With?*

a. The Ombudsman oversees the handling of complaints against solicitors, barristers and licensed conveyancers by the three professional bodies responsible for setting and maintaining standards within the legal profession. His primary function is to investigate the *way* in which complaints have been dealt with by the professional bodies. He does, however, have the discretion to investigate the original complaint itself, when he considers that that is justified.

b. The Ombudsman *cannot* investigate any issue which:

- is being or has been decided by a court or disciplinary tribunal
- is being dealt with by the Legal Aid board
- is being considered by the Solicitors Indemnity Fund

c. You can only refer your complaint to the Legal Ombudsman

if you have already complained to the relevant professional body and given them the opportunity to deal with it. For who to complain to about:

- Solicitors   *see* **Solicitors**
- Barristers   *see* **Barristers**
- Licensed Conveyancers   *see* **Conveyancers**

If you have done this and are still unhappy you can ask the Ombudsman to investigate.

d. On contacting the Ombudsman you will be asked to fill in an application form giving the details of your complaint. This information must be given in writing *within 3 months* of the date the professional body informed you of its decision.

e. When the Ombudsman has received the file on your case from the professional body he will decide whether or not he can carry out an investigation. You will be notified accordingly, and given reasons if the Ombudsman decides not to investigate.

f. The Ombudsman's powers to investigate are limited when, for example:

- a complaint relates to the way a lawyer handled a case in court and the lawyer may therefore have 'advocate's immunity' from actions for damages
- the professional body has not completed its investigations or is considering an appeal

3. *How Independent Is the Complaints Procedure?*

The Ombudsman is appointed by the Lord Chancellor under the **Courts and Legal Services Act 1990**. He is completely independent of the legal profession.

4. *Compensation/Redress?*

a. If the Ombudsman finds your complaint to be justified he can recommend that:

- the professional body should reconsider your complaint, or use its disciplinary or other powers
- the professional body or the lawyer complained of, or both, pay you compensation for loss, inconvenience or distress which you may have suffered

b. The Ombudsman has no power to force compliance with any of his recommendations. The person or professional body against whom the recommendation is made must tell the Ombudsman within 3 months of receiving his report what they have done, or will do, to comply with his recommendation. If they fail to contact him, or refuse to comply with his recommendation, the Ombudsman can require them to publicise their reasons for rejecting the recommendations in whatever way he thinks appropriate (for example, by advertisement in the trade press). If they fail to do so, the Ombudsman can publish the details of the case himself and recover the costs from the lawyer or professional body concerned through the courts.

5. *Any Appeal?*

a. No. The Ombudsman will only re-open a case if he is satisfied that there has been a fundamental error or omission which casts doubt on his conclusion – for example, if important and previously unavailable evidence comes to light.

b. The Ombudsman's investigation does not affect your legal rights. You may, for example, have a civil claim for damages resulting from a lawyer's professional negligence (unless your complaint relates to their behaviour in court, which is covered by advocate's immunity). If you are considering claiming for damages you should take legal advice.

c. If the Ombudsman has been unable to investigate fully because of advocate's immunity you may have a case for judicial appeal, and should take legal advice

see **Where to get help**

6. *Other Options?*

see also **Solicitors**

Barristers

Conveyancers

Local Government

1. *Who Can I Complain To?*

England

Greater London, Kent, Surrey, East Sussex and West Sussex

Local Government Ombudsman
21 Queen Anne's Gate
London SW1H 9BU

Tel: 0171 915 3210
Fax: 0171 233 0396

East Anglia, the south-west, the west, the south and most of central England

Local Government Ombudsman
The Oaks No 2
Westwood Way
Westwood Business Park
Coventry CV4 8JB

Tel: 01203 695999
Fax: 01203 695902

Cheshire, Derbyshire, Nottinghamshire, Lincolnshire and the north of England

Local Government Ombudsman
Beverley House
17 Shipton Road
York YO3 6FZ

Tel: 01904 663200
Fax: 01904 663269

Wales

Local Government Ombudsman
Derwen House
Court Road
Bridgend CF31 1BN

Tel: 01656 661325
Fax: 01656 658317

Scotland

Local Government Ombudsman
23 Walker Street
Edinburgh EH3 7HX

Tel: 0131 225 5300
Fax: 0131 225 9495

Northern Ireland

in writing to:

The Ombudsman
Freepost
Belfast BT1 6BR

Fax: 01232 234912

or in person to:

**Northern Ireland Ombudsman
33 Wellington Place
Belfast BT1 6HN**

or telephone:

Freephone: 0800 282036

2. *What Sort of Complaints Do They Deal With?*

a. Complaints against the following local authorities (LAs):

- district, borough, city, county, Welsh county borough, Scottish islands and Scottish unitary councils (but *not* town, parish or community councils, which have few powers and do not supply services)
- urban development corporations (town and country planning matters only)
- Commissions for New Towns or new town development corporations (housing matters only)
- housing action trusts (but *not* housing associations)
- Scottish Homes (in its role as a direct local landlord only)
- police authorities (but *not* individual police officers)
- fire authorities
- the Environment Agency and the Scottish Environmental Protection Agency (flood defence issues only)
- joint authorities and joint boards of local authorities, including national park boards
- the Land Authority for Wales
- English Partnership
- the Norfolk and Suffolk Broads Authority (flood defence and land drainage matters only)
- education appeal committees, etc.

b. The *Northern Ireland* Ombudsman has a much wider remit, including almost all governmental and public sector bodies in Northern Ireland (see *NB*, below). Unless your complaint is about a government department, you should be able to complain directly to the Ombudsman: contact the Ombudsman's office to confirm this.

c. You can complain to the relevant Ombudsman (as an individual, group or company) if you think you have suffered personal injustice as a result of 'maladministration' by one of these authorities. Maladministration can include such things as:

*   unjustifiable delay
*   discourtesy or harassment
*   failure to follow the authority's own rules or the law
*   bias or discrimination
*   failure to take account of representations
*   mistakes in the handling of claims
*   breaking promises (e.g. appointments)
*   failure to give appropriate advice when asked

The Ombudsmen can only investigate complaints about the *way* an LA has done something; they cannot question what an LA has done simply because you do not agree with it.

d. The Ombudsmen *cannot* investigate complaints about:

*   something you knew about *more than 12 months* before you wrote to the Ombudsman or to an LA, unless the Ombudsman thinks it is reasonable to look into it despite the delay
*   something that you have already gone to court about, or appealed about to a tribunal or to a government minister. If the Ombudsman thinks you could have gone to court or appealed, your complaint will not usually be investigated
*   something affecting all or most of the people living in the LA area, such as a complaint about the council wasting public money
*   court proceedings
*   personnel matters
*   the internal management of schools and colleges
*   contracts for the supply of goods and services to the council (although the sale or purchase of land *can* be investigated)

- *in Scotland*: public passenger transport, docks, har-bours, entertainment, industrial establishments and markets
- anything that happened before: *1 April 1974 in England and Wales*; *16 May 1975 in Scotland*; or *25 November 1969 in Northern Ireland* (when the Ombudsmen were created)
- anything that happened before a particular body was brought under the remit of the Ombudsman

e. The Ombudsmen will only look into your complaint if you have given the LA concerned a chance to resolve it first: if you have not already done so you should contact the depart-ment involved or write to the Chief Executive. If you are still unhappy after going through the LA's internal procedure you can complain in writing to the relevant Ombudsman. You will be informed if the Ombudsman is able to deal with your case.

f. The Ombudsman will first try to settle matters informally, by contacting the LA and asking them to comment. You may be asked to comment on the LA's reply. If the problem cannot be resolved informally, the Ombudsman will conduct a formal investigation and produce a report. This may take several months.

3. *How Independent Is the Complaints Procedure?*

All of the Local Government Ombudsmen and the Northern Ireland Ombudsman were established by Act of Parliament to be completely independent from local government.

4. *Compensation/Redress?*

a. If the Ombudsman decides that there was maladministration by the LA, he will recommend what the LA should do to put things right; this can include financial compensation. The LA must then tell the Ombudsman what it intends to do about it.

b. The Ombudsmen have no powers to force an LA to do anything, although in almost all cases LAs do as the Ombudsman suggests. If an LA does decide not to comply the Ombudsman can have a statement about the refusal published in a local paper.

5. *Any Appeal?*

a. No, the Ombudsman's decision is final. He also has complete discretion to decide whether to investigate a particular case or not.

b. An investigation may only be re-opened if new material evidence comes to light.

c. If you disagree with the Ombudsman's decision, or if the LA refuses to comply with the Ombudsman's recommendations, you may still be able to take the LA to court for compensation. If you are considering legal action, you should get advice   *see* **Where to get help**

6. *Other Options?*

a. Under the **Local Government and Housing Act 1989** each local authority in England, Scotland and Wales must designate a *monitoring officer*, who has a duty to report any actual or likely breaches of the law or codes of practice by the LA, any committee or any officer, as well as any proposal, decision or omission that would give rise to a finding of maladministration as defined by the Local Government Ombudsmen. Once such a report has been made, the LA must suspend any action until after the report has been considered, and consider it within 21 days. The monitoring officer also has to report on whether appointments made to politically restricted posts are properly made. Reports must be made available to the public *if* they have been considered in open session.

If you are concerned about any of the above, particularly if your concern does not fall under the remit of the Local

Government Ombudsman (for example, if you are not personally affected), you may wish to bring it to the attention of the LA's monitoring officer.

b. To complain about government departments, agencies and other public sector bodies   *see* **Government Departments**

c. Advice on how to complain about some specific LA services can be found under separate entries, for example

> *see* **Environment 1**
>
> **Housing**
>
> **Police**
>
> **Schools 1 to 4**

d. For advice on going to court   *see* **Where to get help**

NB

• The remit of the Ombudsman in Northern Ireland is a combination of the remits of the Local Government Ombudsmen and the Parliamentary Ombudsman in England, Scotland and Wales: i.e. he investigates complaints from members of the public about the way they have been treated by local government *and* listed public sector bodies *and* government departments, in Northern Ireland. In the interests of clarity his other functions are described in the separate entry for the Parliamentary Ombudsman

> *see* **Government Departments**

Lottery

1. *Who Can I Complain To?*

Head of Consumer Affairs
OFLOT
2 Monck Street
London SW1P 2BQ

Tel: **0345 125596** (local rate calls)

2. *What Sort of Complaints Do They Deal With?*

a. Complaints relating to the National Lottery, including 'Instants' (scratchcard) Games. You can complain to OFLOT (Office of the National Lottery) if you have already complained to Camelot, the organisers of the Lottery (see *NB*, below), but are still not satisfied.

b. OFLOT's job is to 'protect the interests of participants' and ensure that the Lottery is run with 'due propriety'. It will carry out an impartial review of the facts to find out whether Camelot has complied with the obligations contained in its licence, in the Game Rules and Procedures, in the Player Code of Practice and in the National Lottery Advertising Code of Practice.

c. Complaints regarding, for example:

   - poor service by retailers, e.g. unavailability of lottery tickets and/or instruction leaflets
   - disputed prize claims
   - confidentiality after wins
   - inappropriate advertising (that, for example, appears to encourage under-age gambling, or exaggerates the chances of winning)
   - misleading design of lottery tickets and scratchcards
   - retailers selling tickets to under 16s, etc.

d. OFLOT does *not* handle complaints about the allocation of Lottery funds (see *NB*, below).

e. OFLOT aims to reply to all complaints within 5 working days, and to resolve them within 10 working days of receipt.

3. *How Independent Is the Complaints Procedure?*

OFLOT is an independent, statutory regulator, reporting directly to the Secretary of State for National Heritage.

4. *Compensation/Redress?*

a. If Camelot is found to have failed to comply with any of its obligations OFLOT will ask it to take appropriate action, which may include the payment of a prize. OFLOT has no powers to fine Camelot or direct it to pay compensation, but the Director General of OFLOT has the power to seek High Court injunctions to prevent or remedy licence breaches, and ultimately to revoke a licence if a condition in it has been contravened.

b. It may not always be possible to resolve disputes in a Player's favour, but your experience may cause OFLOT to review the Rules or Codes of Practice.

c. The sale of National Lottery tickets to or by those under 16 is illegal. Reports of sales to children are referred to Camelot and to the relevant police force. Camelot is expected to terminate its contract with any retailer who has knowingly sold tickets to those under 16. Police and Trading Standards officers can prosecute any such sale as a criminal offence (although no prosecutions have yet been brought). OFLOT has no power to bring prosecutions itself.

5. *Any Appeal?*

No.

6. *Other Options?*

Office of Fair Trading   *see* **Goods & Services**

Parliamentary Ombudsman   *see* **Government Departments**

NB

- In the first instance all complaints about the Lottery should be directed to Camelot at:

  **The National Lottery
  PO Box 1010
  Liverpool L70 1NL**

  Tel: 0645 100 000

  Their complaints procedure has several internal stages.
- Copies of all the Rules and Codes of Practice relating to the National Lottery and 'Instants' (scratchcard) Games can be obtained from OFLOT.
- Complaints and queries about the distribution of Lottery funds should be addressed to the relevant distributor.

M

Mail Order

1. *Who Can I Complain To?*

Catalogue mail order

> The Secretary
> The Mail Order Traders' Association (MOTA)
> 100 Old Hall Street
> Liverpool L3 9TD
>
> Tel: 0151 227 4181

Direct marketing

> The Authority of the Direct Marketing Association (DMA)
> Haymarket House
> 1 Oxenden Street
> London SW1Y 4EE
>
> Tel: 0171 738 1625

Protection Schemes:

National daily newspapers

> Mail Order Secretariat
> The National Newspapers' Mail Order Protection
>   Scheme Ltd (MOPS)
> 16 Tooks Court
> London EC4A 1LB
>
> Tel: 0171 406 6806

Magazines

Periodical Publishers' Association Ltd
Imperial House
15–19 Kingsway
London WC2B 6UN

Tel: 0171 404 4166

Regional and local newspapers

The Newspaper Society
74–77 Great Russell Street
London WC1B 3DA

Tel: 0171 636 7014

Scottish daily newspapers

The Scottish Daily Newspaper Society
48 Palmerstone Place
Edinburgh EH12 5DE

Tel: 0131 220 4353

2. *What Sort of Complaints Do They Deal With?*

a. If you have a complaint about the quality of something you have bought by mail order or about the standards of service from the company concerned, and the trader is unable to resolve the matter:

● You can complain to MOTA under their Code of Practice if you have bought or ordered something from a *mail order catalogue* and the trading company is a member of MOTA. MOTA also offers independent low-cost arbitration administered by the Institute of Arbitrators. If you agree to arbitration you will have to pay a registration fee, and you will forfeit the right to claim compensation through the courts.

- You can complain to the Authority of the DMA under their Code of Practice if you have bought or ordered something by mail in response to *direct marketing* through inserts, direct ('junk') mail or by advertisements on television, radio or posters, and the trading company is a member of the DMA. The Authority will always attempt to conciliate a complaint, but when appropriate it will adjudicate on it according to the Code of Practice.

b. If the trader has gone bust or vanished after taking your money but before delivering the goods, and you have ordered from an advertisement in the press, you will be protected against financial loss if the publication is a member of one of the mail order protection schemes mentioned above. If this has happened you should contact the Advertising Manager of the newspaper or magazine in question as soon as possible.

c. The following restrictions apply to all mail order protection schemes:

- you will *not* generally be covered if the advert in question appeared in a 'classified' column
- some schemes state that the trader has to be in liquidation or to have become bankrupt, rather than simply stopped trading
- you are only protected if you have sent the full payment, not just a deposit
- there is usually a time limit within which you should make your claim – ask the publication in question for details

Each of the separate schemes also has its own conditions – for more information contact the publication and/or write to the addresses given above.

3. *How Independent Is the Complaints Procedure?*

a. MOTA is a self-regulatory trade association. The Institute of Arbitrators is completely independent.

b. Complaints addressed to the DMA (which is a trade association) are investigated by the Authority, which is a separate body from the Association with independent representation and an independent chair.

c. The newspaper and magazine mail order protection schemes are completely independent of the mail order industry.

4. *Compensation/Redress?*

a. If MOTA finds that a member company has broken the Code of Practice it may admonish, suspend or ultimately expel a company from membership. This will not, however, stop the company trading. Arbitrators have the power to award compensation, including reimbursement of the registration fee.

b. Similarly, if the Authority of the DMA adjudicates that a member company has broken the Code of Practice it may admonish, suspend or ultimately expel a company from membership. Again, this will not stop the company trading. The Authority of the DMA has no power to award compensation.

c. If your complaint about a mail order advertiser comes under the remit of a mail order protection scheme you will be reimbursed for any financial loss, subject to certain limits.

5. *Any Appeal?*

No.
   Arbitrators' decisions are usually legally binding, although they may be subject to judicial review on a point of law.

6. *Other Options?*

• For more about your rights as a consumer
                                          see **Goods & Services**

- If your mail order purchase is not covered by any of the above schemes, and if the trader is still in business, you may be able to claim damages through the courts (usually via the small claims procedure). If you are considering legal action you should take advice   *see* **Where to get help**
- To complain about direct mail ('junk mail')
                                                        see **Direct Mail**
- To complain about the form or content of a mail order advert   *see* **Advertising**
-                                   *see also* **Video Standards Information 2**
- The Direct Selling Association (DSA) operates a similar code of practice for 'doorstep' and 'party' sales, including full money-back guarantees. If you have a complaint about direct sales and the trading company concerned is a member of the DSA you can contact:

  The Direct Selling Association
  29 Floral Street
  London WC2E 9DP

  Tel: 0171 497 1234
  Fax: 0171 497 3144

NB

- The benefits of the MOTA and DMA codes are *in addition* to your legal rights. When you buy through the post you have as many rights in law as when you buy in person from a shop. If the goods are faulty or not as described when they arrive you are entitled to return them and get your money back, including return postage costs as well as any original posting and package charges.
- If you receive goods you have not ordered you do not have to accept them. If you do nothing and do not hear any more from the trader for six months, the goods become your property. If you write to the trader saying that the goods were 'unsolicited', and the trader does not then collect them

within 30 days, the goods are yours. You must allow a trader to collect the goods at a reasonable time after giving proper notice, and must also take reasonable care of the goods until they are collected.

N

Noise

1. *Who Can I Complain To?*

Who you should complain to about noise depends on where the noise is coming from.

Wherever local government **Environmental Health Officers (EHOs)** are referred to, you should consult the separate entry covering LA environmental responsibilities and complaints procedures   *see* **Environment 1**

a. *General neighbourhood noise*

Barking dogs, hi-fi, noisy parties and noise in the street from vehicles, machinery or equipment, for example, should be reported to an **EHO**.

b. *Loudspeakers in the street*

Complain to the **police** or to an **EHO**.

The **Control of Pollution Act 1974** bans the use of loudspeakers in the street for advertising entertainments, trades or businesses at any time, and restricts the use of loudspeakers used for other purposes in the street to between 8am and 9pm. The LA can consent to the operation of loudspeakers for non-advertising purposes outside these times, but should take local opinion into account. The maximum penalty for illegally using a loudspeaker is £5,000.

c. *Construction noise*

If an informal approach to the **builder or site manager** is not successful, you can contact an **EHO**.

d. *Noise at work*

You should complain to **your employer** about noise created in your own workplace.

If noise from a place of work is affecting the neighbourhood, contact an **EHO**.

e. *Aircraft noise*

   i. Complaints about noise from *civil aircraft* taking off and landing from Heathrow, Gatwick or Stansted should be directed to the airports themselves:

   Heathrow Airport: Freephone 0800 344844

   Gatwick Airport: Freephone 0800 393070

   Stansted Airport: Freephone 0800 243788

   Heathrow, Gatwick and Stansted Airports provide details of complaints received to their respective Consultative Committees on a regular basis.

   see also **Transport 1**

   ii. Complaints about noise from *civil helicopters* can be made to:

   Department of Transport (AED2)
   Zone 2/31
   Great Minster House
   76 Marsham Street
   London SW1P 4DR

   Tel: 0171 271 4913

   You can also ask the trade association for the civil helicopter industry to look into your complaint:

   British Helicopter Advisory Board
   Tel: 01276 856100

   The airports and the DoT operate a 24-hour complaints answering service.

iii. For complaints about aircraft taking off and landing at other airports and aerodromes you should complain to the airport or aerodrome directly, and/or to their Consultative Committee if they have one.

iv. Complaints about noise from *military aircraft* should be addressed to:

> **Ministry of Defence Secretariat (Air Staff) 2B**
> **Room 8249**
> **Main Building**
> **Whitehall**
> **London SW1A 2HB**

v. If your complaint concerns loss, injury or damage that has resulted from military aircraft activities, you should write to the address below, including as many details as possible to help in identifying the aircraft concerned. If you are claiming compensation you should also detail the alleged loss, injuries or damages – your complaint will be helped if you can provide the names of witnesses. If the complaint concerns livestock, veterinary evidence will be required.

> **Ministry of Defence Claims Branch**
> **PL (LS) Claims**
> **First Avenue House**
> **High Holborn**
> **London WC1V 6HE**

vi. If you live near a civil or military airport or aerodrome you may be entitled to a noise insulation grant. Enquiries should be addressed to the appropriate **airport authority** or the **Ministry of Defence** at:

> **Ministry of Defence**
> **DLS Noise**
> **Room B4/2**
> **Government Buildings**
> **Leatherhead Road**
> **Chessington**
> **Surrey KT9 2LT**

f. *Noise from road traffic*

Complain about excessive vehicle noise and illegal motor horns to an **EHO** or the **police** *see* **Environment 1**

Complaints and suggestions about traffic routeing and regulation should be made to your **local traffic authority** (county, district or unitary council in England, unitary council in Wales and Scotland) *see also* **Planning**

You may be entitled to an insulation grant if your property is affected by the construction or use of new or altered roads. For details of how this works and whether you might be entitled to a grant contact the DoE (at the address below) and ask for free leaflet *No 5: Insulation against traffic noise.*

NB

- You may be entitled to compensation if the value of your property depreciates by more than £50 as a result of noise (and other physical factors) arising from the use of public works including new or substantially altered roads and aerodromes. A booklet explaining how the scheme works, *Your Home and Nuisance from Public Development*, is available free of charge from local council offices and Citizens Advice Bureaux.
- More information about all of the above is included in the general booklet *Bothered by Noise?*, available from:

    Department of the Environment
    Publications Despatch Centre
    Blackhorse Road
    London SE9 6TT

P

Pensions

1. *Who Can I Complain To?*

The Pensions Ombudsman
6th Floor
11 Belgrave Road
London SW1V 1RB

Tel: 0171 834 9144
Fax: 0171 821 0065

2. *What Sort of Complaints Do They Deal With?*

a. Complaints of *injustice* caused by the 'maladministration' (see *NB*, below) of both company and personal pension schemes by the trustees or managers of those schemes.

b. Disputes of *fact or law* regarding pensions schemes with trustees, managers or employers.

c. The Ombudsman *cannot* investigate a complaint or dispute:

- already the subject of court proceedings or on which a court has already given a final decision
- about State social security benefits
- about an armed forces pension scheme from a serving member who has a right to go to the Defence Council
- appropriate for other financial services regulators to investigate (see *Other Options?*, below)
- on a point of fact or law about any of the public service

pension schemes *except* the National Health Service Superannuation Scheme for England and Wales

d.   You can complain to the Ombudsman if you are:

- a member of an occupational or personal pension scheme ('member' includes anyone with pensionable service who has left a scheme before retirement age, and also a prospective member)
- the widow, widower or surviving dependant of a deceased member of a scheme
- a relative or other suitable representative, if the person who would otherwise complain is a minor or unable to look after his or her own affairs, or the personal representative if he or she has died

You may also get someone else to act for you with your written authority.

e.   When you have a complaint or dispute, you should first try to sort it out with the trustees or managers of your pension scheme, or with your employer, as appropriate.

f.   If you are not satisfied, you are then normally expected to ask the Occupational Pensions Advisory Service (OPAS) to help you. OPAS is a grant-aided, independent voluntary organisation with a network of experienced local advisers supported by a panel of experts. The name and address of your local OPAS adviser is available from your local Citizens Advice Bureau, or from:

OPAS
11 Belgrave Road
London SW1V 1RB

Tel: 0171 233 8080
Fax: 0171 233 8016

There is no legal requirement to go to OPAS before complaining to the Ombudsman but, unlike the Ombudsman, OPAS can offer advice about how the system works and act on your behalf. Once you have taken your case to the Ombudsman, OPAS cannot become involved. If OPAS cannot solve your problem, they will point you towards the appropriate Ombudsman.

g. A time limit of *three years* applies from the date that you first became aware about the act, or failure to act, that you are complaining about, but is at the discretion of the Ombudsman in exceptional circumstances.

3. *How Independent Is the Complaints Procedure?*

The Pensions Ombudsman is completely independent and acts as an impartial adjudicator. He is appointed under the **Pensions Scheme Act 1993.**

4. *Compensation/Redress?*

If the Ombudsman finds in your favour, he will decide which remedy is appropriate. There is no limit on the maximum financial award, which may include compensation for distress or inconvenience. The decision of the Pensions Ombudsman can be enforced in a county court (England) or the Court of Session (Scotland).

5. *Any Appeal?*

The losing party is given an opportunity to comment on the provisional findings of the Ombudsman, prior to the formal determination. The final decision of the Ombudsman is then binding on all parties, subject to an appeal on a point of law to the High Court or Scottish Court of Session. Very exceptionally, if a new piece of material evidence becomes available, the Ombudsman may, at his discretion, accept it and re-open the case.

6. *Other Options?*

Many complaints about the administration of personal pensions are dealt with by the PIA Ombudsman Bureau *see* **Investment 1**

NB

'Maladministration' has been said to involve 'bias, neglect, inattention, delay, incompetence, ineptitude, perversity, turpitude, arbitrariness and so on'. It is not enough merely to disagree with a decision: you must have reason to believe that the decision was not properly made or implemented.

Planning

a. The 'planning system' is used to make sure that things get built in the right place, and to stop the wrong things getting built. It is supposed to ensure that new uses for land are appropriate for the location, and is used to plan future necessary developments such as schools, roads, homes and hospitals. At the same time it is supposed to protect the natural and man-made environment and make sure that development and growth are 'sustainable'. It does *not* control how buildings are built – this is covered by a separate system of building regulations.

b. **Local planning authorities** – usually local councils – are responsible for most things the planning system does, the most important being:

- the production of a *development plan* for their area
- making decisions about *planning applications* from private developers, including individuals
- the *enforcement* of planning rules when these are broken

About 98 per cent of all planning decisions are taken by local authorities (LAs).

c. The **Secretary of State for the Environment** only gets involved:

- if he formally objects to an LA's development plan
- if he considers that he should decide a particular planning application, or is 'called in' to do so
- with planning appeals against an LA decision

d. In general members of the public have the following rights in relation to the planning system:

- the right to comment on proposed planning policies for your area every time your council revises or replaces its plan, including the right to be informed about the *six-week* period for formal objections to deposited draft plans
- the right to obtain copies of draft plans and other relevant documents at a reasonable price, etc.

e. Most LAs now publish charter statements setting out their target standards of service, which should include target times for deciding planning applications, keeping the public informed and dealing with complaints.

- For more information about the whole complex area of planning, including how to apply for planning permission and how to appeal against planning decisions, contact your **Local Authority** (the address will be in the phone book).
- If you are unhappy about the way your LA has dealt with you in a planning matter, you may be able to complain to the Local Government Ombudsman

see **Local Government**

- If you are unhappy with the way the Secretary of State has dealt with you in a planning matter you may be able to ask your MP to refer your case to the Parliamentary Ombudsman   *see* **Government Departments**
- To find out more about legal ways of challenging planning decisions you should get legal advice

see **Where to get help**

You could also try contacting the environmental pressure groups.

-
see also **Environment 1**

Environment 2

Builders

Plumbers

1. *Who Can I Complain To?*

The Institute of Plumbing (IoP)
64 Station Lane
Hornchurch
Essex RM12 6NB

Tel: 01708 472791
Fax: 01708 448987

England and Wales

The National Association of Plumbing, Heating and
   Mechanical Services Contractors (NAPHMSC)
14/15 Ensign House
Ensign Business Centre
Westwood Business Park
Westwood Way
Coventry CV4 8JA

Tel: 01203 470626
Fax: 01203 470942

Scotland and Northern Ireland

The Scottish & Northern Ireland Plumbing Employers
   Federation (SNIPEF)
2 Walker Street
Edinburgh EH3 7LB

Tel: 0131 225 2255
Fax: 0131 226 7638

2. *What Sort of Complaints Do They Deal With?*

a. The IoP will investigate complaints where there is prima–
facie evidence that an individual registered member of the

Institute has contravened the Institute's Code of Professional Standards. The Code requires IoP members to act professionally, competently and responsibly, and to conform to all the relevant legislation applying to plumbing engineers. Serious complaints may go to a Panel Hearing at which the member and complainant may be present or represented.

b. The Institute *cannot* investigate contractual matters, such as fee disputes.

c. NAPHMSC and SNIPEF operate a Code of Fair Trading, endorsed by the Office of Fair Trading, with which their member firms are required to conform. You can complain to a trade association about any unsatisfactory aspect of a plumber's work. They will initially try to conciliate between the member firm and a complainant, but if this is not possible you will be given the choice of going to independent arbitration. If you agree to arbitration, the member firm must comply, but you will forfeit the right to pursue a claim through the courts. There is a standard fee for arbitration.

d. You can *only* complain to the IoP or one of the trade associations if the contractor concerned is a member of the organisation you are complaining to.

3. *How Independent Is the Complaints Procedure?*

a. The Institute of Plumbing is a self-regulatory professional body maintaining a Register of Plumbers. The IoP's registration, complaints and disciplinary procedures are monitored by the British Standards Institute under BS 5750 (ISO 9000). The IoP Executive Council includes a consumer representative.

b. NAPHMSC and SNIPEF are employer trade associations. Arbitration under a NAPHMSC or SNIPEF scheme is conducted by independent arbitrators.

4. *Compensation/Redress?*

a. If the Institute of Plumbing finds in your favour it may require the member involved to put things right, at no cost to you. If the member is found to have broken the Code of Professional Standards they may be reprimanded, suspended, or ultimately removed from the register.

b. If an arbitrator acting under the NAPHMSC or SNIPEF scheme decides in your favour, he or she has the power to require the member firm to put things right and/or award compensation, including reimbursement of the registration fee. If a firm does not cooperate with its trade association it may also be subject to disciplinary action.

c. In addition, SNIPEF operates a Guarantee of Work scheme which provides customers with an assurance that work will be completed to a satisfactory standard either by the original member firm or by another member at no additional cost to the customer.

5. *Any Appeal?*

a. If you are unhappy with the *way* your complaint has been investigated by the IoP you can appeal to its Executive Council.

b. Arbitration is usually legally binding, although you may be able to apply for judicial review on a point of law.

6. *Other Options?*

* If you are not satisfied with the outcome of either complaints procedure and you decide not to accept arbitration, or if the plumber involved is not a member of either of the above organisations, you may be able to claim compensation through the courts. Your Local Authority Trading Standards Department will be able to advise you on your rights as a consumer   *see* **Goods & Services**
* If you are considering legal action you should always get advice   *see* **Where to get help**

NB

- Copies of the IoP Code of Professional Standards and of the NAPHMSC and SNIPEF Code of Fair Trading are available from the addresses above.

Police

1. *Who Can I Complain To?*

England and Wales only

a. The **Chief Constable of the force concerned,** or in London the **Commissioner of the Metropolitan Police Service** (the address will be in the phone book, or you can ask at any police station). You can also walk into any police station and make a complaint at any time.

b. **The Police Complaints Authority** (PCA)
    10 Great George Street
    London SW1P 3AE

    Tel: 0171 273 6450
    Fax: 0171 273 6401

Note: *For who to complain to in* Scotland *and* Northern Ireland *see* Other Options?, *below.*

2. *What Sort of Complaints Do They Deal With?*

a. Complaints against the conduct of serving police officers in England and Wales, whether on or off duty. These could include complaints about:

- rudeness
- excessive force, including assault
- harassment
- unlawful arrest

- racially discriminatory behaviour
- abuse of your rights
- discreditable conduct
- abuse of authority
- any breach of a statutory Code of Practice (which includes rules about questioning suspects, tape recording of interviews, stop and search, identification procedures, etc.)
- neglect of duty, etc.

The police *cannot* investigate complaints about the direction or control of the police force.

b. You can complain in the first instance either to the Chief Constable of the force concerned or to the PCA, who will forward your complaint to the correct police force. If you make a serious complaint directly to the police they must notify the PCA as soon as it is recorded.

c. When you write you should say:

- when the incident happened
- what happened
- what was done
- what was said
- whether there were any witnesses, other than yourself and the officers
- where the witnesses can be contacted
- what proof exists of any damage or injury

The police force whose officers have been complained about must decide whether to record a complaint.

d. The police can apply for a 'dispensation' *not* to investigate a complaint on the grounds that it is:

- anonymous or repetitious
- vexatious, oppressive or an abuse of the procedures
- made *more than 12 months* after the alleged incident
- not reasonably practical to carry out an investigation

Even so, all such applications are scrutinised carefully by the PCA.

e.   If you would be satisfied with an explanation or an apology the police may be able to resolve your complaint informally. If an informal approach is not acceptable to you, or if the complaint raises more serious allegations, it must be fully investigated by a senior police officer.

f.   The most serious cases will be notified to the PCA, which *must* supervise the investigation of any complaint involving death, serious injury or corruption, and *may* choose to supervise others.

g.   Where the PCA does not supervise, the police force will appoint an officer to investigate the complaint.

h.   Where the PCA supervises a case, it will approve the appointment of the Investigating Officer, decide how the inquiry should be carried out, read all the statements and see all the evidence. The aim is to ensure that the investigation is thorough, impartial and effective. When the investigation is complete the Authority must issue a formal statement indicating whether or not it is satisfied with it and specifying any areas about which it is concerned.

i.   Whether the investigation was supervised or not, the chief officer of the force concerned must submit a memorandum to the PCA stating whether disciplinary charges are to be brought and, if not, the reason for that decision. If after reviewing the case the PCA disagrees with the force recommendations, it has the power to make its own or to direct that disciplinary charges be brought.

j.   The Crown Prosecution Service must decide whether any criminal charges will be brought against police officers. If an officer is tried for a criminal offence, he cannot be charged with a disciplinary charge based on the same facts.

k.   If there is a disciplinary hearing you will hear from the police, and will probably be called as a witness. You can be represented at the hearing by a lawyer or a lay representative (with your authorisation) if you wish. At the time of writing hearings are held by a single chief officer, but this is due to change (see *NB*, below).

3. *How Independent Is the Complaints Procedure?*

a. All complaints are investigated by police officers from the same force.

b. The PCA was set up as an independent watchdog under the **Police and Criminal Evidence Act 1984**: members are full time and come from a variety of backgrounds. None of its members is or ever has been a serving police officer.

c. The Crown Prosecution Service is completely independent of the police.

4. *Compensation/Redress?*

a. Disciplinary action can be taken against a police officer if it can be proved 'beyond reasonable doubt' (i.e. to the stand- ard of proof required by the criminal courts) that they have breached the Police Disciplinary Code. Action can include formal cautions, fines, demotion and dismissal from the force.

b. If the available evidence does not reach this high standard, less formal 'management action' may be taken, ranging from admonishment and warning to advice about future conduct.

c. If there are no disciplinary charges you will receive a per- sonal letter from a member of the PCA explaining the outcome of the complaint.

d. You may receive an apology as well as an explanation, but the PCA has no power to award financial compensation.

(See *NB*, below, for changes in the pipeline.)

5. *Any Appeal?*

a. No. However, a decision of the PCA can be subject to judicial review by the High Court.

b. Making a complaint does not affect your right to take the police to court and sue for damages. If you are considering legal action you should get advice.

c. You *cannot* complain about *how* your complaint was investigated by asking your MP to refer your case to the Parliamentary Ombudsman, as the police do not come under his remit.

6. *Other Options?*

● In *Scotland*

a. Complaints should be addressed to the **Chief Constable of the force concerned**, and will be investigated by the police. There is no equivalent of the PCA in Scotland.

b. If you are unhappy about the *way* your complaint has been investigated (as opposed to the outcome) you can write to:

> **Her Majesty's Inspectorate of Constabulary for Scotland (HMIC)**
> **2 Greenside Lane**
> **Edinburgh EH1 3AH**
>
> **Tel: 0131 244 5614**
> **Fax: 0131 244 5616**

If HMIC decides that a complaint should be reconsidered it will ask the Chief Constable to re-open the case and report back.

c. HMIC is operationally independent of the police and includes a strong lay element, as well as senior officers seconded from the police. It reports to the Secretary of State for Scotland.

d. You can also report a police officer directly to the **Procurator Fiscal** (the equivalent of the Crown Prosecution Service) if you think he or she has broken the law.

- In *Northern Ireland*

a. The equivalent of the PCA is:

> **The Independent Commission for Police Complaints
>   for Northern Ireland
> Chamber of Commerce House
> 22 Great Victoria Street
> Belfast BT2 7LP**
>
> **Tel: 01232 244821
> Fax: 01232 248563**

b. The complaints procedure for the RUC is under review at the time of writing. It is currently similar to that in England and Wales, except that the Commission supervises serious investigations in a slightly more hands-on way, with an individual member of the Commission appointed to take charge of every investigation (although the investigation will still be carried out by an Investigating Officer appointed from the RUC). The police codes of conduct are also different.

c. The RUC does not come under the remit of the Northern Ireland Ombudsman.

- To complain about suspected telephone tapping or mail interception   *see* **Security & Privacy 3**

    (See also *NB* on house bugging, below)

- To complain about alleged investigation by the Security Services (MI5)   *see* **Security & Privacy 1**
- To complain about alleged investigation by the Intelligence Services (MI6)   *see* **Security & Privacy 2**
-

see also **Discrimination**

Solicitors

Barristers

Legal Profession

NB

- You are strongly recommended to get help and advice if you want to make a serious complaint against the police, and/or if you are considering civil action through the courts
  see **Where to get help**
- New discipline procedures and a new code of conduct (replacing the current disciplinary code) for police officers *in England and Wales* are to be introduced in 1997. A 'sliding standard of proof' will also be introduced, to narrow the widely criticised difference between the levels of proof required to win a complainant's case in the civil courts and to prove a case under police disciplinary procedures. This means that minor misconduct will only have to be proved at the level of the 'balance of probabilities', and the standard of proof of 'beyond reasonable doubt' for all cases will be replaced by the test of 'reasonableness' in all disciplinary cases. In the most serious cases, however, the standard of proof will still resemble that applied in criminal cases. Conduct hearings will in future be held before an Assistant Chief Constable (or equivalent) and two Superintendents, and the Investigating Officer in any case involving a Superintendent will be required to be of chief officer rank.
- Investigations of police complaints *in England and Wales* used to be subject to so-called 'Public Interest Immunity', meaning that the contents of complaints investigation files could not be made public unless required by a higher court, and thus that the files could not be used by a complainant taking civil action against a police officer. Since 13 January 1995 this situation has changed, with a Court of Appeal ruling that in future all complaints files should be removed from PII except for the final Investigating Officers' reports. This should make it easier (and cheaper) to take a police officer to court.
- There are no laws governing the use by the police of secret listening devices (bugs) on private property, which can be authorised directly by a senior police officer under the **Police and Criminal Evidence Act 1984**. The police have, however, 'undertaken' not to use these powers in counter-terrorism cases and instead to apply for authorisation from the relevant Secretary of State as the Security and Intelligence Services are already obliged to, but there is still no complaints procedure for suspected bugging by the police.

Post Office

1. *Who Can I Complain To?*

Stage 1

Royal Mail	Tel (local call rate): 0345 740740
Post Office Counters	Tel (local call rate): 0345 223344
Parcelforce	Freephone: 0800 224466

Stage 2

England

**Post Office Users' National Council (POUNC)
6 Hercules Road
London SE1 7DN**

Tel: 0171 928 9458

Scotland

**Post Office Users' Council for Scotland
2 Greenside Lane
Edinburgh EH1 3AH**

Tel: 0131 244 5576

Northern Ireland

**Post Office Users' Council for Northern Ireland
Chamber of Commerce
22 Great Victoria Street
Belfast BT7 7PU**

Tel: 01232 224 4113

Wales

> **Post Office Users' Council for Wales**
> **Caradog House**
> **St Andrew's Place**
> **Cardiff CF1 3BE**
>
> Tel: **01222 374028**

2. *What Sort of Complaints Do They Deal With?*

a. Complaints about:

- Royal Mail delivery services, including problems caused by address changes
- Post Office Counter services
- Parcelforce

b. *Royal Mail*

    i. As long as you follow the Royal Mail's 'conditions of service' – which include the requirements to wrap things properly, use the correct address including postcode and obtain a 'proof of posting' receipt – you are entitled to compensation for items which are lost or damaged in transit, and for avoidable delays if you have paid for a guaranteed delivery service. If you have a complaint you should pick up a form from any post office, or call your local Royal Mail Customer Service Centre on the number given above and have your details ready.

    ii. To complain about the *delay* of an item sent by a guaranteed service (i.e. by Special Delivery, Registered or Registered Plus mail) you must apply *within 14 days*.

    iii. To complain about *loss or damage* to an item sent by any Royal Mail service (i.e. by First Class, Second Class, Recorded, Special Delivery, Registered or Registered Plus mail) you should apply as soon as you can, but in any case *within 12 months* of when the item in question was posted. If you think it will take you a long time to find out the value of an item that was lost or damaged, you should complete the form or call the Customer

Service Centre as soon as you can, and indicate that the value you are quoting may change later.

iv. Completed forms should be returned to your local Customer Service Centre (the Freepost address will be on the form), enclosing a copy of your proof of posting receipt.

v. If you are complaining about a damaged or delayed item you should keep it and the packaging, as these may need to be examined.

vi. You will receive confirmation of your claim within 24 hours, and should receive a full reply within 4 weeks.

c. If you think you have suffered financial loss because you were given insufficient notice of an address change, you can claim compensation from *Royal Mail* for the cost of:

- reprinting stationery and other printed matter
- notifying correspondents
- other related costs

d. Complaints about *Post Office Counters* and *Parcelforce* services should be made on the numbers given above. All sections of the Post Office operate similar internal complaints procedures.

e. If you are unhappy with the *way* your complaint has been handled you can ask the Manager of the Customer Service Centre concerned to look into your case again.

f. If you are still unhappy after this, you can contact the Post Office Users' Council for your part of the country. Local problems (concerning delivery routes, planned address changes, etc.) are also worth referring to your nearest Post Office Advisory Committee (call POUNC for contact details).

3. *How Independent Is the Complaints Procedure?*

a. *Stage 1* of the complaints process is internal.

b. POUNC is the independent statutory body established by the

Post Office Act 1969 to represent users' interests in the Post Office. Members are appointed by the Secretary of State for Trade and Industry. Post Office Advisory Committees are the local voluntary extensions of POUNC.

4. *Compensation/Redress?*

a. You are entitled to compensation for items lost or damaged in transit in the post, but only if you follow the conditions of service described. Amounts vary according to the service you have bought, from a maximum of 100 times the cost of a first-class stamp (currently £26) for First Class, Second Class, Recorded or Special Delivery mail, to up to £2,200 if you have used Registered Plus and paid the extra fee for cover against consequential loss. If you have sent something by a guaranteed delivery service and it has been delayed you should get double the fee back, and will also get compensation if you have paid for extra cover.

b. If you can prove that you have suffered financial loss as a result of inadequate notice of an address change, you may be eligible for compensation of up to 2,000 times the cost of a first-class stamp (currently £520).

c. Other complaints will be assessed on their merits and may result in you receiving an explanation, an apology and/or occasionally a modest *ex gratia* payment depending on the problem.

d. POUNC will take up your complaint and try to negotiate a resolution, but has no powers to make the Post Office do anything.

5. *Any Appeal?*

a. The Post Office will reconsider your complaint if any relevant new information comes to light.

b. If you are still unhappy after complaining to POUNC you have the option of taking court action against the Post

Office, or seeking arbitration through the Chartered Institute of Arbitrators. For details of how to apply for arbitration, for which you will have to pay a fee, contact:

**Chartered Institute of Arbitrators
24 Angel Gate
City Road
London EC1V 2RS**

Tel: 0171 837 4483

Arbitrators can award compensation, and may also refund your application fee if you win your case. If you decide to go to arbitration you must accept the arbitrator's decision, and will forfeit the right to go to court.

c. If you decide to bring a court action or go to arbitration you should do so *within 12 months* of the incident you are complaining about.

6. *Other Options?*

● If you want to complain against a private postal service provider your options are the same as for other commercial services *see* **Goods & Services**

NB

● Taking the Post Office to court is not straightforward, as it is publicly owned and therefore not covered by ordinary goods and services legislation. POUNC will be able to advise you of your rights in this situation and/or point you in the right direction for advice.

Press

1. *Who Can I Complain To?*

Press Complaints Commission
1 Salisbury Square
London EC4Y 8AE

Tel: 0171 353 1248
Fax: 0171 353 8355
Helpline (for urgent information/complaints):
    0171 353 3732

2. *What Sort of Complaints Do They Deal With?*

a. You can complain to the PCC about any item in a news-
    paper or magazine which you believe breaches the indus-
    try's Code of Practice. The Code sets out standards of
    acceptable journalistic behaviour in relation to:

    - accuracy
    - subjects' opportunity to reply
    - the need to distinguish between comment, conjecture
      and fact
    - privacy
    - the use of clandestine listening devices
    - making enquiries in hospitals
    - the use of subterfuge
    - intimidation and harassment
    - payment for articles
    - intrusion into grief or shock
    - protecting the privacy of innocent friends and relatives of
      persons convicted or accused of crimes
    - interviewing or photographing children
    - protecting the privacy of children in sex cases
    - protecting the privacy of victims of crime
    - discrimination
    - probity in financial journalism
    - protection of confidential sources

Copies of the full Code are available from the PCC.

b. Several clauses of the Code create exceptions where some-thing otherwise considered unacceptable is allowed if it can be justified 'in the public interest'. For the purposes of the Code this is taken to mean the journalist was primarily engaged in:

   i. detecting or exposing crime or a serious misdemeanour
   ii. protecting public health and safety
   iii. preventing the public from being misled by some state-ment of an individual or organisation

c. The PCC *cannot* deal with any complaint which is a matter of court, tribunal or other proceedings.

d. It is a good idea to complain to the editor of the publication concerned in the first instance. You should give them at least 7 days to reply. If you wish to complain to the PCC you should do so *within one month* of either publication date or the editor's reply to a complaint.

e. Whenever possible, you should identify the clause in the Code of Practice which you believe has been broken. You should also enclose both a dated copy of the item you are complaining about and copies of any relevant correspondence.

f. The Commission usually only deals with complaints from people or organisations directly affected by the matters about which they complain. It will however consider third-party complaints where there has been a breach of the Code which significantly affects the public interest and which has not been previously resolved.

g. If a complaint cannot be resolved informally, the Commis-sion will proceed to a formal adjudication. In any case raising issues of public interest beyond the three definitions given above, the PCC will require the editor of the publica-tion involved to demonstrate how the public interest was served.

h. The Commission has appointed one of its members to act as a 'Privacy Commissioner' with special responsibility to investigate urgent complaints about privacy. The Privacy Commissioner can act even when a complaint has not been received to ensure that self-regulation is effective in the face of gross or calculated breaches of the Code of Practice.

3. *How Independent Is the Complaints Procedure?*

The PCC is a non-statutory self-regulatory body financed by a levy on the industry. It was set up in 1991 to replace the Press Council, following the first Calcutt Report into press self-regulation. Its Code of Practice was drawn up by a committee of newspaper and magazine editors and ratified by the PCC. The Commission has sixteen members, of which the majority, including the Chairman, have no connection with the press.

4. *Compensation/Redress?*

a. You will be sent a copy of the adjudication. The publication concerned is required to publish the adjudication in full whenever a complaint is upheld. A monthly report is also published which contains a summary of all complaints received, however they have been resolved. The vast majority of complaints to the PCC are resolved through the publication of corrections or apologies.

   In rare cases, usually involving children or intrusion into privacy, the Commission may agree not to publish an adjudication or the identities of some or all of those involved.

b. Instances of severe or calculated breaches of the privacy clauses of the Code are brought to the attention of publishers so that disciplinary action may be considered against the editor or journalist concerned.

c. The Commission has no power to award compensation, nor to fine publications.

5. *Any Appeal?*

No.

6. *Other Options?*

You retain the right to sue a publisher for libel in the High Court if you are not satisfied with a PCC adjudication and/or with a simple apology, and think you have been libelled. Legal aid is not available for libel cases, which can be very expensive to pursue.

● *see also* **Advertising**

Mail Order

NB

● It is becoming increasingly common to incorporate the PCC Code of Conduct, with associated sanctions, in editors' and journalists' contracts.

Prisons

1. *Who Can I Complain To?*

England and Wales

> **The Prisons Ombudsman**
> **St Vincent House**
> **30 Orange Street**
> **London WC2 7HH**
>
> **Tel: 0171 389 1527**
> **Fax: 0171 389 1492**

Scotland

> **Scottish Prisons Complaints Commission (SPCC)**
> **Government Buildings**
> **Broomhouse Drive**
> **Edinburgh EH11 3XA**
>
> **Tel (local call rate): 0345 023402**

2. *What Sort of Complaints Do They Deal With?*

a. Complaints by prisoners about almost any aspect of imprisonment, and which cannot be resolved by the Prison Service's internal complaints procedure. Complaints might be about, for example:

- security category decisions
- disciplinary hearings and punishments
- food
- visits
- work party allocation
- restoration of lost remission/rescinding of additional days, etc.

b. The SPCC and the Ombudsman *cannot* consider complaints about:

- wrongful conviction
- decisions about parole or lifer release/life licence
- outside agencies like the police, the courts or the Immigration Department
- professional judgements by doctors, social workers, psychologists, etc.
- any matter which is the subject of legal proceedings in the courts

c. Decisions which have been personally taken by Home Office Ministers, including advice given to Ministers by Prison Department officials, have also been removed from the remit of the Prisons Ombudsman.

d. Complaints *cannot* normally be considered if they come from third parties (for example, from a relative on behalf of a prisoner). In practice, prisoners will be asked if they wish to pursue such complaints themselves.

e. All prisoners should be issued with a copy of the prisoners' information handbook when they arrive in prison. This sets out the full internal complaints procedure, including how to complain to the Governor, the Board of Visitors and the Area

Manager (in England and Wales) or to the Area Governor and Visiting Committee (in Scotland).

f. If you want to complain to the *Prisons Ombudsman* you should write to him *within one month* of receiving a final reply from Prison Service HQ or as soon as the time limit for the HQ's reply (currently 6 weeks) has expired. You should be told within 5 days whether the Ombudsman can investigate your complaint; if he can you should normally receive a full reply within 4 weeks.

g. If you want to complain to the *SPCC* you should do so *within 3 months* of the last decision complained about. You should be told within 5 days whether the Commission can investigate your complaint; if it can you should normally receive a reply within 4 weeks.

h. If you mark your letter to the Ombudsman or the SPCC 'Confidential Access', no one should open it before it leaves the prison. The SPCC or Ombudsman will preserve confidentiality in their dealings with you, but will probably not be able to keep your name secret when they investigate your complaint. You should include your prison number in the letter.

3. *How Independent Is the Complaints Procedure?*

a. The Prisons Ombudsman is completely independent of the Prisons Service.

b. The SPCC is completely independent of the Scottish Prisons Service.

4. *Compensation/Redress?*

a. If the Ombudsman or SPCC finds your complaint to be justified, they will make an appropriate recommendation to the chief executive of the relevant Prisons Service: for example, that you should be recategorised, granted or reassessed for home leave, transferred, or receive an apology.

b. The Prisons Ombudsman and the SPCC have no statutory powers to force the Prisons Services to comply with their recommendations, although they usually do comply.

c. If the Ombudsman/SPCC decides not to uphold your complaint, you will be sent a letter explaining why not.

5. *Any Appeal?*

a. There is no formal appeal against a decision of the Ombudsman or SPCC.

b. If you are unhappy with the Ombudsman's or SPCC's decision, or if they decided they were unable to investigate your complaint, you may wish to refer your complaint to someone outside the prison. For example, you can ask your MP to refer your case to the Parliamentary Ombudsman, petition the Queen, Parliament or the European Parliament, notify the police if you think an offence has been committed, or apply to the European Commission for Human Rights. More information about all of these options and others is available in the prisoners' information pack.

6. *Other Options?*

see also **Discrimination**

Police

Courts

Solicitors

Barristers

Government Departments

European Union

NB

- There is *no* equivalent to the Prisons Ombudsman or SPCC in *Northern Ireland*. The same alternative options apply if you have exhausted the internal complaints procedure of the Prison Service (see *Any Appeal?*, above). The most common next step is to refer your complaint via your MP to the Northern Ireland Ombudsman

see Government Departments

- You do not have to write to the Ombudsman or the SPCC in English.

R

Rent

1. *Who Can I Complain To?*

Who you can complain to about your rent, and in which circumstances, depends on the kind of tenancy you hold. For more information about the different kinds of tenancies see *NB*, below.

a. The first person to contact if you are a 'regulated' tenant, or if you are any kind of tenant and you are claiming Housing Benefit (HB), is your local **Rent Officer** (listed in the phone book under 'Rent Officer').

b. The second stage if you are a 'regulated' tenant, and the only option if you are an 'assured' or 'assured shorthold' tenant (and are *not* claiming HB), is to appeal or apply to a **Rent Assessment Committee**, which will be drawn from the relevant **Rent Assessment Panel**:

  - *England*

    For the address of your local **Rent Assessment Panel** contact:

    Housing Private Rented Sector
    Department of the Environment
    Room N11/02
    2 Marsham Street
    London SW1P 3EB

    Tel: 0171 276 3000
    Fax: 0171 276 0531

- *Wales*

> Secretary
> Rent Assessment Panel for Wales
> Block B, West Wing
> 1st Floor
> Southgate House
> Wood Street
> Cardiff CF1 1JJ
>
> Tel: 01222 237687
> Fax: 01222 236146

- *Scotland*

> Secretary
> Rent Assessment Panel for Scotland
> Mulberry House
> 16 Picardy Place
> Edinburgh EH1 3JT
>
> Tel: 0131 557 0555

c. In *England and Wales only* there are certain circumstances in which tenants with old-style 'restricted contracts' (i.e. resident landlords) can still apply to a **Rent Tribunal**. Rent Tribunals are also drawn from the Rent Assessment Panels and can be contacted at the addresses above.

2. *What Sort of Complaints Do They Deal With?*

a. If you are a 'regulated' tenant (see below) either you or the landlord can apply to the Rent Officer for a 'fair rent' to be registered. Once a rent is registered it is the maximum the landlord can charge until it is reviewed or cancelled (this usually means for at least two years). The Rent Officer will give you an application form, and will send a copy of the completed application to the landlord (and *vice versa* if it is the landlord who applies).

b. When deciding fair rents for regulated tenancies Rent Officers must follow the rules laid down in the Rent Acts, and must *consider*:

- all the circumstances except the personal circumstances of the landlord and the tenant
- the state of repair of the house or flat, its character, locality and age, how much furniture is provided and what it is like
- any premium lawfully paid

They must *ignore*:

- any disrepair for which the tenant is responsible
- any improvements that the tenant has made which he did not need to under the terms of the tenancy
- any possible pressures of supply and demand in the local market (i.e. they must assume that the rent would not be forced up by shortage)

The registered rent will *not* include the community charge (although if the landlord pays any of this, this information will be noted on the rent register), but it *will* include any sum payable for furniture and services provided by the landlord.

c.   Rent Assessment Committees have two main functions:

  i. to consider objections to 'fair rents' fixed by Rent Officers for 'regulated' tenancies under the Rent Acts (as for 'assured' and 'assured shorthold' tenancies for Housing Benefit purposes)
  ii. to determine 'market rents' for 'assured' and 'assured shorthold' tenancies under the **Housing Act 1988** ('short assured' and 'statutory assured' tenancies under the **Housing (Scotland) Act 1988**)

d.   A Rent Assessment Committee will *not* fix the rent of a regulated tenant if:

- the landlord has got a Certificate of Fair Rent and the rent registered is the same as the Certificate
- the Rent Officer accepted and registered the rent for which both landlord and tenant had jointly applied

e. If you want to appeal against a Rent Officer's decision you should do so *within 28 days* of being told about it.

f. If you are an 'assured shorthold' tenant (and not claiming Housing Benefit) you can *only* apply to a Rent Assessment Committee during the initial term of your tenancy (usually the first six months) or, when this period has expired, if the landlord serves notice of increase of rent.

g. If you are an 'assured' tenant (and not claiming Housing Benefit) you can *only* apply to a Rent Assessment Committee if your tenancy agreement does *not* specify how and when your rent will go up. If the agreement does not say anything about rent increases, the landlord must propose the rent increase on a special form, and give appropriate notice (which can be up to at least six months if the tenancy is yearly). You then have *this period of notice* to apply to the Rent Assessment Committee and ask it to decide the rent.

h. Assured tenants or landlords can also ask the Rent Assessment Committee to decide the *terms* of a tenancy agreement, if one party has proposed changes which the other cannot agree to. If either party wants to do this, they must apply to the Committee *within three months* of the 'notice' to change the terms being served.

i. A Rent Assessment Committee may decide a case by considering the papers, or may hold an informal hearing. Both the tenant and the landlord may request a hearing which both may attend.

j. In England and Wales Rent Tribunals have the power to fix 'reasonable rents' and in some cases deal with applications to suspend notices to quit under 'restricted contracts' (lettings by resident landlords), although they are being phased out under the **1980 Housing Act**.

3. *How Independent Is the Complaints Procedure?*

a. Rent Officers are independent officials who do not work for either local or central government.

b.   There are 14 Rent Assessment Panels covering England and Wales, and 2 in Scotland. They operate independently of local and central government and of the Rent Officers. Members are appointed by the relevant Secretary of State or by the Lord Chancellor. Committees (and Tribunals) are always chaired by a member with legal expertise and usually include another member with surveying or other relevant property expertise as well as a lay member.

4. *Compensation/Redress?*

a.   If a Rent Officer decides that the registered rent is *lower* than the rent a tenant has been paying, the landlord must reduce the rent to the registered rent as from the 'effective date' (i.e. usually from the date an application was made to the Rent Officer). The landlord will have to reimburse the tenant for any money paid over and above the registered rent after this date.

b.   If the Rent Officer decides that the registered rent is *higher* than the rent previously payable the landlord can increase the rent from the effective date if:

●   the tenancy is statutory
●   the tenancy is protected (i.e. still subject to an agreement) and the agreement allows for increases

In the case of statutory tenancies the landlord will have to serve a 'notice of increase', which cannot be backdated for more than four weeks.

c.   If a tenancy is protected and the agreement does *not* allow the landlord to raise the rent, he cannot do so until the tenancy comes to an end. The landlord can end a 'periodic' tenancy by serving a notice to quit, but this must give the tenant the proper length of time in which to leave.

d.   If a Rent Officer decides that accommodation is 'too expensive' to be fully covered by Housing Benefit (HB) you will only receive help up to the Rent Officer's assessment of a 'reasonable' rent. The Rent Officer will also decide whether, according to the law, the accommodation is 'too large' to be eligible for full HB, and whether or not the rent is 'reasonable' for its size; in this case you will only receive HB up to the Rent Officer's assessment of a reasonable rent for appropriate accommodation, *unless* the local authority chooses to award more.

e.   If a Rent Assessment Committee changes a Rent Officer's decision relating to a regulated tenancy (or to an HB assessment on an assured or assured shorthold tenancy) the new rent will be chargeable from the date of the Committee's decision. The rent that was chargeable between the Rent Officer's decision and the Rent Committee's decision is *not* affected (i.e. if the Rent Officer put it up and the Committee subsequently reduced it, the tenant will still have to pay the higher rent for the interim period). You cannot, however, be evicted while an appeal against a Rent Officer's decision is pending before a Rent Assessment Committee.

f.   If a Rent Assessment Committee fixes a rent for an assured tenancy which is *less* than the rent previously payable, the landlord must reduce it from the date of the Committee's decision *unless* the tenant agrees to the higher rate (i.e. it is not a legal maximum). If the Committee fixes a *higher* rent than before, the landlord can apply this from the date of the decision. If the Committee decides the terms of the rent agreement should change, it will specify the date from which the new terms should apply.

5. *Any Appeal?*

a.   There is no appeal against a Rent Assessment Committee's decision, except to the High Court on a point of law.

b.   If you are unhappy about the *way* your case has been handled by a Rent Assessment Committee you can ask your MP to refer your case to the Parliamentary Ombudsman
see **Government Departments**

6. *Other Options?*

a.   Tenants of registered Housing Associations (HAs) are almost always either 'secure' (i.e. regulated) or assured tenants, depending on when their tenancy started, with additional rights in regard to security of tenure. The rents of registered HAs are covered by the Tenants' Guarantee (and equivalent schemes in Wales and Scotland) which requires registered associations to set and maintain rent levels within the reach of people in low-paid employment. For more about how to complain about HAs   *see* **Housing Associations**

b. Council tenants cannot apply to either a Rent Officer or a Rent Assessment Committee. For more information
                                           see **Housing 2**

●   *see also* **Housing 1**

                              Housing Benefit/Council Tax Benefit

                                        Where to get help

NB

a. *'Regulated' tenancies*

Most lettings by private landlords who do not live in the same property as their tenants and which began *before 15 January 1989* are 'regulated' tenancies under the Rent Acts (also called 'Rent Act tenancies'). A tenancy will also be a regulated tenancy after this date if:

● it is a new tenancy granted to an existing regulated tenant, other than a shorthold tenant, by the same landlord
● a court has directed that it should be a regulated tenancy
● in certain cases, where the landlord is a new town development corporation or the Commission for New Towns

A letting will *not* normally come under the Rent Act protections if it is not actually a tenancy but a *licence to occupy*, for example because you share part of the accommodation with other people or because the occupier has to live there because of their job, etc.

Almost all 'controlled' tenancies were converted into regulated tenancies by the Housing Acts.

b. *'Assured' and 'assured shorthold' tenancies*

Most new lettings made *after 15 January 1989* by private landlords who do not live in the same property as their tenants will be assured tenancies or assured shorthold tenancies. The main difference between these kinds of tenancies and regulated tenancies is that it is easier for the landlord to gain repossession, particularly in the case of assured shorthold tenancies where there is usually a fixed initial term of six months followed by a 'periodic' tenancy which can be terminated by either party at any time as long as the required notice (usually two months) is served.

c. In *Northern Ireland* the legislation relating to private rented housing is significantly different. For more information about rent regulation and appeals, etc. contact:

> **The Rent Officer for Northern Ireland**
> **Room 542**
> **Clarence Court**
> **10–18 Adelaide Street**
> **Belfast BT2 8GB**
>
> **Tel: 01232 540540**

The Rent Officer for Northern Ireland comes under the remit of the Northern Ireland Ombudsman

see Government Departments

S

Schools 1
(Admissions)

1. Who Can I Complain To?

Stage 1

The **Admissions Authority** (AA) of the school you are complaining about. This is the **Local Education Authority** (LEA) for 'maintained' (ordinary, state) schools as well as for most 'voluntary aided' (usually religious) schools. It is always the **governing body** for grant-maintained schools.

Stage 2

An **Education Appeal Committee**.

2. What Sort of Complaints Do They Deal With?

a. If your child is not offered a place at the school of your choice, and informal dialogue fails to change the AA's decision, you have a statutory right to appeal to an Appeals Committee. This right of appeal will be mentioned on the AA's refusal letter.

b. Schools must publish their admissions criteria and are expected to allocate places according to them (for example, 'siblings of children already at the school' may have priority over 'children living within a defined catchment area'). All admissions criteria must be clear, lawful and reasonable (it is, for example, illegal to refuse to admit children because of racial discrimination).

c.   You have a right to appeal an AA decision on *any* grounds, for example if:

- you think your child should have been admitted to the school, according to its published admissions criteria
- you think the admissions authority is applying unacceptable criteria
- your child was ill on the day of the entry exam and you think they would otherwise have passed
- all your child's friends are going to the school in question and you think your child would be significantly unhappy if they could not go there too, etc.

You can appeal regardless of the age of your child, or the number of schools you have applied to.

d.   Appeals Committees do not have to restrict themselves to applying the school's own admissions criteria when considering an appeal.

3. *How Independent Is the Complaints Procedure?*

a.   The process is internal until you get to Stage 2.

b.   Appeal Committees are set up by the AAs but are independent of them and include a majority of lay members. All Appeal Committees are overseen by the independent Council on Tribunals which ensures that the procedures are as open, fair and impartial as possible.

4. *Compensation/Redress?*

If you win your appeal then your child will be able to attend the school of your choice.

5. *Any Appeal?*

If you are not satisfied with the way any education appeal was held you can:

a. Complain to the **Local Government Ombudsman**. The Ombudsman can also investigate complaints about how admissions authorities have handled your application in the first place   *see* **Local Government**

   If the Ombudsman finds in your favour, he or she can reprimand the school and/or the AA, and recommend them to admit the child in question and/or pay you financial compensation. The Ombudsman has no power to impose any recommendations, but schools do normally back down and comply.

b. Complain to the relevant **Secretary of State**, who can only overrule the AA if he or she is satisfied that one of two conditions apply: *either* the authority has acted 'unreasonably' by refusing to offer your child a place, *or* they have failed to carry out a statutory duty by, for example, turning away children even though the school was not full.

   If either of these conditions applies, the Secretary of State can require the school to admit your child.

c. Apply *on a point of law only* to the **High Court** for judicial review.

6. *Other Options?*

● If you are unhappy about the *way* the Secretary of State (i.e. the relevant government department) has looked into your complaint the final option is to contact the Parliamentary Ombudsman, via your MP
                                   see **Government Departments**

NB

● Although you have an absolute right to appeal any admissions decision, it is obviously a good idea to be careful about meeting any stated deadlines and other conditions such as obtaining religious reports, entering the child for the correct examinations, etc. If you are applying for several very popular schools you should also be aware that parents giving a higher 'preference vote' to a particular school are likely to be given priority there.

Appendix

The Secretary of State you should complain to depends on which part of the UK the school is in. The relevant addresses are as follows:

The Department for Education and Employment
Sanctuary Buildings
London SW1P 3BT

Tel: 0171 925 5000

The Scottish Office
Education Department
New St Andrew's House
Edinburgh EH1 3TG

Tel: 0131 556 8400

The Welsh Office
Education Department
Cathays Park
Cardiff CF1 3NQ

Tel: 01222 825111

Government of Northern Ireland
Education Department
Rathgael House
Balloo Road
Bangor
County Down
BT19 7PR

Tel: 01247 279279
Fax: 01247 279100

Schools 2
(Exclusions)

1. *Who Can I Complain To?*

Stage 1

> The **governing body** of the school and/or the **Local Education Authority** (LEA).

Stage 2

> An **Education Appeal Committee** (the governing body or LA will be able to tell you about this).

2. *What Sort of Complaints Do They Deal With?*

a. Parents of pupils from county, controlled and maintained special schools may complain to the governing body and/or the LEA if their child has been excluded either permanently, or for more than five days, or in circumstances in which they would lose the opportunity to take a public examination.

b. There are similar complaints mechanisms available for parents of excluded children in aided, grant-maintained (GM) and special agreement schools. In such schools only the governing body has powers to order reinstatement after a permanent exclusion; the LEA's powers are limited to fixed period exclusions (suspensions).

c. If after complaining to the governing body or LEA your child is still permanently excluded you have the right of appeal to an independent Appeal Committee established by the LEA for county, controlled and maintained special schools and by the governing body for aided, GM and special agreement schools.

3. *How Independent Is the Complaints Procedure?*

a. The initial procedure (to the governing body or the LEA) is internal.

b. Education Appeal Committees are set up by the LEA or governing body but are independent of them and include a majority of lay members. All Appeal Committees are overseen by the independent Council on Tribunals which ensures that the procedures are as open, fair and impartial as possible.

4. *Compensation/Redress?*

If the governing body or LEA finds in your favour, then your son or daughter will be allowed to return to the school.

5. *Any Appeal?*

If you are not satisfied with the way any education appeal was held you can:

a. Complain to the **Local Government Ombudsman**. The Ombudsman can also investigate complaints about how exclusions were handled in the first place

see **Local Government**

   If the Ombudsman finds in your favour, he or she will recommend that the school readmits the child in question. The Ombudsman has no power to impose any recommendations, but schools do normally comply.

b. Complain to the relevant **Secretary of State**, who can only overrule a decision if he or she is satisfied that one of two conditions apply: *either* the authority has acted 'unreasonably' by excluding your child, *or* they have failed to carry out a statutory duty to, for example, tell you about your right to appeal.

   If either of these conditions applies, the Secretary of State can require the school to readmit your child.

c. Apply *on a point of law only* to the **High Court** for judicial review.

6. *Other Options?*

- Exclusion cases may be referred by the Appeal Committee to a Special Education Needs Tribunal if this is considered more appropriate   *see* **Schools 4**
- If you are unhappy about the *way* the Secretary of State (i.e. the relevant government department) has looked into your complaint the final option is to contact the Parliamentary Ombudsman, via your MP   *see* **Government Departments**

NB

- The particular arrangements will depend on the school you are dealing with. They have a duty to explain these mechanisms to you.
- For the addresses of the relevant Secretary of State see the *Appendix* to **Schools 1**.

Schools 3
(National Curriculum)

1. *Who Can I Complain To?*

Stage 1

The **governing body** of the school concerned.

Stage 2

The **Local Education Authority** (for state schools) or the relevant **Secretary of State** (for maintained schools).

2. *What Sort of Complaints Do They Deal With?*

a. You can complain to the governing body of a school if the headteacher has decided that, for special reasons, your child should *not* follow the full national curriculum for the moment and you disagree, or if you think the headteacher *should* decide this and she or he refuses to do so.

b. Complaints about

- the teaching of the National Curriculum
- religious education
- collective worship
- unapproved external qualifications or syllabuses
- the provision of information

in your child's school.

3. *How Independent Is the Complaints Procedure?*

School governing bodies and LEAs are both part of the education system, although LEA complaints procedures are external to individual schools.

Secretaries of State are government ministers: appeals to them will be investigated by the appropriate government department.

4. *Compensation/Redress?*

If the school's governing body, or the LEA, or the Secretary of State finds in your favour then the matter you have complained about will be put right.

5. *Any Appeal?*

a. If you are unhappy about the *way* the LEA has dealt with your complaint you can complain to the Local Government Ombudsman   *see* **Local Government**

b. Parents of children at state schools can also complain to the appropriate Secretary of State if they are still unhappy after appealing to the LEA.

6. *Other Options?*

- If you are unhappy about the *way* the Secretary of State (i.e. the Department for Education and Employment, etc.) has

looked into your complaint the final option is to contact the
Parliamentary Ombudsman, via your MP

see **Government Departments**

NB

● Each school prospectus must explain how you can complain
   about the curriculum.
● For the address of the relevant Secretary of State see the
   Appendix to **Schools 1**.

Schools 4
(Special Needs)

1. *Who Can I Complain To?*

Special Education Needs Tribunal (SENT)
71 Victoria Street
London SW1H 0HW

Tel: 0171 925 6925
Fax: 0171 925 6926

2. *What Sort of Complaints Do They Deal With?*

a. The SENT considers parents' appeals against the decisions of
   Local Education Authorities (LEAs) about a child's special
   educational needs, if you have already tried to sort the matter
   out with the LEA and are still unhappy.

b. You can appeal to the Tribunal if the LEA:

   ● refuses to make a formal assessment of your child's
      special educational needs

- refuses to issue a statement of your child's special educational needs, after making a formal assessment

If the LEA has made a statement of your child's special educational needs, or has changed a previous statement they have made, you can appeal against:

- the description in the statement of your child's special educational needs
- the description in the statement of the special educational help that the LEA thinks your child should get
- the school named in the statement for your child to go to
- the LEA's not naming a school in the statement

You can also appeal if the LEA:

- refuses to change the school named in the statement
- refuses to re-assess your child's special educational needs if they have not made a new assessment for at least six months
- decides not to maintain the statement

c. You *cannot* appeal to the Tribunal against:

- the way the LEA carried out the assessment, or the length of time it took
- the way the LEA is arranging to provide the help set out in your child's statement
- the way the school is meeting your child's needs
- the description in the statement of your child's non-educational needs or how the LEA plans to meet those needs

d. If you think you have grounds on which to appeal you should obtain the relevant leaflet (see *NB*, below) and fill in the attached form. Appeals should be made *within two months* of the LEA decision you are appealing against (although if the end of the two months is in August, you will have until 1 September). You will need to include copies of:

- the LEA's letter which gives the decision you are appealing against

- your child's statement of special educational needs and all the papers attached to it, if one has been made
- any other documents you think may be useful

e. The LEA may decide to oppose your appeal. If they do, a Tribunal hearing will take place at which you should be present. You will be given 10 days' notice to attend the hearing, and you are allowed to take a representative and a maximum of two witnesses. Your representative may be a barrister or solicitor if you wish, but you will not get legal aid for this.

f. Your child does not have to attend the hearing, but can if you or your child want his or her views to be taken into account separately from your own.

g. You will be sent the Tribunal's formal decision, together with the reasons for it, within 10 working days of the hearing. The whole process should be completed within four or five months.

3. *How Independent Is the Complaints Procedure?*

The SEN Tribunal is independent of both government and the LEAs. The Lord Chancellor appoints the president and the chairman; the Secretaries of State for Education and Employment and for Wales appoint the other members.

4. *Compensation/Redress?*

Whatever the Tribunal decides, both you and the LEA must accept the decision.

The Tribunal cannot award compensation, but you (and your child if attending) will be able to claim travel expenses for attending the hearing.

5. *Any Appeal?*

a. You (and the LEA) can appeal to the **High Court**, but *only on points of law.*

b. If the LEA does not keep to the Tribunal's decision, you can complain to the appropriate **Secretary of State**.

6. *Other Options?*

*   If you are unhappy about any of the things listed in 2c, above, you can complain to the appropriate Secretary of State that the school or LEA is acting unreasonably or failing to carry out its duties. If the Secretary of State agrees with your complaint, he may direct the school or LEA to put things right.
*   If you are unhappy about the *way* the Secretary of State (i.e. the Department for Education and Employment, etc.) has looked into your complaint the final option is to contact the Parliamentary Ombudsman, via your MP

    see **Government Departments**
*   If your complaint is about matters the Tribunal cannot deal with, you can sometimes complain to the Local Government Ombudsman   *see* **Local Government**

NB

*   This information is based upon the Department for Education and Employment leaflet: *Special Educational Needs Tribunal – How to Appeal.* You should get hold of this free leaflet before making an appeal. It is available from:

    DfEE Publication Centre
    PO Box 6927
    London E3 3NZ

    Tel: 0171 510 0150

*   For the address of the relevant Secretary of State see the *Appendix* to **Schools 1**.

Security & Privacy 1 (Security Service)

1. *Who Can I Complain To?*

Security Service Tribunal
PO Box 18
London SE1 0TZ

Tel: 0171 273 4095

2. *What Sort of Complaints Do They Deal With?*

a. You can complain to the Tribunal about anything you believe that the Security Service (also known as MI5) has done to you or your property, for example if you believe that:

  * your house has been bugged or burgled for information
  * you are being kept under surveillance
  * the Service has given vetting information about you to your employer or to someone to whom you have applied for a job

  Anyone can complain to the Tribunal, as an individual or as an organisation, and a complaint about interference with property can be about where you live and/or where you work.

b. The Tribunal *cannot* investigate complaints about:

  * the alleged actions of police officers, whether or not those actions are thought to have been undertaken in order to assist the work of the Security Service
  * telephone bugging or mail interception
  * anything done *before 18 December 1989* (when the **Security Service Act 1989** came into force) unless you believe the activity in question continued after that date

c. If you want to complain to the Tribunal you should get hold of their complaints leaflet from the above address and fill in the attached form.

d. If the Tribunal find that you have been the subject of inquiries they will determine whether the Service has 'reasonable grounds' for continuing them. If the inquiries have stopped, they will determine whether there were reasonable grounds for starting them. The Service is only allowed to gather information which it needs to carry out its functions, which are:

- the protection of national security, in particular from espionage, terrorism, sabotage, subversion and the agents of foreign powers
- to safeguard the economic well-being of the United Kingdom

Under the **Security Service Act 1996** the Service has the additional function of:

- supporting the police and other law enforcement agencies in the prevention and detection of serious crime

e. If your complaint concerns the disclosure of vetting information, the Tribunal will establish whether the Service has disclosed such information, and if so, whether it had reasonable grounds for believing the information disclosed was true. The Service can only disclose information in order to carry out its functions (as above).

f. If your complaint refers to action against your property, the Tribunal will refer your case to the Security Services Commissioner. The Commissioner will find out whether a 'property warrant' has been issued against your property, and if so, whether the Secretary of State who issued it was acting in accordance with the law in doing so.

3. *How Independent Is the Complaints Procedure?*

The Tribunal is completely independent of government and is made up of senior members of the legal profession. The Commissioner is a senior Judge.

4. *Compensation/Redress?*

a. If the Tribunal find in your favour they will notify you and may also order one or more of the following remedies:

- the Service to end its inquiries about you
- the Service to destroy any records it holds about those inquiries
- the quashing of a property warrant
- payment of financial compensation

They will not, however, explain what went wrong.

b. If the Tribunal or Commissioner do not find in your favour, you will be notified of this, but you will not be told why.

c. You have no legal right to see your MI5 files.

5. *Any Appeal?*

Under the **Security Service Act 1989** there is *no* right of appeal or right to apply for judicial review against a decision of the Tribunal. It has, however, been argued (by Mr Justice Kennedy) that in certain circumstances the Appeal Court could have jurisdiction despite these exclusory provisions. The law relating to appeals has yet to be seriously tested in court.

6. *Other Options?*

- If you think your telephone is being bugged or your mail is being intercepted   *see* **Security & Privacy 3**
- To complain about the Secret Intelligence Service (MI6)
  see **Security & Privacy 2**
- For more about your rights to information
  see **Information 1** *and* **2**
- To complain about the police   *see* **Police**

NB

- You cannot be prosecuted under the Official Secrets Act for anything you disclose to the Security Services Tribunal.

- Property warrants are issued by the Home Secretary, the Foreign Secretary and the Secretaries of State for Scotland and for Northern Ireland. They are applied for by the Metropolitan Police Special Branch, National Criminal Intelligence Service, HM Customs and Excise, GCHQ, the RUC, the Scottish Police Forces and by MI6 as well as by the Security Services.

Security & Privacy 2
(Intelligence Services)

1. *Who Can I Complain To?*

Intelligence Services Tribunal
PO Box 4823
London SW1A 9XD

Tel: 0171 273 4096

2. *What Sort of Complaints Do They Deal With?*

a. Under the **Intelligence Services Act 1994** you can complain to the Tribunal about anything you believe that the Secret Intelligence Services (SIS, also known as MI6), or Government Communications Headquarters (GCHQ) have done in relation to you or your property. The functions of the two agencies are as follows:

- SIS: to provide intelligence and perform other tasks relating to the actions or intentions of persons outside the British Isles
- GCHQ: to produce intelligence derived from communications and other emissions

Both functions can only be exercised:

- in the interests of national security

- in the interests of the economic well-being of the UK
- in support of the prevention or detection of serious crime

Complaints could therefore relate to any kind of audio bugging, visual surveillance, investigation, burglary for information, etc. and can also relate to wireless telegraphy transmissions.

b. Anyone can complain to the Tribunal, as an individual or as an organisation, and from outside the UK as well as inside. Complaints about interference with property can be about where you live and/or where you work.

c. The Tribunal *cannot* investigate complaints about:

- telephone bugging or mail interception
- anything done *before 15 December 1994* (when the Act came into force) unless you believe the activity in question continued after that date

d. If you want to complain to the Tribunal you should get hold of their complaints leaflet from the above address and fill in the attached form.

e. The Tribunal will find out whether SIS or GCHQ have obtained or provided information or performed any other task in relation to you or your property. If so, the Tribunal will determine whether the agency concerned had 'reasonable grounds' for its actions, according to its functions (see above).

f. If your complaint involves property, or the Tribunal wishes to know whether an authorisation has been given by a Secretary of State, they will refer the matter to the Commissioner. If the Commissioner discovers that an authorisation has been issued, he will go on to consider whether it was properly done.

3. *How Independent Is the Complaints Procedure?*

The Tribunal is completely independent of government and is made up of senior members of the legal profession. The Commissioner is a senior Judge.

4. *Compensation/Redress?*

a. If the Tribunal finds in your favour they may order one or
    more of the following remedies:

    - the agency to end its activities in relation to you or your
      property
    - the agency to destroy any records it holds about those
      activities
    - the quashing of any outstanding warrants or authorisa-
      tions
    - financial compensation

    The Tribunal will notify you and a report of their findings
    will be made to the Secretary of State. However, they are *not*
    permitted to tell you the reasons for their decision.

b. You will also be notified if the Tribunal or the Commissioner
    do not find in your favour, but you will not be told whether
    either of the agencies has, in fact, taken any action concern-
    ing you or your property.

c. You have no legal right to see your Intelligence Services files.

5. *Any Appeal?*

Under the **Intelligence Services Act 1994** there is *no* right of
appeal or right to apply for judicial review against a decision of
the Tribunal. The law relating to appeals has, however, yet to be
seriously tested in court.

6. *Other Options?*

- If you think your telephone is being bugged or your mail is
  being intercepted   *see* **Security & Privacy 3**
- To complain about the Security Service (MI5)
                               see **Security & Privacy 1**
- For more about your rights to information
                               see **Information 1** *and* **2**
- To complain about the police   *see* **Police**

NB

- You cannot be prosecuted under the Official Secrets Act for anything you disclose to the Intelligence Services Tribunal.
- Property warrants are issued by the Home Secretary, the Foreign Secretary and the Secretaries of State for Scotland and for Northern Ireland. They are applied for by the Metropolitan Police Special Branch, National Criminal Intelligence Service, HM Customs and Excise, GCHQ, the RUC, the Scottish Police Forces and by MI5 as well as by the Intelligence Services.

Security & Privacy 3
(Interception of Communications)

1. *Who Can I Complain To?*

Interception of Communications Tribunal
PO Box 44
London SE1 0TX

Tel: 0171 273 4096

2. *What Sort of Complaints Do They Deal With?*

a. Complaints about the interception of any letters or packages sent through the Royal Mail or of any phone calls made through a public telecommunications operator.

b. Unauthorised interception of communications is a criminal offence under the **Interception of Communications Act 1985**. Authorisations for interceptions can only be issued by the appropriate Secretary of State, according to certain legal guidelines. If you think your communications may have been intercepted there are two courses of action open to you:

  i. You can report your suspicions to the police, who will

investigate the matter. If evidence is found that someone has been illegally tapping your telephone or intercepting your mail this may lead to a criminal prosecution. The police cannot, however, investigate questions relating to interceptions authorised by a Secretary of State – and they cannot tell you if they discover that there is an authorisation applying to your property.

ii. You can ask the Interception of Communications Tribunal to investigate whether a Secretary of State has authorised any interception against you. The Tribunal must investigate all complaints.

c. The Tribunal will first find out if an interception of your mail and/or phone calls has been authorised. If it has, they will go on to consider whether such authorisation was properly given, according to the requirements of the Act. Secretaries of State can only issue interception warrants where they consider it necessary for one of the following reasons:

- in the interests of national security
- for the prevention or detection of serious crime
- in order to safeguard the economic well-being of the United Kingdom

d. If you want to complain to the Tribunal you should get hold of their complaints leaflet from the above address and fill in the attached form.

3. *How Independent Is the Complaints Procedure?*

The Tribunal is completely independent of government and is made up of senior members of the legal profession. The President is a senior Judge.

4. *Compensation/Redress?*

a. If the Tribunal find in your favour they may order one or more of the following remedies:

- quashing of the relevant authorisation
- destruction of copies of material intercepted under the authorisations concerned
- payment of financial compensation

You will be notified of their conclusion and of the effect of any order made.

b. If the Tribunal do not find in your favour, you will be notified 'that there has been no contravention of sections 2–5' of the Interception of Communications Act. You will not be told why – i.e. you will not be told whether your communications are being intercepted and the Tribunal has decided this is justified, or whether your suspicions were unfounded.

5. *Any Appeal?*

Under the **Interception of Communications Act 1985** there is *no* right of appeal or right to apply for judicial review against a decision of the Tribunal. However, the law relating to appeals of this kind has yet to be tested in court.

6. *Other Options?*

- To complain about the Security Service (MI5)
  see **Security & Privacy 1**
- To complain about the Secret Intelligence Service (MI6)
  see **Security & Privacy 2**
- To complain about the police   *see* **Police**

Security & Privacy 4 (Data Protection Tribunal)

1. *Who Can I Complain To?*

Data Protection Tribunal
Room 978
E Division
Home Office
Queen Anne's Gate
London SW1H 1HT

2. *What Sort of Complaints Do They Deal With?*

a. The Tribunal deals with appeals by *data users* (i.e. organisations or individuals which hold and use computerised information about living individuals) against decisions of the Data Protection Registrar. It does *not* deal with complaints by individual data subjects (i.e. living individuals whose personal information is held on computer). The Data Protection Registrar deals with those complaints

see **Information 2**

b. Under section 13 of the **Data Protection Act 1984**, a data user may appeal to the Tribunal against the Registrar's refusal of registration or of alteration of registered particulars; or against an enforcement notice, de-registration notice or transfer prohibition notice which has been served on him/her by the Registrar. The procedure for hearing appeals is set out in the **Data Protection Tribunal Rules 1985**. The appeal is triggered by a notice of appeal being served on the Tribunal *within 28 days* of the notification of the Registrar's decision being served on the appellant.

3. *How Independent Is the Complaints Procedure?*

The Tribunal is completely independent of the Data Protection Registrar.

4. *Compensation/Redress?*

The Tribunal has the power to award costs in favour of either party. This includes the power to award costs against the Registrar where it considers that the Registrar's decision was manifestly unreasonable.

5. *Any Appeal?*

Any party may appeal against the decision of the Tribunal on a point of law to the appropriate court. If you are considering further legal action you should get advice

see **Where to get help**

6. *Other Options?*

●

see also **Security & Privacy 1** *to* **3**

Information 2

Social Security

The procedures for appealing against social security benefit decisions are complex and under comprehensive review at the time of writing. The following is a highly simplified summary of the basic stages involved in appealing against decisions relating to non-contributory benefits.

For how to appeal against other kinds of benefit decision see *Other Options?*, below.

1. *Who Can I Complain To?*

Stage 1

Ask an **Adjudication Officer** to *review* the decision of the Adjudicating Authority in your case, or *appeal* to a **Medical Board**.

Stage 2

> *Appeal* to a **Tribunal.**

Stage 3

> *Appeal* on a point of law only to a **Social Security Commissioner** (or a Tribunal of Commissioners).

2. *What Sort of Complaints Do They Deal With?*

a. *Reviews/appeals to medical boards*

> i. If you disagree with a decision about any non-contributory benefit apart from Disability Living Allowance (DLA), Attendance Allowance (AA) or Disability Working Allowance (DWA) you can ask for an Adjudication Officer to review the decision on the grounds that:
>
> - the decision was given in ignorance of a material fact
> - the decision was based on a mistake about a material fact
> - there has been, or there is about to be, a relevant change of circumstances since the decision was made
> - the decision was based on an error in law
> - the decision was based on another Adjudicating Authority's decision, and that decision has since been revised
>
> If you decide to apply for a review you should do so *within 3 months* of the decision letter being sent to you.
> ii. If you disagree with a decision about DLA, AA or DWA you are automatically entitled to a review; the only condition being that you apply *within 3 months* of the decision letter being sent to you.
> iii. If you disagree with the medical aspects of any decision you have *3 months* to appeal to a Medical Board. The Medical Board will then notify the Adjudication Officer in your case of the outcome of your appeal, so that the

decision about your benefit can be reviewed as appropriate.

b. *Appeals to a Tribunal*

    i. If you are still unhappy after the decision in question has been reviewed, or reconsidered by a Medical Board, or if your application for a review is denied, you have a right to appeal to the appropriate Tribunal.

- appeals about Adjudication Officer decisions except for those on DLA, AA or DWA are heard by a Social Security Appeal Tribunal (SSAT)
- appeals about Adjudication Officer decisions on DLA, AA or DWA are heard by a Disability Appeal Tribunal (DAT)
- appeals about Adjudicating Medical Authority decisions are heard by a Medical Appeal Tribunal (MAT)

If you decide to appeal you should write to the same DSS or Employment Service office that sent you the decision letter *within 3 months* of it being sent to you.

    ii. You will be asked to attend the Tribunal hearing, but you can be represented by anyone you feel can best put forward your views (although it is a good idea to attend yourself even if you choose to be represented). You are allowed to take a friend, and can call any witnesses you like.

c. *Appeals to a Social Security Commissioner*

    i. If you are unhappy with the decision of an SSAT, DAT or MAT you have a right to appeal to a Social Security Commissioner (SSC), but only on a point of law. An error in point of law is where, for example, the Tribunal:

- made a mistake in applying the law to your case
- took irrelevant matters into account or failed to consider relevant matters
- failed to give proper or sufficiently clear reasons for its decision

- breached the rules of natural justice, etc.

ii. If you want to appeal to an SSC you need to ask either the chairman of the tribunal or the SSC for 'leave of appeal'.
iii. Most appeals to an SSC are decided without an oral hearing.
iv. SSCs have no power to deal with medical questions.

3. *How Independent Is the Complaints Procedure?*

a. Adjudication Officers are appointed by the Secretary of State to make decisions independently of the DSS and Employment Service, but they are allowed to review their own and other officers' decisions.

b. Medical Boards consist of two or more Adjudicating Medical Practitioners (i.e. doctors).

c. A Social Security Appeal Tribunal is made up of a chairperson, who is a lawyer, and two other people.

d. A Disability Appeal Tribunal is made up of a chairperson, who is a lawyer, a doctor – normally a GP – and a person who knows about dealing with the needs of disabled people.

e. A Medical Appeal Tribunal is made up of a chairperson, who is a lawyer, and two doctors who are consultants.

   SSATs, DATs and MATs are run by the Independent Council on Tribunals.

f. Social Security Commissioners are lawyers who are independent of the DSS, the Employment Service and Tribunals.

4. *Compensation/Redress?*

a. If an Adjudicating Officer decides to revise a decision (after his or her own review, or after a Medical Board appeal) and awards you benefit or increases your benefit, the decision will be backdated for different lengths of time depending on the benefit in question. You may be eligible for up to 12 months of arrears if you were entitled to benefit throughout that period *and* you had 'good cause' for not making your application for review earlier. The 'good cause' provision does *not*, however, apply to Income Support, Child Benefit, Social Fund (Maternity and Funeral Payments), Mobility Allowance or Family Credit.

b. If a Tribunal decides in your favour the Social Security Office or Jobcentre will usually act on the decision as soon as they receive a copy of it, *unless* the Adjudication Officer decides to appeal to the SSC, in which case you will have to wait for the decision of the Commissioner. The Tribunal can require benefits or benefit increases to be backdated.

If you go to a Tribunal you can get your expenses paid.

c. Similarly, if the SSC decides in your favour the decision will be implemented immediately, and may be backdated as appropriate.

5. *Any Appeal?*

a. You have no right to appeal a refusal of leave to appeal to an SSC. However, if you think this decision is wrong you should take legal advice, as it may be possible to seek judicial review.

b. There is a further right of appeal against a decision of the SSC on a *point of law only* to the Court of Appeal (Court of Session in Scotland).

c. Any decision by a Medical Board, a Tribunal, the Social Security Commissioner or the Secretary of State may be 'corrected' if any accidental error is made, or 'set aside' on the grounds that:

- a document relating to the proceedings was not sent to you or your representative
- you or your representative did not receive a document relating to the proceedings at all or received it only after the decision was made

- the Board/Tribunal, etc. did not receive a document relating to the proceedings before the decision was made
- you, your representative or another party's representative were not present at the inquiry
- it is in the interests of justice

If you think you have grounds for applying to have a decision set aside you must write to the appropriate authority *within 3 months* of being notified of the decision. There is no appeal against a decision not to set aside a decision.

6. *Other Options?*

a. If you think a decision relating to a *contributory benefit* (for example, Jobseekers Allowance, Incapacity Benefit, Maternity Allowance or Retirement Pension) has been based on incorrect National Insurance contribution records, you can apply to the Secretary of State for a formal decision. Your Social Security Office or Jobcentre will be able to give you an application form. The Office for the Determination of Contribution Questions (ODCQ) will then investigate your case on behalf of the Secretary of State and may decide to hold an inquiry, to which you will be invited. You have a right of appeal against a decision of the Secretary of State, *on a point of law only*, to the High Court (Court of Session in Scotland).

b. The Secretary of State is also responsible for certain decisions about the *way* benefit is paid: if you disagree with such a decision the appeals procedure is the same as above.

c. If you think that a decision about a *War Pension* is wrong, see leaflet WPA 8 *Can I claim?* or leaflet WPA 1 *Notes about war pensions and allowances.*

d. If you disagree with a decision about a *Maternity Payment, Funeral Payment* or *Cold Weather Payment* from the Social Fund you can appeal to an SSAT (see above).

e. If you disagree with a decision about a *Community Care Grant, Budgeting Loan* or *Crisis Loan* from the Social Fund you can ask the Social Fund Officer to review your case. To find out more see leaflet SB 16 *A guide to the Social Fund*.

f. To appeal against *Housing Benefit* and/or *Council Tax Benefit* decisions   *see* **Housing Benefit/Council Tax Benefit**

NB

- For more information ask your Social Security Office or Employment Service Jobcentre. Leaflets NI 260 *A guide to reviews and appeals* and leaflet NI 246 *How to appeal* are particularly useful (although this information may be out of date by the time you read this – if in doubt check with your benefit office).
- For who else to turn to for help and advice in this complex area   *see* **Where to get help**

Social Services 1 (General)

1. *Who Can I Complain To?*

Stage 1

The **Complaints Officer** at the **Social Services Department** of your Local Authority (the address and contact number will be in your local phone book).

Stage 2

A **Review Panel** appointed by the Local Authority.

2. *What Sort of Complaints Do They Deal With?*

a. Complaints about the actions, decisions or apparent failings of a Local Authority (LA) Social Services Department (SSD), including comments on the availability, nature, quality, appropriateness, delivery and/or non-delivery of social services. Services provided by SSDs include:

- social workers
- home care and home help services
- meals-on-wheels
- community care – including sheltered housing, residential care homes and nursing homes
- foster services and children's homes, etc.

When you complain you should say what result you would be happy with.

b. For more information about complaints relating to children and the Children Act (concerning, for example, care orders and children's homes)   *see* **Social Services 2**

c. For more information about complaints relating to residential care and nursing homes   *see* **Social Services 3**

d. You can complain to your SSD if:

- the LA in question has a power or a duty to provide or to secure the provision of a social service for you (this usually just means you must be a resident of the LA area) *and*
- your need or possible need for such a service has (by whatever means) already come to the attention of the LA

You may also authorise someone else to complain on your behalf.

e. All LAs are required by law to have an effective and efficient complaints mechanism in place for social services. The LA will usually try to resolve your complaint in an informal manner first. If this is unsuccessful you can make a 'registered complaint' (i.e. a complaint in writing) and the complaints officer (together with an independent person, if the complainant is a child) will look into your concerns and report back to you. You should receive a response within 28 days or, where this is not possible, an explanation of the position within 28 days and a full answer within 3 months.

f. If you are unhappy with the outcome of the complaints officer's investigation you can ask the LA to appoint a review panel to reconsider your case. If you decide to ask for a review you should do so *within 28 days* of receiving the complaints officer's final response. You will be invited to submit written evidence to the panel, and to attend its meeting to give oral evidence. You may call witnesses to give evidence on your behalf, and you may be represented by another person if you feel they are better able to present your case than you – although this must not be a legal professional, and you should still attend the meeting yourself. You will be sent the panel's decision, and the reasons for it, within 24 hours of the meeting.

3. *How Independent Is the Complaints Procedure?*

a. Social Services Department complaints officers are Local Authority employees.

b. Complaints made by or on behalf of children are initially investigated by a complaints officer together with an independent person appointed by the LA.

c. Review panels are groups of at least three people appointed by the LA, at least one of whom is independent. Independent panel members are appointed from lists drawn up by LAs in consultation with voluntary groups and other agencies, and should have experience relevant to the subject matter of the complaint.

4. *Compensation/Redress?*

a. If the review panel finds in your favour, it will make recommendations about what the LA should do to put things right. The LA is required to reconsider its decision in the light of the panel's findings to decide what action it ought to take, although it is not obliged to accept a review panel's recommendations. You will be notified of the outcome of the LA's reconsideration within 28 days of the date of the panel's recommendation.

b. LAs may decide to reverse or change a decision and/or pay compensation. You may also be reimbursed for travelling and other expenses.

c. Allegations suggesting that a criminal offence may have been committed will always be referred to the police.

5. *Any Appeal?*

a. If you are unhappy with the review panel's recommendations, or with the decision of the LA after its reconsideration of your case in the light of the panel's recommendations, you can try writing to your local councillor and/or your MP.

b. If you are unhappy with the *way* the LA has handled your complaint you can refer your case to the Local Government Ombudsman   *see* **Local Government**

6. *Other Options?*

a. For more about how to complain about Social Services if you are under 16 (or under 21 and still living in a children's home)   *see* **Social Services 2**

b. For more about how to complain about a residential care or nursing home   *see* **Social Services 3**

●   *see also* **Health Service 1** *and* **3**

Health (Mental)

Social Security

Information 1 *and* **2**

Discrimination

Social Services 2
(Children)

Social Services Departments

a. Children have a number of specific rights to care and protec-
    tion under the **Children Act 1991.** Under the Act, local
    authority Social Services Departments (SSDs) must help chil-
    dren if they will suffer without help, or if they have a
    disability and need help. They must provide a range and level
    of services appropriate for children in need in their area, in
    partnership with parents, and taking into account the child's
    race, religion, culture and language.

b. Specific rights of children under the Act include:

    • the right to have your views listened to and taken into
      consideration when decisions about you are being
      taken
    • the right to refuse a medical examination over the age
      of 16, or under this age if you understand what it
      means
    • the right to have a court decide various questions about
      where you will live, who will take care of you, and who
      can stay in contact with you if your parents cannot agree
      or are incapable of taking care of you (see below)
    • *when in care*: the right not to be locked up without
      official permission from a court or from the Secretary of
      State, the right not to be punished in a number of specific
      ways, and the right to complain if you are being hurt or
      harmed by anyone caring for you
    • the right to continuing accommodation between the ages
      of 16 and 21 if you would be in serious danger without it

c. If you are *in care*, unless there are exceptional circumstances
    and/or the relevant permission has been given, SSDs *must
    not*:

    • change your religion
    • change your name
    • take you abroad for more than one month at a time

There are many other rights under the Act – see *NB*, below, for how to find out more.

d. If you are under 16, or under 21 but still in care, and you are either unhappy with the way you have been treated by Social Services or you have not been given help when you have asked for it, you should complain to the SSD of your local authority. Complaints made by or on behalf of children will go through the standard Social Services complaints procedure, with the difference that an independent person will be involved from the very first stage.

● For how to complain   *see* **Social Services 1**

The Courts

The **Children Act 1991** also gives children (and parents) a number of legal rights, for example the right to apply for, and to appeal against, court orders relating to contact, residence, care, etc. Free legal representation and advice is available for children.

see also **Where to get help**

Courts

Solicitors

Barristers

Legal Profession

NB

a. For more information about:

- services available in your area
- children's rights under the Act
- how children can complain when things go wrong
- organisations offering free specialist help and advice including legal advice and representation

contact your local authority SSD or a Citizens Advice Bureau (the numbers will be in the phone book). Copies of the booklets *Getting Help from Social Services*, *Living Away From Home: Your Rights* and *The Children Act & the Courts* (written for children) are also available from:

> **BAPS**
> **Health Publications Unit**
> **Storage & Distribution Centre**
> **Heywood Stores**
> **Manchester Road**
> **Heywood**
> **Lancashire OL10 2PZ**

b. Boarding schools with pupils resident all year round are treated as children's homes under the Children Act.

Social Services 3
(Residential & Nursing Homes)

1. *Who Can I Complain To?*

There is no unified procedure specifically covering people living in residential and nursing homes. Who you should complain to depends on the nature of your complaint.

Residential Homes

a. Complaints about care homes run by the Local Authority (LA) should be directed to the **Social Services Department** (SSD) of the LA   *see* **Social Services 1**

b. Registered residential care homes – i.e. voluntary or private-sector homes providing care services with financial support from the LA – are legally obliged to have their own 'in-house' complaints procedure. Complaints about care services in these types of home should therefore be directed to **the management of the home in question** ('the service provider') in the first instance.

If you are still unhappy after exhausting the internal complaints procedure of the service provider, or if for some reason you do not wish to complain to them, you can then refer your case to the SSD   *see* **Social Services 1**

c.   You can also complain to the **Local Authority** in its capacity as the registering authority if you think the home may have broken the terms of its registration, although registering authorities are not obliged to investigate residents' complaints.

d.   Complaints about the accommodation and service in private residential care homes should similarly be directed to **the management of the home**.

Nursing Homes

Nursing homes are under no obligation to provide an in-house complaints procedure.

a.   If you are a resident of a nursing home and your medical care is being funded by the NHS you can use the NHS complaints procedure   *see* **Health Service 1**

b.   If you have been placed in a nursing home by Social Services you can also use their complaints procedure
see **Social Services 1**

Complaints about nursing homes made to Social Services Departments will be copied to the Health Authority registration officer responsible for registration and inspection of the home. Either or both of the authorities will then investigate the complaint, or different aspects of the complaint, in liaison with each other. You can also complain directly to the **Local Health Authority** in its capacity as a registration authority if you think a nursing home may have broken the terms of its registration.

2.   *Other Options?*

see **Social Services 1**

Health Service 1 *and* **3**

Health (Mental)

Solicitors

1. *Who Can I Complain To?*

Office for the Supervision of Solicitors (OSS)
Victoria Court
8 Dormer Place
Leamington Spa
Warwickshire CV32 5AE

Tel: 01926 820082/3
Fax: 01926 431435
Helpline: 01926 822007/8/9

Note: The OSS only deals with solicitors practising in England
and Wales. *Complaints about solicitors in* Scotland *and* Northern Ireland *are handled directly by the relevant* **Law Societies** –
for addresses   *see* **Where to get help**

2. *What Sort of Complaints Do They Deal With?*

a. Complaints which cannot be solved by the solicitor in question, about:

- the quality of professional service supplied by a solicitor
  to a client, including: unjustifiable delay, lack of information about costs, failure to keep you informed, failure to
  reply to phone calls and letters, and/or failure to follow
  instructions
- allegations of professional misconduct, including: failure
  to release papers, failure to account
- the level of a solicitor's fees

If you are not sure if you have grounds to complain, you can
call the Helpline number to discuss your problem.

When you make your complaint you should say what you
want to happen, bearing in mind the powers of the OSS (see
below).

b. The OSS *cannot* investigate:

- complaints of professional negligence (but see *Other Options?*, below)
- any complaint which is not about a solicitor or his or her staff
- complaints about the outcome of a court case, or of a Legal Aid Board decision

It may also be unable to investigate formally the handling of a matter which has not yet been completed, as this may, for example, hamper court proceedings. It may, however, be able to help restore communications between you and your solicitor.

c. The OSS will usually only investigate complaints from a solicitor's client, not a third party. If you want to complain about someone else's solicitor, your complaint should be supported by your own solicitor.

d. The OSS will first attempt to resolve a complaint relating to service through conciliation. If this is not possible, a formal investigation will be carried out. This may take several months, but you will be kept informed of the progress of your case.

e. Allegations of serious professional misconduct or breaches of the Solicitors Investment Business Rules will be handled by the Office for Professional Regulation within the OSS. The OSS will prosecute the most serious allegations of professional misconduct before the Solicitors Disciplinary Tribunal.

f. If you think your solicitor's charges are too high there are two ways you can have them checked to see if they are fair and reasonable. You can ask your solicitor to apply for a Remuneration Certificate, which means the Law Society will review your bill. Alternatively, you can ask the court to assess whether your bill is fair and reasonable; this is called applying to the court for 'taxation' and is the only method you can use if the work concerned involved court proceedings. You should be aware that there are *strict time limits* involved for both processes.

- For more information about Remuneration Certificates, call: **01926 822022**.
- For a free information sheet on the process of 'taxation', call: **0171 936 6093**.

If either method results in a judgment that a solicitor has overcharged, the OSS can then look into this as a misconduct complaint. Complaints about charges will not be investigated while either of these two processes are continuing.

3. *How Independent Is the Complaints Procedure?*

The Office for the Supervision of Solicitors was established by the Law Society on 1 September 1996, and is funded by solicitors. It replaces the Solicitors Complaints Bureau as the organisation responsible for regulating the solicitors' profession, guarding professional standards and investigating complaints about solicitors' service and conduct.

The powers of the OSS are given to it by the Law Society, which guarantees its independence in carrying out its duties. It is overseen by a committee of the Law Society with 23 members, 10 of which are lay members appointed by the Master of the Rolls.

4. *Compensation/Redress?*

a. The OSS has the power, where appropriate, to:

- reduce a solicitor's bill in whole or in part
- require the solicitor to pay compensation of up to £1,000 (but only if the solicitor's bill is dated after 1 April 1991)
- order a solicitor to correct a mistake at his or her own expense
- discipline a solicitor for misconduct

b. In cases of severe professional misconduct a solicitor may have his or her registration suspended or made conditional, and may ultimately be struck off the legal register. Solicitors cannot legally practise unless they are registered.

c.   The OSS *cannot*:

- require a solicitor to stop acting for a particular client
- appoint another solicitor for you (although see below)

5. *Any Appeal?*

a.   If you disagree with the OSS adjudication, or are unhappy with the way it handled your complaint, you can complain to the Legal Services Ombudsman. If you want to do this, you should do so *within three months* of the OSS's final decision

see **Legal Profession**

b.   If you want to complain about the service you received from the OSS you can write to the **Quality Manager** at the address above. The OSS is a member of a Quality Assurance Scheme, registered to ISO 9002.

6. *Other Options?*

a.   Although the OSS cannot investigate allegations of professional negligence it does offer advice about how to proceed in such cases. The deciding factor as to whether the matter can be dealt with by the OSS is (with very few exceptions) the amount of potential financial loss you think your solicitor has caused you: if the amount exceeds £1,000 the OSS will not be able to investigate. However, if it thinks there is a possible negligence case to be answered it will offer you an hour's *free* legal advice from a member of its Negligence Panel.

If a panel solicitor advises you that you may have a claim for negligence against your solicitor, the matter will then be referred to the **Solicitors Indemnity Fund Limited (SIF)**. SIF is not connected with the OSS, and acts on behalf of the solicitor against whom the claim is made. You can also contact SIF directly, in which case you should set out the details of your claim (but you are still advised to get legal advice before doing so). Their address is:

Solicitors Indemnity Fund (SIF)
100 St John Street
London EC1M 4EH

Tel: 0171 566 6000

SIF will carry out their own investigations and may offer to settle your claim.

b. If the SIF decide not to settle the claim, or if you are not satisfied with their offer, or if the OSS panel member advises you in advance that the SIF may reject your claim, you still retain the right to claim for damages through the courts. If you are considering legal action you should get advice

see **Where to get help**

see also **Barristers**

Conveyancers

Legal Profession

NB

●   The OSS produces a standard Complaint Resolution Form which can be used to make your initial complaint to a solicitor. Call the Helpline number above to obtain a copy.

Subsidence

1. *Who Can I Complain To?*

The Office of the Subsidence Adviser (OSA)
Severns House
20 Middle Pavement
Nottingham NG1 7DW

Tel: 0115 959 6363
Fax: 0115 959 6360

2. *What Sort of Complaints Do They Deal With?*

a.   You can contact the Subsidence Adviser (SA) if you have already made a claim against a mine owner (which will be either a mining company or the Coal Authority) for coal mining subsidence damage, and you think the administration of your claim has been mishandled. Possible complaints include:

- unreasonable delays
- the failure to reply to letters or return telephone calls
- the abuse of discretionary powers, such as the unjustified use of stop notices

b.   The Subsidence Adviser *cannot*:

- make a claim on your behalf
- intervene in complaints about the execution of claims (for example, about the quality of repairs or amount of compensation offered)

c.   Generally only owners of damaged property can claim compensation from the mine owner, although tenants may also claim if their tenancy agreement makes them responsible for any repair and maintenance.

d.   If you decide to claim you should do so as soon as possible from the date of any damage becoming apparent, and in any case *no longer than six years* after this.

3. *How Independent Is the Complaints Procedure?*

The Subsidence Adviser is an independent person appointed by the Secretary of State for Trade and Industry.

4. *Compensation/Redress?*

a. If the Subsidence Adviser finds your complaint to be justified he will recommend the mine owner take appropriate steps to put things right.

b. Private and business property owners, farmers and owners of movable property are all legally entitled to compensation and redress of various kinds for subsidence damage according to the individual circumstances. To find out about your rights, contact the OSA.

c. The SA's recommendations are not legally enforceable, but they may be taken into account by an arbitrator or the Lands Tribunal (see *Other Options?*, below).

5. *Any Appeal?*

Not against the decision of the SA, although there are other ways to resolve disputes (see *Other Options?*, below). The Adviser also has complete discretion over whether and when to investigate complaints.

6. *Other Options?*

a. If you have a dispute with a mine owner about, for example, the amount of compensation offered, the quality of repairs carried out or whether the mine owner is legally obliged to buy your home, you have the right to take the matter to the **Lands Tribunal**. There are also two independent **arbitration schemes** run by the Chartered Institute of Arbitrators specifically designed to deal with disputes about subsidence damage. Contact the OSA for more details of these options.

b.   If you need help in making a claim you should seek professional advice, for example from a surveyor, solicitor or
architect. If your claim is successful their fees will be paid by
the person responsible for the damage

see **Where to get help**

NB

a.   The Office of the Subsidence Adviser provides information
and advice on:

- your statutory rights in relation to coal mining subsidence damage
- how to identify who is responsible for subsidence damage
- how to make a claim against a mine owner

b.   Copies of the official 'Damage Notice' you should send to
the mine owner to make your initial claim are available from
the OSA.

Surveyors
(Chartered)

1.   *Who Can I Complain To?*

Professional Conduct Department
Royal Institution of Chartered Surveyors (RICS)
12 Great George Street
Parliament Square
London SW1P 3AD

Tel: 0171 222 7000
Fax: 0171 222 9430

2. *What Sort of Complaints Do They Deal With?*

a. Only complaints against members of the RICS, who are entitled to call themselves 'Chartered Surveyors'. They can be recognised by the letters ARICS or FRICS after their names.

b. The RICS will investigate allegations of professional misconduct, including complaints about:

- unjustifiable delay in dealing with your affairs
- failure to reply to your letters
- disclosure of confidential information
- failure to disclose conflicts of interest, such as a conflict with the private interests of the surveyors, or with the interests of another client
- failure to look after your money properly, i.e. to keep it in a separate account and maintain a record of all transactions

c. It *cannot* investigate complaints where the law provides a remedy, such as allegations of professional negligence or breach of contract, or where you think you have a legal claim to financial compensation (but see e, below). Nor can it investigate or comment upon the actions of anyone other than a Chartered Surveyor, although in certain circumstances it may hold a Chartered Surveyor responsible for the actions of partners or employees who are not RICS members.

d. Complaints should be made in writing, and include permission for the RICS to send a copy of the complaint, as well as any documents you enclose, to the Chartered Surveyor involved.

e. Claims against Chartered Surveyors which cannot be resolved informally may, with the consent of both parties, be taken to arbitration, under the Chartered Surveyors Arbitration Scheme. The arbitrator's decision is legally binding.

3. *How Independent Is the Complaints Procedure?*

The RICS complaints procedure is self-regulatory.
  The Chartered Surveyors Arbitration Scheme is independently

administered by the Chartered Institute of Arbitrators (see *NB*, below).

4. *Compensation/Redress?*

a. If a Chartered Surveyor is found to have breached the RICS by-laws or code of conduct they can be reprimanded, suspended or expelled from membership. The RICS has no powers to assess or award financial compensation.

b. In cases where professional negligence is found to have occurred the Chartered Surveyors Arbitration Scheme has the power to award financial compensation.

5. *Any Appeal?*

No. If you decide not to go to arbitration, you retain the right to go to court.

6. *Other Options?*

● For more information about going to court
see **Where to get help**
● For general information about consumer rights
see **Goods & Services**

NB

● Details of the Arbitration Scheme are available from either the RICS at the above address or from:

> **Chartered Institute of Arbitrators**
> **24 Angel Gate**
> **City Road**
> **London EC1V 2RS**
>
> **Tel: 0171 837 4483**

The scheme does not yet operate in Scotland.

T

Tax

1. *Who Can I Complain To?*

The Adjudicator's Office
Haymarket House
28 Haymarket
London SW1Y 4SP

Tel: 0171 930 2292
Fax: 0171 930 2298

Note: You should only complain to the Adjudicator after you have exhausted the internal complaints procedure of the tax agency in question. Contact details of the final stage for each agency are given at the end of this entry.

2. *What Sort of Complaints Do They Deal With?*

a. Complaints about the *way*:

- the Inland Revenue, including the Valuation Office Agency
- the Contributions Agency
- Customs and Excise

have handled your affairs, and which cannot be resolved by the internal complaints procedure of the agency in question.

b. Complaints should be about, for example:

- excessive delay

- errors
- discourtesy
- the way in which any of the taxation agencies has exercised its discretion (for example, the way in which an agency dealt with a request for additional time to handle a bill)
- the way Customs and Excise searched you or your property
- the way the Contributions Agency dealt with a request for information under the government's **Code of Practice on Access to Information**.

c. The Adjudicator *cannot* deal with:

- appeals on matters of law relating to your tax liability
- appeals against property valuations, including Council Tax bandings
- disputes relating to National Insurance liability
- anything which is or has been the subject of criminal proceedings or may be the subject of a legal appeal (although some matters relating to criminal prosecutions can be considered by the Adjudicator when proceedings are completed)
- any complaint relating to something which happened *before 5 April 1993* (or *before 31 March 1993* for companies) for Inland Revenue and Valuation Office Agency complaints, or *before 1 April 1995* for Customs and Excise and Contribution Agency complaints
- complaints which have already been investigated by the Parliamentary Ombudsman

d. The Adjudicator will not normally look at complaints made *more than 6 months* after you have received a final reply from the tax agency in question.

e. Complaints should be made in writing (you can ask for help to do this) and should include:

- your tax reference number and National Insurance number
- what you want the agency to do to settle your complaint

- details of any costs you have incurred as a result of the agency's action

f. The Adjudicator will try to settle most complaints informally first. If this is not possible, she will make a formal recommendation.

3. *How Independent Is the Complaints Procedure?*

The Adjudicator is completely independent of the taxation agencies.

4. *Compensation/Redress?*

a. The agencies have agreed to accept the Adjudicator's recommendations in all but exceptional circumstances. If an agency does not do so, the Adjudicator will want to know why, and will report the fact (without identifying you) in her published annual report.

b. If the Adjudicator finds in your favour she may recommend that the agency in question should:

- pay interest on late repayments of tax or National Insurance to you
- not collect tax (or interest on tax) that is strictly due
- reimburse any costs incurred as a result of the delay or mistake

5. *Any Appeal?*

If you are unhappy with the outcome of the Adjudicator's investigation you can ask your MP to refer your case to the Parliamentary Ombudsman   *see* **Government Departments**

6. *Other Options?*

a. If you are unhappy with the Inland Revenue's assessment of your tax liability (for any direct tax) you can appeal to the Special Commissioners of Income Tax. The main office contact is:

Clerk to the Special Commissioners
Combined Tax Tribunal Centre
15–19 Bedford Avenue
London WC1B 3AS

Tel: 0171 631 4242
Fax: 0171 436 5151

b.   If you are unhappy about a decision of HM Customs and Excise relating to the amount of tax or duty to be paid, penalties, etc., you can appeal to the VAT and Duties Tribunal. If you want to do this you should write to the **Registrar** at the **Combined Tax Tribunal Centre**, at the address above.

c.   If you are unhappy with the Contributions Agency's decision or ruling on your National Insurance liability you have the right to ask for the matter to be decided by the Secretary of State for Social Security. For more information contact your local Social Security or Contributions Agency office, and
see also **Social Security**

NB

●   You can ask your MP to refer your case to the Parliamentary Ombudsman without first going to the Adjudicator, but if you are unhappy with the Ombudsman's decision you cannot then ask the Adjudicator to intervene
see **Government Departments**
●   The contact addresses for the *final* stages of the internal complaints procedures of the separate tax agencies are as follows:

Inland Revenue

There is no central Head Office finally responsible for complaints. You should write to the **IR Controller** for the office or unit dealing with your affairs – the address will be on their correspondence and in the phone book.

Valuation Office Agency

Director of Customer
  Services
Valuation Office Agency
Chief Executive's Office
New Court
Carey Street
London WC2A 2JE

Tel: 0171 324 1110/1157

Customs and Excise

HM Customs and Excise
Quality Service Branch
11th Floor
New King's Beam House
22 Upper Ground
London SE1 9PJ

Contributions Agency

The Chief Executive
Room C1837
Contributions Agency
Newcastle upon Tyne
NE98 1YX

Telecommunications

1. *Who Can I Complain To?*

England

Consumer Representation Section
Room 1/1
Office of Telecommunications (OFTEL)
50 Ludgate Hill
London EC4M 7JJ

Scotland

The Secretary
Scottish Advisory Committee on Telecommunications
Greenside Lane
Edinburgh EH1 3AH

Wales

The Secretary
Welsh Advisory Committee on Telecommunications
Caradog House (1st Floor)
St Andrews Place
Cardiff CF1 3BE

Northern Ireland

The Secretary
Northern Ireland Advisory Committee on
    Telecommunications
7th Floor
Chamber of Commerce and Industry
22 Great Victoria Street
Belfast BT2 7QA

Disabled and elderly consumers

You can also write to the **Advisory Committee on Telecommunications for Disabled and Elderly People** (DIEL) at the address for OFTEL, above.

Textphone telephone: 0171 634 8769 (Minicom) *or*
                    0171 634 8771 (text, 300 BAUD)

Small businesses

You can also write to the **Advisory Committee on Telecommunications for Small Businesses** (BACT) at the address for OFTEL, above.

Lo-call number for all telephone complaints: 0345 145000

2. *What Sort of Complaints Do They Deal With?*

a. Complaints about telephone and other telecommunication services or apparatus which cannot be resolved by the company concerned. Under their operating licences all telecommunications companies (e.g. British Telecom, Mercury, cable companies, etc.) are required to produce a Consumer Code of Practice including details of their complaints procedure. Your telephone company will be able to send you a free copy of their Code. The British Telecom (BT) Code of Practice is in the back of the standard telephone directory.

b. Complaints addressed to BT are handled progressively by a Customer Services Adviser, Customer Services Manager and the Complaints Review Service. As a last resort BT offers free arbitration administered by the Chartered Institute of Arbitrators. This is an alternative to legal action, and legal action cannot be pursued once a dispute has been referred to arbitration.

c. If your telephone company is unable to resolve your complaint to your satisfaction, you may refer the matter to OFTEL or the relevant Advisory Committee (there is an Advisory Committee for England, too, but day-to-day complaints are handled by OFTEL). Neither OFTEL nor the Advisory Committees can investigate complaints which have been taken to arbitration or are the subject of legal action.

d. Complaints and comments about local issues, including phone box placement and directory coverage, may be directed to your nearest local **Telecommunications Advisory Committee** (TAC) – the address should be in your phone book, or you can call the lo-call number for details.

e. The Advisory Committees will refer complaints to OFTEL and/or the DGT, and OFTEL may pass complaints on to the DGT, if it appears that the statutory powers of the regulator may need to be exercised.

3. *How Independent Is the Complaints Procedure?*

a. OFTEL is a non-ministerial government department set up under the **Telecommunications Act 1984** to regulate the telecommunications industry. It has sole responsibility for the monitoring and enforcement of licences. OFTEL is completely independent of the telecommunications industry and the Director General of Telecommunications is independent of ministerial control.

b. The national Advisory Committees and the two specialist Advisory Committees were set up under the Telecommunications Act and have a duty to advise the Director General of Telecommunications (DGT) whenever he seeks their advice, although they have no statutory, specific consumer remit. Members of all the national and specialist Advisory Committees are appointed by the appropriate Secretaries of State. TACs form a (rather patchy) local voluntary network. The Advisory Committees are independent of the telecommunications industry.

4. *Compensation/Redress?*

a. If OFTEL or an Advisory Committee decides that your complaint is justified it will recommend your phone company takes appropriate action to put things right, such as reconnection or the adjustment of a bill. It has no power to award financial compensation. Neither OFTEL nor the Advisory Committees have the power to force a company to comply with their recommendations, although companies usually do.

b. If the DGT finds that a telephone company is in breach of its licence conditions he can order the company to fall into line, and can take civil action to enforce an order if necessary. In theory the DGT has the power to refuse to renew the licence of a persistent offender.

c. OFTEL will also consider and can make changes to the regulatory framework if an operator's policy or practice gives rise to widespread concern.

5. *Any Appeal?*

a. There is no formal appeal against a finding by OFTEL or one of the Advisory Committees, although both will reconsider a complaint if new information comes to light.

b. If you go to arbitration the outcome will be legally binding.

c. If you are unhappy with the *way* OFTEL has handled your complaint you can ask your MP to refer your case to the Parliamentary Ombudsman   *see* **Government Departments**

6. *Other Options?*

a. If you are not satisfied after complaining to OFTEL and do not wish to go to arbitration, you have the right to take your telephone company to court for breaches of contract and/or to claim compensation for loss or damages incurred as a result of their negligence. You may also wish to complain to a local Trading Standards Officer. For more information on how to complain about inadequate services
    see **Goods & Services**

b. If you are considering legal action you should get advice
    see **Where to get help**

c. Complaints about *premium rate telephone services* including live chatlines and 'one-to-one' services should be addressed *within one month* to the **Independent Committee for the Supervision of Standards of Telephone Information Services** (ICSTIS) at:

> **ICSTIS**
> **3rd Floor**
> **Alton House**
> **177 High Holborn**
> **London WC1V 7AA**

> Tel: (24-hour Freephone): **0800 500 212**

Copies of their Code of Practice are also available from this address. You can claim compensation for the unauthorised use of your telephone to call premium rate services, and may also be able to claim part or all of the cost of installing a call-barring facility on your line. If a premium rate service provider is found to be breaking the ICSTIS Code of Practice it will be asked to stop, may be fined, and the network operator may be asked to (and in practice always will, if asked) bar access to the relevant numbers until further notice.

●   *see also* **Appointments**

Trade Unions 1

1. *Who Can I Complain To?*

The Commissioner for the Rights of Trade Union Members
1st Floor
Bank Chambers
2A Rylands Street
Warrington
Cheshire WA1 1EN

Tel: 01925 415771
Fax: 01925 415772

2. *What Sort of Complaints Do They Deal With?*

a. The Commissioner exists to help protect certain statutory rights of trade union members. You can apply to the Commissioner for assistance in taking your union to court if your union:

- has, without the support of a properly conducted secret ballot, authorised or endorsed industrial action in which you and other members are likely to be (or have been) induced to take part

- has broken the law in the way it has conducted elections to its principal executive committee
- has spent money for party political purposes without proper authorisation
- has failed to comply with the rules approved by the Certification Officer in any ballot, or proposed ballot, on the use of funds for party political purposes
- has caused or allowed, or intends to cause or allow, any unlawful use of the union's funds or property
- has refused to allow you to inspect the union's accounting records
- has refused to allow you to look at your entry on the union's membership register

b. You can also apply to the Commissioner for assistance if you think your union has failed to observe the requirements of its rule book in relation to:

- the appointment or election of a person to, or the removal of a person from, any office
- disciplinary proceedings by the union (including expulsion)
- the authorising or endorsing of industrial action
- the balloting of members
- the application of the union's funds or property
- the imposition, collection or distribution of any levy for the purpose of industrial action
- the constitution or proceedings of any commitment, conference or other body

although the Commissioner will only be able to help you if the breach of rule you are complaining about also affects other members of your union.

c. If the Commissioner decides to help you she can:

- pay for you to get legal advice from a solicitor
- pay for you to take your union to court, including paying for you to be represented in court

d. The Commissioner *must* agree to help you if your application relates to a declaration against your union by the

Certification Officer about a union election, political fund ballot or membership register, *and* it appears to the Commissioner that you have a good chance of obtaining a court order on the same matter.

e.   In other circumstances, the Commissioner has wide discretion whether or not to grant assistance, but is more likely to do so if your case:

- raises a point of principle
- involves a matter of substantial public interest
- is sufficiently complex that it would be unreasonable to expect you to be able to deal with it on your own

f.   The Commissioner *cannot* provide assistance for:

- proceedings brought by an employer against a trade union
- pursuing complaints to the Certification Officer, to an industrial tribunal or to the Employment Appeal Tribunal

g.   If the Commissioner grants you assistance you will be given a choice about the arrangements – for example, you can choose to use your own legal advisers and representatives and be reimbursed, or to have the Commissioner arrange this for you.

3. *How Independent Is the Complaints Procedure?*

The post of Commissioner was created by the **Employment Act 1988**. The Commissioner is appointed by the Secretary of State for Education and Employment, but is independent of government control and of all trade unions.

4. *Compensation/Redress?*

a.   The Commissioner has no power to award financial compensation or redress; this will depend on the court's decision.

b.   You may be offered an 'out-of-court' settlement by the union which you can choose to accept. If you win your case the court may award you costs and/or expenses. In either case, the Commissioner is entitled to recover the value of assistance that has been provided.

c.   If the Commissioner helps you to take a case to court and you lose, the Commissioner will still pay your costs.

5. *Any Appeal?*

a.   There is no right of appeal against the Commissioner's decision.

b.   You have a right to appeal a decision of the court, and in appropriate cases the Commissioner's assistance can be extended to help you do this.

c.   If your union refuses to obey a court order arising out of your case, the Commissioner may also provide assistance for contempt of court proceedings against them. This may lead to enforcement action, such as fines and ultimately sequestration of the union's assets.

6. *Other Options?*

see also **Trade Unions 2**

Employment

NB

●   It is illegal for your union to discipline you for complaining to the Commissioner. If it does, you can complain to an industrial tribunal   *see* **Employment**

Trade Unions 2

1. Who Can I Complain To?

**The Commissioner for Protection Against Unlawful
   Industrial Action**
2nd Floor
Bank Chambers
2A Rylands Street
Warrington
Cheshire WA1 1EN

Tel: 01925 414128
Fax: 01925 415772

2. What Sort of Complaints Do They Deal With?

a. You can apply to the Commissioner for financial assistance
to take legal action against a union if you think that you have
been, or are likely to be, deprived of goods or services (or if
the quality of goods and services has been or is likely to be
reduced) as a result of industrial action unlawfully organised
by a trade union.

b. Industrial action is illegal if:

- it does not have the support of a properly conducted
  secret ballot
- the purpose is to promote any closed shop practice
- the aim is to support an employee dismissed whilst
  taking part in unofficial industrial action
- the action is 'secondary' action (by workers not in dispute with their own employer, in support of a dispute
  involving workers of another employer)
- it is done in the course of, or involves calls for, unlawful
  picketing – which would include picketing which is not
  peaceful, or picketing by workers at any place other than
  their own place of work
- it is not done 'in contemplation or furtherance of a trade
  dispute'

c.   If the Commissioner decides to help you she can:

   - pay for you to get legal advice from a solicitor
   - pay for you to take your union to court, including paying for you to be represented in court

d.   The Commissioner has wide discretion whether or not to grant assistance, but is more likely to do so if your case:

   - involves a matter of substantial public interest
   - is sufficiently complex that it would be unreasonable to expect you to be able to deal with it on your own

e.   If the Commissioner grants you assistance you will be given a choice about the arrangements – for example, you can choose to use your own legal advisers and representatives and be reimbursed, or to have the Commissioner arrange this for you.

3. *How Independent Is the Complaints Procedure?*

The post of Commissioner was created by the **Trade Union Reform and Employment Rights Act 1993**. The Commissioner is appointed by the Secretary of State for Education and Employment, but is independent of government control and of all trade unions.

4. *Compensation/Redress?*

a.   The Commissioner has no power to award financial compensation or redress; this will depend on the court's decision.

b.   If a court finds your complaint to be justified it will make an order restraining the unlawful organisation of the industrial action. A court also has discretion to award costs or expenses to you. You may also be offered an 'out-of-court' settlement by the union which you can choose to accept. In either case, the Commissioner is entitled to recover the value of assistance that has been provided

c. If the Commissioner helps you to take a case to court and you lose, the Commissioner will still pay your costs

5. *Any Appeal?*

a. There is no right of appeal against the Commissioner's decision.

b. You have a right to appeal a decision of the court, and in appropriate cases the Commissioner's assistance can be extended to help you do this.

c. If the union refuses to obey a court order arising out of your case, the Commissioner may also provide assistance for contempt of court proceedings against it. This may lead to enforcement action, such as fines and ultimately sequestration of the union's assets.

6. *Other Options?*

●
see also **Trade Unions 1**

Goods & Services

Transport 1
(Air)

1. *Who Can I Complain To?*

Air Transport Users Council (AUC)
5th Floor
Kingsway House
103 Kingsway
London WC2B 6QX

Tel: 0171 242 3882
Fax: 0171 831 4131

2. *What Sort of Complaints Do They Deal With?*

a. Complaints about airline or airport services that have not been satisfactorily resolved by the airline or airport concerned.

b. Complaints about *airline services* could be about:

- in-flight service
- check-in and security procedures
- over-booking
- lost or damaged baggage
- flight delays, diversions and cancellations
- an airline going bust, etc.

c. Complaints about *airport services* could be about:

- airport information
- car parking and travel to and from the airport
- quality of airport facilities and/or service, including complaints about duty-free shops
- lost or damaged baggage, etc.

If your complaint about airport services cannot be resolved on the spot or by the airport's management you should then contact the relevant Airport Consultative Committee (ACC) by writing to the ACC secretary at the airport's address. All British Airport Authority airports and the larger local authority airports have ACCs.

d. Problems with *lost or damaged baggage* (which may be the airline's or the airport's fault) should be reported immediately, and claims for compensation made in writing *within seven days*. In general it is important to keep all travel documents and receipts for expenses incurred when things have gone wrong.

e. Failing the above, unresolved complaints of *any kind* about air transport services, regarding both British and foreign carriers, can be referred to the AUC.

f. The only aspect of package holidays the AUC can deal with is the air transport aspect. It does *not* handle complaints about travel agents or tour operators

see **Holidays 1** *and* **2**

3. *How Independent Is the Complaints Procedure?*

The AUC is funded by the Civil Aviation Authority (CAA), but its independence and authority are well recognised. Members are recruited through advertisements and represent a wide range of air transport users. It was set up to make reports and recommendations to further the interests of all UK air transport users.

4. *Compensation/Redress?*

a.   The AUC's powers are purely persuasive. It has no legal status and cannot arbitrate on claims for refunds or compensation if the service provider refuses to budge.

b.   Airlines have a legal obligation to pay compensation for lost or damaged luggage (if you have complained immediately), but the amount is based on *weight*, not the cash value of your possessions, and is currently about £14 per kilogram for international flights, less for domestic journeys. You should bear this in mind when considering travel insurance.

c.   The main form of consumer protection of *package* air travellers in cases of company insolvency, also administered by the CAA, is the Air Travel Organisers' Licensing (ATOL) Scheme. Under this scheme, anyone except an airline taking money for air travel must immediately give the customer either an airline ticket which is valid for travel or a document confirming that the sale is protected by an ATOL. Before it gets a licence, a tour operator has to provide a financial guarantee to the CAA; if the operator then fails, this will be used to compensate customers. If any individual guarantee is insufficient to meet all a company's liabilities after its failure, a Reserve Fund managed by the Air Travel Trust is available to meet those claims. If you are in any doubt as to whether a tour operator holds an ATOL, or whether you may be covered in another way, contact:

Civil Aviation Authority
CAA House
45–49 Kingsway
London WC2B 6TE

Tel: **0171 832 6000**

d. Other (less watertight) safeguards exist if you are making your own flight arrangements   *see* **Holidays 1** *and* **2**

5. *Any Appeal?*

No.

6. *Other Options?*

●   *see also* **Holidays 1** *and* **2**

NB

●   The CAA is the statutory body responsible for the safety regulation of British aircraft, approves British airline tariffs and promotes the provision of airline services which satisfy public demand. It is not a complaints handling organisation, but uses the AUC as its channel for receiving consumer views.

Transport 2 (Sea Ferries)

- There is no regulatory body for sea ferries.
- If you are unhappy with a ferry operator's response to a complaint about *ferry services or facilities* (e.g. timetabling, fares, cleanliness, etc.), then in most cases the only other option is to take legal action for compensation. It is particularly important to get legal advice before doing this if the ship or company is registered abroad   *see* **Where to get help**
- If your complaint is about *safety standards or procedures* on board, you can write to the Chief Executive of the Marine Safety Agency or to the Department of Transport:

Chief Executive	**Minister for Aviation and**
Marine Safety Agency	**Shipping**
Spring Place	**Department of Transport**
105 Commercial Road	**2 Marsham Street**
Southampton SO15 1EG	**London SW1P 3EB**
Tel: 01703 329100	**Tel: 0171 271 5000**

- If you have a complaint about a ferry in a *metropolitan county area*, it is quite likely that the service is the responsibility of the area's Passenger Transport Executive (PTE)

    see **Transport 7**
- The Rail Users' Consultative Committee (RUCC) for *Scotland* has a special remit to handle complaints about Caledonian MacBrayne ferries (CalMac ferries)

    see **Transport 5**
- Any service to, or from, *Northern Ireland* is the responsibility of the General Consumer Council of Northern Ireland – for the address of the GCCNI

    see **Goods & Services**
- To complain about canal and river boat operators

    see **Goods & Services**

    Holidays 1 *to* **3**

- To complain about canal and river navigability

    see **Environment 2**

Transport 3
(Taxis)

1. *Who Can I Complain To?*

In London only

Public Carriage Office (PCO)
15 Penton Street
London N1 9PU

Tel: 0171 230 1631
Fax: 0171 230 1662

Note: for who to complain to outside London, *see* Other Options?, *below.*

2. *What Sort of Complaints Do They Deal With?*

a. Passenger complaints about Licensed London Taxis and Licensed Drivers. The PCO operates to a Code of Practice which licensed cab drivers and operators are expected to comply with.

b. Complaints might include such matters as: abusive or otherwise unacceptable behaviour; overcharging; lack of knowledge; failure to complete a hiring; taking a devious route; the mechanical condition and general fabric of the vehicle, including excessive emissions of smoke. London taxi drivers must, unless they have a reasonable excuse, accept a hiring up to six miles (twenty miles from Heathrow), provided the destination is in the Metropolitan Police District. All hirings which begin and end in the Metropolitan Police District and City of London must be done on the taxi meter. Fares for hirings which take a driver outside this area must be negotiated in advance. You are not legally entitled to a receipt for a taxi journey.

c. A significant number of complaints relating to licensed taxis are in fact criminal offences, for example: demanding more than the proper fare; refusing fares; restrictions on where taxis may ply for hire; refusal to carry a reasonable quantity of luggage; the length of journeys up to which a driver must take a passenger, etc. etc. However, many of these are covered by the so-called 'seven-day process' rule which requires papers to be served at court *within seven days* of the alleged offence and which effectively prevents most such offences ever coming to court. Failure to take court action where it may have been appropriate does not affect the PCO complaints procedure.

d. If you have *ordered* a licensed cab, you should in the first instance complain to the radio circuit company involved, particularly if the complaint relates to charges made over and above the fare (if you have ordered a minicab see *Other Options?*, below). If the company cannot resolve the complaint to your satisfaction you may still refer it to the PCO. Complaints about abusive behaviour, lack of knowledge or failure to complete a hiring should always be reported to the PCO.

e. You should try to note down the licence number, vehicle registration number and driver's badge number if at all possible. The licence number is displayed on a white enamel plate inside the passenger compartment, and also on the exterior of the vehicle on the boot lid. The driver should be wearing his badge somewhere clearly visible.

f. The PCO promises to provide a substantive response to complaints against licensed taxi drivers within 30 working days of receipt or send a letter telling you the reasons for the delay and giving a date for a full reply.

3. *How Independent Is the Complaints Procedure?*

The Public Carriage Office is a civilian branch of the Metropolitan Police, and acts on behalf of the Assistant Commissioner of Police, who is the legal Licensing Authority. It has independent statutory responsibility for the licensing and regulation of London taxis and is not an employer or an operator (licensed drivers are self-employed).

4. *Compensation/Redress?*

The PCO has no power to award compensation. In theory, serious complaints may be passed on to the Cab Law Enforcement branch of the Metropolitan Police, which can, with the complainant's agreement, summons the driver to court. In practice, the seven-day process prevents this happening, but a conviction is not necessary for disciplinary action to be taken against a driver. Every complaint received is noted on the driver's individual record, which is then considered as a whole when complaints are made. The PCO will warn drivers when it sees fit, and has the power to suspend, limit the use of or revoke a driver's taxi licence.

5. *Any Appeal?*

a. If you are unhappy with the outcome of a complaint to the PCO about an individual taxi driver, you can write directly to the Officer-in-Charge of the PCO, asking him to look further into the matter. You will receive a reply within 10 working days of receipt.

b. Complaints about a member of PCO staff, procedure or action can be referred sequentially to the Officer-in-Charge, then to either the Assistant Commissioner of the Metropolitan Police, Territorial Operations, or to the Director of Support and Administration Territorial Operations at Scotland Yard.

c. If you are still unhappy with the *way* the PCO has handled your complaint you may raise the matter with the Parliamentary Ombudsman   *see* **Government Departments**

d. If the Cab Law Enforcement branch decides not to take your case to court, and/or it is too late under the seven-day process to bring a criminal prosecution, you may still be able to bring a civil action for compensation yourself.

6. *Other Options?*

● *Outside London*, taxis have to be licensed by the district council   *see* **Local Government**

- *Minicab* journeys must be pre-booked, and so are subject to the law of contract. It is illegal for them to ply for hire. The minicab trade *in London* is not licensed, so there are no controls on drivers and vehicles other than those which apply to any driver and vehicle. There are no controls on operators either, apart from planning permission and radio licence fee requirements. *Outside London*, minicab vehicles, drivers and operators do have to be licensed by the district council, if it has adopted relevant legislation (95 per cent of councils have done so); in these areas unlicensed minicabs are therefore illegal   *see* **Goods & Services**

NB

- By 1 January 2000, all London's taxis will have to be able to accommodate a person in a wheelchair in the passenger compartment.
- Drivers are currently *not* allowed to refuse passengers who insist on smoking, although legislation is planned which will change this.

Transport 4 (Buses & Coaches)

General tips for complaining about buses and coaches

Buses

- If you have a complaint about a local bus service you should take it up with the bus operator first. Serious complaints about safety and persistently poor timekeeping should be copied to the local Traffic Commissioner (see below).

- Over 80 per cent of bus services are commercially run with little effective independent regulation. If the service you are complaining about is on a *tendered* (subsidised) route, how-ever – or you are not sure if it is a tendered service or not – you should write to the transport co-ordinating officer of the county council (in Scotland, the regional council), or in metropolitan areas to the Passenger Transport Executive (PTE)   *see* **Transport 7**
- Local government bodies may be able to exert some influ-ence over *privately run services* if your complaint is about bus routeing or design, and they are also the people to approach about the reinstatement or establishment of bus services   *see* **Local Government**
- For complaints about *buses in London* (including Victoria Coach station)   *see* **Transport 6**

Coaches

- All coach services in the UK are privately run, and there are no independent passenger bodies for handling complaints. As with privately run buses, complaints should be directed first to the service operator and, if serious enough, copied to the Traffic Commissioner.

Traffic Commissioners

- The Traffic Commissioner for each area is responsible for setting and enforcing safety standards for buses and coaches before issuing licences to operators. They can limit or revoke a licence if an operator breaks the law or persistently fails to run the service it is registered to run.
- Traffic Commissioners do *not* have the remit or resources to deal with individual complaints.
- For the address and phone number of your local Traffic Commissioner see your local phone book or call the **Depart-ment of Transport** on **0171 276 3000**.

Transport 5 (Railways)

1. *Who Can I Complain To?*

Stage 1

The **Rail Users Consultative Committee** (RUCC) for the region concerned.

Midlands

Secretary
RUCC for the Midlands
77 Paradise Circus
Queensway
Birmingham B1 2DT

Tel: 0121 212 2133
Fax: 0121 236 6945

East

Secretary
RUCC for Eastern England
Midgate House
Midgate
Peterborough PE1 1TN

Tel: 01733 312188
Fax: 01733 891286

North West

Secretary
RUCC for North Western England
Fifth Floor
Boulton House
17–21 Chorlton Street
Manchester M1 3HY

Tel: 0161 228 6247
Fax: 0161 236 1476

North East

> Secretary
> RUCC for North Eastern England
> Hillary House
> 16 St Saviour's Place
> York YO1 2PL
>
> Tel: 01904 625615
> Fax: 01904 643026

West

> Secretary
> RUCC for Western England
> 13th Floor
> Tower House
> Fairfax Street
> Bristol BS1 3BN
>
> Tel: 01272 265703
> Fax: 01272 294140

South

> Secretary
> RUCC for Southern England
> Fourth Floor
> 35 Old Queen's Street
> London SW1H 9JA
>
> Tel: 0171 222 0391
> Fax: 0171 222 0392

Scotland

> Secretary
> RUCC for Scotland
> 249 West George Street
> Glasgow G2 4QE
>
> Tel: 0141 221 7760
> Fax: 0141 221 3393

Wales

> Secretary
> RUCC for Wales
> St Davids House (East Wing)
> Wood Street
> Cardiff CF1 1ES
>
> Tel: 01222 227247
> Fax: 01222 223992

Stage 2

> The **Central Rail Users Consultative Committee** (CRUCC)
>
> **Central Rail Users Consultative Committee**
> **Clements House**
> **14–18 Gresham Street**
> **London EC2V 7NO**
>
> Tel: 0171 505 9090
> Fax: 0171 505 9004

2. *What Sort of Complaints Do They Deal With?*

a. Regional RUCCs keep watch on such issues as:

- punctuality and reliability of train services
- timetabling changes
- overcrowding
- cleanliness
- fares
- quality and design of trains
- tickets – purchase facilities and ticket inspection
- station facilities
- provision of information at stations, on trains and by telephone

b. Your complaint should first be made to the train or station operator providing the service. If you live in a metropolitan area covered by a Passenger Transport Executive you may also complain to them (*see* **Transport 7**). If you are not satisfied with the response you can then refer the matter to your RUCC, which will take the case further on your behalf.

c. RUCCs also have a special responsibility to report to the Regulator on hardship likely to be caused by proposed station and line closures.

d. If you are unhappy about the *way* a Regional RUCC has handled your complaint, you can ask the CRUCC to intervene.

e. If the problem you wish to complain about affects rail users *nationally*, you should write directly to the CRUCC.

3. *How Independent Is the Complaints Procedure?*

a. RUCCs are independent statutory bodies set up under the **Railways Act 1993** to protect the interests of rail users. They are established and funded by the Rail Regulator who appoints their members and provides their resources. Members represent a wide cross-section of rail users and the Committees meet in public.

b. The CRUCC is the RUCC representing the interests of rail users nationally. It also co-ordinates the regional RUCCs. Its members include the Chairs of the RUCCs and the London Regional Passengers' Committee (LRPC).

4. *Compensation/Redress?*

a. Neither RUCCs not the CRUCC have the power to award compensation – they can only make recommendations, and have no powers to force a rail operator to do anything. They will, however, ask the Rail Regulator to use his powers where necessary, a specific example of this being where an RUCC recommends that the Regulator take action to lessen the impact of a proposed closure.

b. RUCCs also monitor the extent to which franchise standards are being achieved for the Franchising Director. The Franchising Director has the power to sanction franchise holders and to refuse to renew a rail franchise.

5. *Any Appeal?*

No.

6. *Other Options?*

- If the rail operator simply refuses to budge, your only option may be to take legal action (although see *NB*, below). If you are considering legal action you should get advice
  see **Where to get help**
- In and around *London*, the London Regional Passengers' Committee represents rail users' interests   *see* **Transport 6**

NB

- The RUCC for *North Western England* also has responsibility for Greater Manchester Metrolink Services.
- The RUCC for *Scotland* also has responsibility for shipping services operated by Caledonian MacBrayne.
- The RUCC for *North Eastern England* also has responsibility for Tyne & Wear Metro Services.
- Before privatisation British Rail offered arbitration for unresolved disputes through the Chartered Institute of Arbitrators. If you are engaged in a dispute over compensation it may still be worth asking if the operator in question has set up its own arbitration scheme.

Transport 6
(London Area)

1. *Who Can I Complain To?*

The Secretary
London Regional Passengers' Committee (LRPC)
Clements House
14–18 Gresham Street
London EC2V 7PR

Tel: 0171 505 9000
Fax: 0171 505 9003

2. *What Sort of Complaints Do They Deal With?*

a. Complaints about all services and facilities provided by:

- all mainline railways
- London Transport (London Underground; bus services; Victoria Coach Station) *and*
- the Docklands Light Railway

within the London area, and which cannot be resolved by the operating company concerned, i.e. by Network South-East, London Transport Buses, Docklands Light Railway, London Underground or Victoria Coach Station as appropriate (contact details for all of these are in the phone book).

b. The London area is taken to extend from Gatwick (South) to Dartford (East) to Bedford (North) to Bicester North and Windsor (West). All mainline trains running through the London area come under the LRPC's remit, i.e. Inter City as well as the former Network South-East.

c. The Committee will look into all complaints about:

- frequency and timing of services

- punctuality
- cleanliness of stations, trains and buses
- conditions of travel
- information about services, fares and facilities
- special offers
- catering
- conduct of staff
- ticket arrangements
- new bus routes
- vehicle design
- passenger safety and security

d. The LRPC also has a special responsibility to report to the Rail Regulator on hardship likely to be caused by proposed station and line closures.

3. *How Independent Is the Complaints Procedure?*

The LRPC is an independent body set up under the **London Regional Transport Act 1984**. It is autonomous both of the government and of the public transport operators.

4. *Compensation/Redress?*

The LRPC has no powers to award compensation; its main job is to make recommendations to the operating companies, the Rail Regulator and the government. It will, however, press strongly for recompense in appropriate cases, if it considers the complaint is justified. The LRPC will keep you informed of progress with your case by letter at least every 20 working days.

5. *Any Appeal?*

If you are not satisfied with the way the LRPC has handled your case you can ask a senior member of the Committee to review it.

6. *Other Options?*

- You have the right to take a transport operator to court to claim compensation. If you are considering legal action you should get advice   *see* **Where to get help**

NB

- Many transport operators now operate Customer Charters, under which you are entitled to set amounts of compensation for delays, etc. You should always keep your receipt and make a note of any relevant vehicle and/or personnel registration numbers when making a complaint.

Transport 7 (Metropolitan Areas)

1. *Who Can I Complain To?*

Greater Manchester

> **Greater Manchester Passenger Transport Executive**
> **Freepost**
> **Manchester M1 8DT**
>
> **Tel: 0161 242 6000**
> **Fax: 0161 242 6295**

Tyne & Wear

> **Tyne & Wear Passenger Transport Executive**
> **Cuthbert House**
> **All Saints**
> **Newcastle upon Tyne NE1 2DA**
>
> **Tel: 0191 261 0431**
> **Fax: 0191 203 3180**

West Midlands

> **West Midlands Passenger Transport Executive** (Centro)
> **16 Summer Lane**
> **Birmingham B19 3SD**
>
> Tel: 0121 214 7214/7085
> Fax: 0121 214 7033

West Yorkshire

> **West Yorkshire Passenger Transport Executive** (Metro)
> **Wellington House**
> **40–50 Wellington Street**
> **Leeds LS1 2DE**
>
> Tel: 0113 251 7272
> Fax: 0113 251 7333

South Yorkshire

> **South Yorkshire Passenger Transport Executive**
> **Exchange Street**
> **Sheffield S2 5YT**
>
> Tel: 0114 276 7575
> Fax: 0114 275 9908

2. *What Sort of Complaints Do They Deal With?*

a. You should complain to the relevant Passenger Transport Executive (PTE) rather than your local council if you live in one of the listed metropolitan areas and have a problem with public transport. PTEs will investigate complaints about:

- subsidised local rail services
- subsidised local bus services

- education transport arrangements
- services provided directly by them to the public

within their areas. Tyne and Wear PTE is also responsible for the Metro (underground) and the Shields Ferry, and South Yorkshire PTE is also responsible for the Supertram.

b. Services provided directly to the public by PTEs include:

- concessionary travel schemes
- the sale and administration of pre-paid tickets
- the issue of school bus passes
- facilities at bus stations, bus stops and shelters and station car parks
- timetables for local bus and rail services
- public transport information services
- transport services for elderly and disabled people

c. Complaints could be about, for example:

- punctuality and reliability of services
- timetable changes
- route changes
- fares
- quality of services
- access and other problems experienced by disabled people
- provision of timetables and other public information
- the condition and/or adequacy of passenger facilities provided at bus stations
- problems with the siting and condition of bus stops and shelters
- lost, damaged or invalid pre-paid tickets

d. The PTEs will also try to help with complaints falling outside their remit – concerning, for example, commercial bus and rail and mainline rail services – or will pass your complaint on to the relevant body.

e. You can complain to a PTE whether or not you have already contacted the transport operator in question, but should complain to a PTE about rail services *before* contacting your regional RUCC.

3. *How Independent Is the Complaints Procedure?*

a. The Passenger Transport Executives are the professional co-ordinating bodies responsible for implementing the policies of the metropolitan Passenger Transport Authorities (PTAs).

b. The PTAs consist of councillors nominated by the District Councils within the metropolitan areas (so, for example, the West Yorkshire PTA is made up of councillors from Bradford, Calderdales, Kirklees, Leeds and Wakefield Councils). The Authorities decide public transport policy for their region as well as providing the money for it from government grants and a levy on the District Councils.

c. All districts also have their own Passenger Consultative Committees, made up of local public transport users, which keep the PTAs informed of passengers' concerns and interests.

4. *Compensation/Redress?*

a. The PTEs can sometimes refund tickets if these have been bought through them, and may offer compensation if incorrect information has led to serious passenger inconvenience, but they have no power to make commercial operators do anything.

b. PTEs can report any incident to the relevant Traffic Commissioner or Vehicle Examiner if the operator's response proves unsatisfactory. This could result in enforcement action or in an operator's licence being revoked or not renewed.

c. An increasing number of operators have their own passenger charters, under which you may be able to claim compensation for delays and cancellations.

5. *Any Appeal?*

Complaints can be referred progressively as follows:

a. You can ask for your case to be reviewed by a more senior manager within the PTE.

b. You can complain to the Director General of the PTE.

c. You can write to the Chairman of the PTA (the PTE will be able to give you the address).

d. If you are unhappy with the *way* the PTA has looked into your complaint (rather than the outcome) you may then refer your case to the Local Government Ombudsman
see **Local Government**

6. *Other Options?*

- For how to complain about bus services   *see* **Transport 4**
- For how to complain about rail services   *see* **Transport 5**
- If you are dissatisfied with the response from a transport operator you may wish to take them to court for damages under consumer law. If you are considering legal action you should get advice   *see* **Goods & Services**

Where to get help

NB

- If you are complaining about a local bus service you need to be very specific about when and where you experienced a problem – as many bus companies operate both subsidised and commercial services on the same routes, at different times of the day and days of the week.

V

Valuers & Auctioneers

1. *Who Can I Complain To?*

Professional Services Department
The Incorporated Society of Valuers and Auctioneers (ISVA)
3 Cadogan Gate
London SW1X 0AS

Tel: 0171 235 2282
Fax: 0171 235 4390

2. *What Sort of Complaints Do They Deal With?*

a. Complaints about the professional misconduct of any ISVA member, which cannot be resolved by the firm or practitioner concerned. Members are expected to comply with the Society's Rules of Professional Conduct, copies of which are available from the address above.

b. The ISVA *cannot* investigate allegations of professional negligence, or any complaints about auctioneers or valuers who are not members of the Society.

c. Complaints are initially investigated by the Professional Services Department, which passes them on to the Professional Practice Committee if it decides there is a prima-facie case to answer. Serious complaints which cannot be resolved by the Professional Practice Committee are referred to the Disciplinary Committee.

3. *How Independent Is the Complaints Procedure?*

The ISVA is a professional body operating a voluntary self-regulatory complaints procedure. Both the Disciplinary and Appeals Committees have one lay member (out of four) who are recommended by the Consumers' Association.

4. *Compensation/Redress?*

a.   If one of the Committees decides in your favour, the ISVA member may be warned, reprimanded and ultimately expelled from membership of the Society. Expulsion does not stop someone practising as an estate agent, auctioneer or property manager, although it does effectively prevent them from acting as a professional valuer.

b.   The ISVA has no power to award compensation.

5. *Any Appeal?*

No, only the ISVA member has a right to appeal to the Appeals Committee against the decision of the Disciplinary Committee.

6. *Other Options?*

If you wish to claim damages for professional negligence you will have to go to court. If you are considering legal action you should get advice   *see* **Where to get help**

●   *see also* **Estate Agents 1** *and* **2**

Surveyors

Goods & Services

Auctioneers

Advertising

NB

- An arbitration scheme is being negotiated at the time of writing – ask the ISVA for more details of this.
- Negotiations are also in progress at the time of writing for an Ombudsman to cover residential estate agency. Again, ask the ISVA or any residential estate agent for details.

Video Standards
(Videos & Computer Games)

1. *Who Can I Complain To?*

a. The **Trading Standards Department** of your local council (see your local telephone directory for contact details).

b. **The Video Standards Council (VSC)**
Kinetic Business Centre
Borehamwood
Hertfordshire

   Tel: 0181 387 4020
   Fax: 0181 387 4004

2. *What Sort of Complaints Do They Deal With?*

a. You should complain to a Trading Standards Officer (TSO) of your local council if you think a video or computer game retailer has sold or hired or attempted to sell or hire:

- a legally classified video or computer game to someone too young
- an unclassified video or game which should have been classified
- counterfeit videos or games

as all of these things are illegal. Similar laws apply to video and computer game distributors and manufacturers.

b. You can complain to the Video Standards Council if you have bought or hired, or considered buying or hiring, a video or computer game from, distributed by or made by, one of its member companies and:

- you object to the content of the game or video
- you object to the packaging, labelling, promotion or advertising of the game or video
- the game or video is faulty or damaged
- the retailer was showing age-rated material (for example an 18-rated video or trailer) in a public place to which minors have access
- a member company sells or hires, or attempts to sell or hire, a video game classified under the VSC or European Leisure Software Publishers Association (ELSPA) voluntary classification system to someone too young
- a member company has in any other way contravened the VSC Code of Practice Rules (available from the address above)

Alleged breaches of the VSC Rules are investigated by the Complaints Board. The Council is obliged to pass on all allegations of illegal activity to a TSO.

3. *How Independent Is the Complaints Procedure?*

a. Trading Standards Officers are employees of local government and completely independent of the video and computer games industry.

b. The VSC is a non-profit-making company managed by a committee of representatives from all segments of the video and games industries, an independent Secretary General, and an Operations Manager. Its Code of Practice Rules were developed together with a Consultative Committee made up of representatives from a number of bodies concerned with children and the family who consider and advise on matters of public concern.

The Complaints Board includes members of the Consultative Committee.

4. *Compensation/Redress?*

a. Trading Standards Officers will prosecute if they think an offence has been committed. The penalties for illegal supply of videos and/or computer games include fines and imprisonment.

b. If the VSC finds that a member company has broken the Code of Practice Rules it can discipline and ultimately expel the company from membership (although this will not stop the company from trading). The council may also recommend that a member offers compensation or replacement goods if, for example, a video or game is of unacceptable quality.

5. *Any Appeal?*

No.

6. *Other Options?*

●

see **Advertising**

Broadcasting 1 *to* **5**

Goods & Services

NB

Most video games do not have to be legally classified. The VSC administers and expects all its members to comply with the European Leisure Software Publishers Association (UK) Ltd *voluntary* age-rating system.

W

Water 1

1. *Who Can I Complain To?*

The **OFWAT Customer Service Committee** for your area –
for the address see your phone book under 'Office of Water
Services'.

For more information, or to complain directly to the **Director General of Water Services**, contact OFWAT Head Office
at:

Office of Water Services (OFWAT)
Centre City Tower
7 Hill Street
Birmingham B5 4UA

Tel: 0121 625 1300

*Note: OFWAT only covers England and Wales. For who to
complain to in Scotland and Northern Ireland, see Other
Options?, below.*

2. *What Sort of Complaints Do They Deal With?*

a. Complaints about water supply and sewerage services which
    cannot be resolved by the water company concerned. Every
    water company must have a procedure for dealing with complaints, which will have been subject to consultation by the
    relevant Customer Service Committee (CSC), and must be
    approved by the Director General of Water Services (DGWS).
    You can ask your company for a free copy of its procedure.

b. If you do not receive a reply to your written complaint within 10 days, you will normally be entitled to £10 compensation from the company under the Guaranteed Standards Scheme (see *NB*, below). It may, however, take 20 days to reply to your complaint if they need to visit you or make further enquiries.

c. If the water company is unable to satisfy your complaint you can then approach the CSC responsible for your water company. Any customer or potential customer, domestic or non-domestic, can complain to OFWAT. You will be kept informed of the progress of any investigation.

d. Complaints may be about, for example:

    ● water supply
    ● water quality
    ● sewerage problems
    ● water pressure
    ● billing
    ● charges
    ● debt and disconnection

e. Neither the DGWS nor the CSCs can deal with any complaint about:

    ● non-regulated activities of water companies such as plumbing services, waste management, engineering and consulting services, hotels, vehicle leasing, media interests, fish farming or any overseas activities
    ● river or coastal water pollution, fisheries, recreation, navigation, water resource management and river management
    ● any event that occurred *before 1 September 1989* (when OFWAT was set up), unless the problem continued beyond that date
    ● any matter which has been, is in the process of being, or could best be resolved through the courts

f. The DGWS will consider your complaint if:

    ● the CSC cannot resolve your complaint to its satisfaction

(when it will automatically refer it to the DG)

- you are unhappy with the *way* the CSC has investigated your complaint (not simply the outcome), and refer it to the DG yourself
- it falls into one of the categories which must, by law, be investigated by the DG. These include alleged contraventions by water companies of any condition of their licences or any statutory or other enforceable requirement

g. Under the **Water Services Act 1991** you can also refer certain disputes with a water company (about terms and conditions of supply, sewerage arrangements, payments under the guaranteed standards scheme, etc.) to the DGWS, whose determination is binding on both parties. For more information see *OFWAT Information Note 21* (available free from your local CSC office).

h. Finally, there are some cases in which statutory provisions exist for disputes to be determined formally by an independent arbitrator appointed by agreement between the customer and the company (or, if they cannot agree, by the Institute of Civil Engineers, the Secretary of State or the DGWS). These are disputes over:

- certain conditions relating to water main requisition
- costs of installation and the location of meters installed at the customer's expense
- certain conditions relating to sewer requisition
- compensation for street works and sewerage works

Arbitration is not free.

3. *How Independent Is the Complaints Procedure?*

a. OFWAT is a non-ministerial government department headed by the Director General of Water Services, set up to ensure that the water and sewerage companies in England and Wales provide their customers with a good-quality, efficient service at a reasonable price. It is independent of the water companies.

b. The DGWS is the economic regulator of the water industry. He is appointed by the Secretaries of State for the Environment and for Wales, and is himself responsible for appointing the members of the ten regional Customer Service Committees. The CSCs have the status of non-departmental public bodies (NDPBs, also known as quangos) and have statutory duties to represent the interests of customers at a regional level and to ensure their complaints are dealt with properly.

c. Arbitration is independent.

4. *Compensation/Redress?*

a. If OFWAT agrees that your complaint is justified, it will ask the water company to take action to put the matter right. This may include an explanation, an apology or a change in policy and procedure. It may also include a rebate of charges where you have not received the service you have paid for, or compensation where you have suffered financial loss (including loss of interest), damage, distress, inconvenience, or where you have been put to unreasonable trouble and expense by the company in pursuing the matter.

b. If OFWAT decides that no investigation is necessary, for example because the complaint is about something it has already looked into and agreed is reasonable (such as the continued use of rateable values until the year 2000 as a basis for charging) it will write to you and explain why it cannot help.

c. OFWAT has no statutory powers to require the water companies to act on its recommendations, but in practice they usually do.

d. If the DGWS or an independent arbitrator is called in to arbitrate on a dispute, you may be awarded compensation as well as any costs.

5. *Any Appeal?*

a. If you are unhappy with the *way* the DGWS has handled

your case you can ask your MP to refer the matter to the Parliamentary Ombudsman   *see* **Government Departments**

b. Arbitration decisions are usually legally binding on both sides.

c. If you are still unhappy about the quality of your drinking water after complaining to the water company and to OFWAT you can ask your local authority to check it, and may wish to complain to the Drinking Water Inspectorate
see **Water 2**

6. *Other Options?*

● To complain about the quality of rivers, lakes and coastal waters   *see* **Environment 2**
● The Local Government Ombudsman may be able to investigate complaints about action or inaction of a former water authority or statutory water company *before 1 September 1989*   *see* **Local Government**
● If you decide not to accept arbitration you retain the right to take a water company to court for damages. If you suffer loss or damage amounting to more than £275 as a result of a company supplying water which does not meet the required standards, you have a right of redress under the Consumer Protection Act. You can also claim compensation through the courts if loss or damage has occurred as a result of a water company's negligence. If you are considering legal action you should get advice   *see* **Where to get help**
● In *Scotland* water and sewerage services are now run by three regional water authorities: **East of Scotland Water, North of Scotland Water** and **West of Scotland Water.** Complaints can be made to them (their numbers are in the phone book) and/or to the **Scottish Water and Sewerage Customers Council** (**Tel** (lo-call): **0345 023049**). The water authorities still come under the remit of the Local Government Ombudsman   *see* **Local Government**
● In *Northern Ireland* complaints about water and sewerage services should be directed to the nearest **Customer Service Unit** of the **Water Service** – the address will be in your phone book, or you can contact Head Office at:

Water Service
Northland House
3 Frederick Street
Belfast BT1 2NR

Tel: 01232 244711
Fax: 01232 330790

You can also contact the Chief Executive at this address if you are unhappy with the *way* your complaint has been dealt with by your regional office. The Water Service is a 'Next Steps' (i.e. arm's-length) agency of government staffed by civil servants. If you are still unhappy with the way your complaint has been investigated after complaining to the Chief Executive, you can refer your complaint to the Northern Ireland Ombudsman   *see* **Government Departments**

NB

a. The guaranteed standards which all water companies are legally required to meet, and to pay compensation (normally £10) for when they don't, cover:

- making and keeping appointments
- answering questions and complaints
- warning you of planned interruptions to the water supply that are likely to last more than 4 hours
- the time it takes to get your water back on after an interruption
- the time it takes to put in a meter after the company receives your payment
- making a payment if your property is flooded from the company sewer

Contact your local water company for more details.

b. If you are a landowner wishing to complain about pipelaying or other works by a water or sewerage company you should get hold of *OFWAT Information Note 22* from your local CSC office.

Water 2

1. *Who Can I Complain To?*

Drinking Water Inspectorate (DWI)
Room B155
Romney House
43 Marsham Street
London SW1P 3PY

Tel: 0171 276 8808/8666

Note: The DWI only covers England and Wales. For who to complain to about all aspects of water supply in Scotland *and* Northern Ireland   *see* **Water 1**

2. *What Sort of Complaints Do They Deal With?*

a.   Complaints about water quality which cannot be resolved by the supply company concerned or by OFWAT   *see* **Water 1**

b.   Both water supply and drinking water quality in England and Wales are now the responsibility of the privatised water companies, but drinking water quality is further safeguarded because Local Authority (LA) Environmental Health Departments have a duty to monitor its quality, and the water quality regulations are ultimately enforced by the DWI.

c.   If you are worried about the quality of your own supply and are still unhappy after complaining to OFWAT, you can ask your LA to test your water. If the LA is not satisfied with the water's quality they will tell the company concerned, and will report the company to the DWI if they are not happy with its response. You can also complain directly to the DWI yourself.

d.   The DWI enforces the **Water Supply (Water Quality) Regulations 1989** which lay down three main standards relating to:

- the presence of bacteria
- the presence of chemical substances such as nitrates, pesticides and lead
- how water looks and tastes

3. *How Independent Is the Complaints Procedure?*

The DWI is the government body responsible for checking that water companies supply water that is wholesome and fit to drink when it reaches your home, and for monitoring how LAs fulfil their duties with regard to water quality. On health matters, the DWI is advised by the Government's Chief Medical Officer.

It is independent of the water companies.

4. *Compensation/Redress?*

If the DWI finds that a water company is failing to meet the required standards it will order it to take appropriate action to put things right. It has no power to award compensation.

5. *Any Appeal?*

a. If you are unhappy about the way the DWI has dealt with your complaint you can ask your MP to refer your case to the Parliamentary Ombudsman   *see* **Government Departments**

b. If you are unhappy about the *way* your LA has dealt with your complaint you can complain to the Local Government Ombudsman   *see* **Local Government**

6. *Other Options?*

- If a company has supplied water which is unfit to drink, you may be able to claim damages through the courts
  see **Water 1**
- To complain about pollution and environmental problems   *see* **Environment 2**

- To complain about the quality of water from a *private supply* (e.g. a well, spring, borehole, pond or stream) contact your local authority. LAs have similar powers to the DWI in relation to private water supplies, and can order the person(s) responsible to improve the supply. In severe cases where water quality is unimprovable and/or posing a significant health hazard, the LA can insist that properties served by a private supply are connected to a public supply from a water company   *see* **Environment 1**

Where to get help

If you need help in taking up a complaint, or you want to get advice or more information, there are a number of people and places you can turn to:

- Top of the list is the **Citizens Advice Bureau** (CAB). Your local CAB (the address and telephone number will be in the phone book) will have information about most of the areas covered here and will be able to advise you on how to make a complaint. The national contact point is:

  National Association of Citizens Advice Bureaux
  Myddleton House
  115–123 Pentonville Road
  London N1 9LZ

  Tel: 0171 833 2181

- Your local **library** is an invaluable resource centre and its reference section will have leaflets and books on what your rights are in relation to many different areas, and on what you can do when things go wrong. It should, for example, keep a copy of the *Directory of Trade Associations*.
- Your local **MP** is a one-person ombudsman, who can often help you with complaints when you seem to be getting nowhere yourself. (S)he may have a local office and should hold regular advice surgeries. MPs are usually listed in the phone book, but in case of difficulty can always be contacted at:

  House of Commons
  London SW1A 0AA

  Tel: 0171 219 3000

- Your local **councillor** should be able to help with issues concerning the local council. The council office should provide you with a name, address and telephone number.

- Some areas have a local **law centre** or **advice centre** offering free services to local communities. Libraries or council offices should know about these if they exist in your area, as well as about other sources of help and expertise such as **citizens' advocacy schemes** and local **charities**.
- If you need a **solicitor**, the Law Society produces regional directories of solicitors with a guide to what they specialise in. This should be available from your local library, but you can also contact:

> **The Law Society**
> **50 Chancery Lane**
> **London WC2A 1SX**
>
> **Tel: 0171 242 1222**

> *or*

> **Law Society of Scotland**
> **26 Drumsheugh Gardens**
> **Edinburgh EH3 7YR**
>
> **Tel: 0131 226 7411**

> *or*

> **Law Society of Northern Ireland**
> **98 Victoria Street**
> **Belfast BT1 3JZ**
>
> **Tel: 01232 231614**

The Law Society also produces leaflets about the services (including the flat-fee consultations) and charging procedures of solicitors.

- Information about the **small claims** (and in Scotland the **summary cause**) **procedure** (where you do not need a solicitor) can be obtained from your local County Court (Sheriff Court in Scotland), library or CAB. In case of difficulty, contact:

in England and Wales

Customer Service Unit
Court Service
Southside
105 Victoria Street
London SW1E 6QT

Tel: 0171 210 8500

in Scotland

Administration Unit
Scottish Court Service
Hayweight House
23 Lauriston Street
Edinburgh EH3 9DQ

Tel: 0131 229 9200

in Northern Ireland

Communications Unit
The Northern Ireland
  Court Service
Windsor House
9-15 Bedford Street
Belfast BT2 7LT

Tel: 01232 328594

- The **Trading Standards** (or **Consumer Protection**) Department of the council (in England: county, metropolitan district, London borough) will be able to help or advise on many problems relating to goods and services. The contact number will be in the phone book. The **environmental health** department of the council may be able to assist with a number of other problems   *see* **Goods & Services**
- The **Office of Fair Trading** is the official body concerned with consumer protection issues. It produces a range of leaflets and runs a consumer information telephone line – 0345 224499. A list of its publications can be obtained from:

OFT
PO Box 2
Central Way
Feltham
Middlesex TW14 0TG

Tel: 0181 398 3405

- Many of the **trade schemes** involve conciliation or **arbitration** arrangements. To find out which trades are covered, and how the schemes work, contact:

The Chartered Institute of Arbitrators
International Arbitration Centre
24 Angel Gate
City Road
London EC1V 2RS

Tel: 0171 837 4483

In Scotland:

Scottish Council for Arbitration
27 Melville Street
Edinburgh EH3 7JF

Tel: 0131 220 4776

Finally, there are a number of **publications** which are helpful on different aspects of taking up complaints. Particularly to be recommended are:

- *120 Letters that Get Results* and the new *Which? Way to Beat the System*, both from the Consumers' Association. The first provides sample letters of complaint, with good advice, for a whole range of goods and services. The second looks at how to get the best out of public services. Both are available from:

   Which? Books
   2 Marylebone Road
   London NW1 4DF

- *A Buyer's Guide*, Office of Fair Trading. An excellent free booklet from OFT on basic consumer rights in relation to goods and services and how to complain. Available from OFT (address above).
- *Resolving Disputes Without Going to Court*, Lord Chancellor's Department. A recent and very useful free booklet on the different options for resolving disputes and pursuing complaints without using the courts. This should be available at courts, libraries and CABs, but in case of difficulty contact the Court Service at one of the addresses above.

Index

INTRODUCTION

The North West of England saw some of the very earliest main line railway development but the failure of the 'established' railway companies to provide a connection with the mill towns of east Lancashire prompted local communities to take matters into their own hands by establishing companies to promote railways to serve the needs of their particular area. One such company was the Manchester, Bury and Rossendale Railway, later renamed as the East Lancashire Railway, whose aim was to construct a railway from Clifton, on the Manchester to Bolton line, along the scenic valley of the River Irwell via Bury and Ramsbottom to Rawtenstall. Public services began in 1846.

The frantic railway closures that followed the Beeching Report in 1963 saw the demise of many lines in the area, although passengers were able to use the Bury to Rawtenstall line until June 1972. The spirit and persistence of those early railway pioneers has now been matched by a group of volunteers keen to ensure that not all of the area's railway heritage was lost.

Formed in 1968, the East Lancashire Railway Preservation Society set about preserving a section of the original East Lancashire Railway. Initially the intention was to restore a section of line around the town of Helmshore, but this was unsuccessful. The cessation of services between Bury and Rawtenstall saw their focus redirected to centre on Bury with the aim of preserving that line intact. Work began in earnest in 1980, following the end of coal traffic and the transfer of the electric train service away from Bolton Street Station as part of the introduction of the Manchester Metrolink tram system.

The Society would have struggled to succeed without the not inconsiderable help and assistance of the local authorities of the area with whom a partnership was formed. Their first success was the re-introduction of passenger services over the first 4 miles of track to Ramsbottom on 25 July 1987. Rawtenstall was reached in 1992 and more recently the extension to Heywood, where a connection with the main rail network remains, was re-opened on 6 September 2003.

The general perception of Lancashire is one of an over-developed industrial landscape, with dark satanic mills and an inclement climate to match. In reality even when in the heart of a city you are never more than half an hour from a green and very scenic countryside, occasionally bathed in sunshine, as I trust the following photographic journey along the East Lancashire Railway will show. Operationally the line is a relative newcomer in the preservation movement, but has quickly established itself as a very popular tourist attraction. I hope that this book adequately conveys the reasons for the success. A visit is highly recommended.

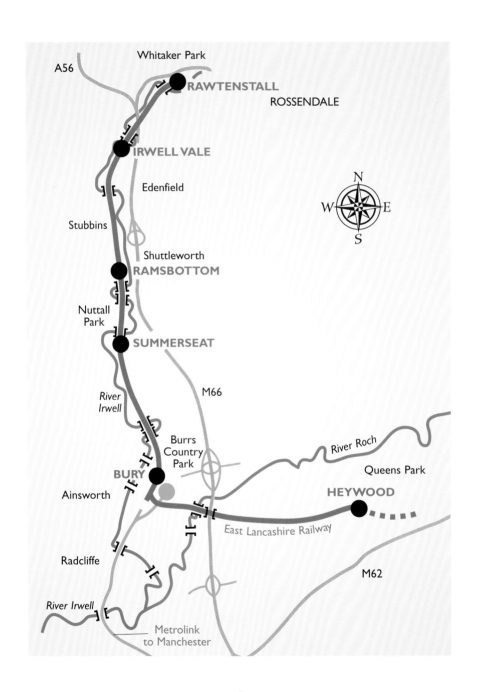

Whitaker Park

A56

RAWTENSTALL

ROSSENDALE

IRWELL VALE

Edenfield

Stubbins

Shuttleworth

RAMSBOTTOM

Nuttall
Park

SUMMERSEAT

M66

*River
Irwell*

Burrs
Country
Park

River Roch

Queens Park

BURY

HEYWOOD

Ainsworth

East Lancashire Railway

Radcliffe

M62

River Irwell

Metrolink
to Manchester

N
W E
S